D1498018

The First Guidebook

to Prisons and Concentration Camps

of the Soviet Union

AVRAHAM SHIFRIN

The First Guidebook

to Prisons and Concentration Camps

of the Soviet Union

BANTAM BOOKS
TORONTO · NEW YORK · LONDON · SYDNEY

THE FIRST GUIDEBOOK TO PRISONS AND
CONCENTRATION CAMPS OF THE SOVIET UNION
*A Bantam Book / published by arrangement with
Stephanus Edition Verlags GMBH*

PRINTING HISTORY
Stephanus Edition published September 1980
*Commissioned by THE RESEARCH CENTER FOR
PRISONS, PSYCHPRISONS AND FORCED-LABOR
CONCENTRATION CAMPS OF THE USSR*
Translated from the Russian
Illustrations and drawings by Jorge Martines
Bantam edition / June 1982

Library of Congress Cataloging in Publication Data
Shifrin, Avraham.
  The First guidebook to prisons and concentration camps
of the Soviet Union.
  Translation of Putevoditel′po lageriam, tiuŕmam i
psikhiatricheskim tiuŕmam v SSSR.
  Bibliography: p. 373
  Includes index.
  1. Prisons—Soviet Union—Guide-books. 2. Concen-
tration camps—Soviet Union—Guide-books. I. Title.
HV9712.S4913   365′.947   81-17543
ISBN 0-553-01392-0 pbk.   AACR2

Published simultaneously in the United States and Canada

*Bantam Books are published by Bantam Books, Inc. Its
trademark, consisting of the words "Bantam Books" and
the portrayal of a rooster, is Registered in U.S. Patent
and Trademark Office and in other countries. Marca
Registrada. Bantam Books, Inc., 666 Fifth Avenue, New
York, New York 10103.*

PRINTED IN THE UNITED STATES OF AMERICA

0 9 8 7 6 5 4 3 2 1

CONTENTS

PREFACE TO THE SECOND EDITION

My work on this book has been a continuing torture; the constant imaginative return to the camp zones is most unpleasant.

While preparing this Second Edition, I have come across a tremendous quantity of new material which bears witness to the increasingly cruel persecution of dissidents and religious persons as well as harsher treatment for political prisoners in the U.S.S.R. At the end of this edition, I have added a certain amount of this new material.

The intense response of readers of the Guidebook and their letters have helped me find the strength to plunge again into the never-ending hell of the Soviet camps. Some readers in Europe, the United States, and Africa have written that this book has given them the opportunity to understand the essence of the Soviet regime in Russia for the first time.

It is a sad thing for me to acknowledge that even today after books on the experience of the camps by Evgeniia Ginzburg, Noble Solonevich, Yury Margolin, Alexander Marchenko, and others, there is still someone who does not understand the zverskoi essence which is hidden behind the beautiful if false slogans and promises of the Kremlin.

There has also been response to the material in this book from within the U.S.S.R. In many newspapers, its author has been called a liar and even a "new Goebbels", although the Guidebook itself has not been mentioned nor has there been any information given about my work in publicizing the Gulag system in the U.S.S.R.

There has even been a television film vilifying me in the U.S.S.R., but again there was no mention made of the Guidebook.

It is clear to me why the Soviet regime is afraid to mention this book: the undeniable existence of millions of prisoners is a forbidden topic in the U.S.S.R.

I have also received word from the U.S.S.R. that the regime has taken measures to close those camps and prisons whose addresses in the Guidebook are noted as being conveniently located for photographing. For example, the children's camp at Valuiki station has been closed and the children imprisoned in it have been transported to other camps. In Kishinev, the psychiatric prison on Kuznechnaya Street has been closed. But the regime has not destroyed the camp barracks there or the barbed wire. One is reminded of the attempt by the Nazis at the close of World War Two, to blow up the crematoriums in their death camps.

I hope that this Guidebook will be of use to those who desire to find the many prison and camp sites during their travel in the U.S.S.R. Unfortunately, closing them all will not be possible while the Communist system continues to exist there.

A. Shifrin

PREFACE TO THE FIRST EDITION

You are holding an unusual book in your hands. It is a *Guidebook* and the first work of its kind that contains detailed information on more than 2000 penal institutions in the Soviet Union. This figure, however, does not represent a complete list of camps and prisons in the U.S.S.R., but includes only those facilities for which we have an address.

Most of the addresses in this book refer to concentration camps currently in operation. (The official Soviet designation for such camps is *ispravitel'no-trudovaya koloniya* in singular form, corrective labor colony or ITK, the Russian acronym-*trans*.) The Soviet state began the construction of its camp system as early as 1917 and has maintained it to this day.

The *Guidebook* lists not only the penal colonies set aside for political prisoners, but also those where ordinary criminals are held as well. In every Soviet camp of the latter variety, the authorities conceal scores of *de facto* political prisoners from the eyes of the world by placing them among the ranks of common offenders. The *Guidebook* will introduce to you some of these prisoners by their real names.

The *Guidebook* contains information on penal institutions located in all parts of the Soviet Union. The maps and the notes accompanying them will provide you with all the necessary instructions for reaching the camps, prisons, and psychiatric prisons – exact address, numbers of tram, bus, and trolley bus lines, and road directions, too.

The *Guidebook* will introduce you to a world of camps, watchtowers manned by guards bearing machine guns, and electrically charged barbed-wire fences. You will see columns of prisoners, prisoners in transport vehicles, dogs sicked on prisoners, prisoners in striped or in black camp uniforms with numbers across their chests, women prisoners, child and teenage prisoners.

The photographs of camps and prisons taken with hidden cameras by our courageous friends and reproduced for this book will help you locate these frightful dens of innocent human suffering.

We are speaking of innocent human beings persecuted

for thinking differently; reading "forbidden" philosophical, political, or religious books; posting up notices; putting up a flag; demanding religious instruction for their children; or undertaking a private commercial initiative. These are the "crimes" for which a Soviet citizen can be imprisoned.

The photographs in the *Guidebook* will also show you some receipts, for example, for fines levied against those penalized for "belief in God" or for possession of "anti-Soviet literature" – in this case, the Bible. You may find it difficult to believe that these things still take place in the Soviet Union today, long after Stalin's death. This is precisely why this *Guidebook* has been written.

In the notes to the maps of the camps, you will read the testimony of former political prisoners, of the hunger they experienced, and the beatings and humiliations they suffered at the hands of the camp guards. Is this the kind of treatment accorded to the inmates in your country's prisons?

You are now invited to undertake an unusual journey to the prison camps – to the Gulag Archipelago – of the Soviet Union. Rest assured that you will not be running the risk of an indefinite stay in the process. Soviet law does not, after all, prohibit tourists from visiting its camps, prisons, or psychiatric prisons. Feel free, therefore, to approach those thronging the gates of a Soviet camp or prison in the hope of obtaining a visit with an imprisoned relative. Tell the visitors about yourself and have them pass on a few words of encouragement to those suffering in their dismal torture chambers. Request permission from the administration of the penal facility to meet with those political prisoners whose names are listed in this *Guidebook*. Your request will be denied, of course, but word of your visit will reach the prisoners, and give them encouragement and moral support. The administration, however, will be alarmed, because, more than anything else, it fears that evidence of the camps will reach the free world. It may, as a result, even feel compelled to ease prison conditions for some of the inmates. Do not forget to ask for the names of administration officials or to take photographs of everything you see.

You should not be surprised by the fact that the slogan, "Honest labor: the road home!", posted at the entrance of Soviet penal settlements bears a strong resemblance to the catchword, "Arbeit macht frei!" (Work shall set you free), placed by the Nazis over the gates of their own concentration camps. We do not know who learned from whom. But we do know that posters of this kind can be found in Soviet camps today. Our *Guidebook* contains a photograph of the Soviet slogan, posted at the gates of a children's camp in *Orël*.

And so, our trip begins. Allow us to suggest an itinerary not found in Soviet guidebooks.

In *Moscow,* for example, you can visit and photograph *"Lubyanka",* the central K.G.B. prison, and *"Lefortovo",* the special prison where Aleksandr Solzhenitsyn spent his last two nights in the Soviet Union before his expulsion from the country and where Anatolii Shcharanskii was held for more than two years. Some 30 additional camps, prisons, and psychiatric prisons are included in our Moscow city program as well.

In *Leningrad,* we recommend the famous *"Kresty",* the central K.G.B. prison of the city, and at least another dozen penal facilities.

In downtown *L'vov,* you can visit six camps and prisons. In *Novosibirsk,* you will easily find 15 camps and four prisons within the city limits. Your guide from "Intourist" will "forget" to show you the women's and children's camps in *Odessa,* but our *Guidebook* will take you on a tour of these and nine other penal facilities in this health resort. And so on for the entire country.

Wherever your travels in the Soviet Union take you, consult our *Guidebook,* and you will find the addresses of the camps, prisons, and psychiatric prisons in your area: Slaves are building Communism... Visit them!

The author

5

ACKNOWLEDGMENTS

I am greatly indebted to my most diligent assistant, Mr. Ariel Cohen, who personally sought out and interviewed hundreds of new arrivals from the Soviet Union and thus supplied me with highly valuable information for this book; to Mrs. Hedi Fluri, without whose unfailing friendship, support and encouragement this book would probably never have been written; to Rev. Richard Wurmbrand and Mr. Michael Wurmbrand, the directors of the "Jesus to the Communist World" – one of the most active anti-Communist organizations in the West – for providing me with a wealth of information and material on the Soviet state's persecution of its religious citizens; and to Mr. Paul Klavinc, whose help was enormous in assembling information on Latvian camps and prisons. I am very grateful to Mrs. Tsiva Krapivskaya, who spent long hours in helping me to process information for the book; to the hundreds and hundreds of witnesses of the Soviet prison system who sent me their testimonies from all over the world or who submitted their statements to me in Israel; and especially to those men and women who took an active part in gathering information on the camps and prisons of the U.S.S.R.: A. Vudka, A. Feldman, M. Klabin, M. Kharitonskii, L. and G. Birin, P. Medinsh, L. Lubarskii, I. Levinstein, M. Milman, D. Kustanovich, B. Podolskii, E. Devaltovskaya, I. Zandelevich, E. Multyaner and many others. I owe a great debt of gratitude to my wife, Eleonora Poltinnikova-Shifrin, who has worked with me all these years as permanent editor and translator of the text of the *Guidebook* and selflessly applied her knowledge and energy towards helping me to compile this book.

Finally, the greatest debt of gratitude, which cannot be repaid even with a simple listing of names, is owed to those of our friends in the U.S.S.R. who risked their freedom and their families' well-being by assembling and sending us information on the Soviet prison system and by submitting to us pictures of Soviet camps, prisons and psychiatric prisons – many of which are shown here in this book.

23 January 1980

Administrative Divisions ot the Soviet Union (1979)
15 Union Republics

1. R.S.F.S.R.	16 autonomous S.S.R.'s, 5 autonomous regions, 10 autonomous districts (until 1977, national districts), 6 territories, 49 regions
2. Ukrainian S.S.R. (full member of United Nations)	25 region; each region is divided into 10–20 districts
3. Belorussian S.S.R. (White Russia; full member of United Nations)	6 regions; each region is divided into districts
4. Uzbek S.S.R.	a) Kara-Kalpak A.S.S.R. b) 11 regions c) 58 cities, 88 settlements of urban status, 116 districts
5. Kazakh S.S.R.	19 regions a) 81 cities b) 175 settlements of urban status c) 205 districts
6. Georgian S.S.R.	a) Abkhazian A.S.S.R. b) Adzharian A.S.S.R. c) South Ossetian Autonomus Region
7. Azerbaidzhan S.S.R.	a) Nakhichevan' A.S.S.R. b) Nagorno-Karabakh Autonomus Region
8. Lithuanian S.S.R.	a) 92 cities b) 23 settlements of urban status c) 44 districts
9. Moldavian S.S.R.	a) 20 cities b) 33 settlements of urban status c) 32 districts
10. Latvian S.S.R.	a) 56 cities b) 34 settlements of urban status c) 26 districts
11. Kirghiz S.S.R.	3 regions: 1) Issyk-Kul', 2) Naryn, 3) Osh a) 15 cities b) 35 settlements of urban status c) 32 districts
12. Tadzhik S.S.R.	2 regions: 1) Leninabad, 2) Kulyab Gorno-Badakhshan Autonomous Region a) 18 cities b) 47 settlements of urban status c) 40 districts
13. Armenian S.S.R.	a) 23 cities b) 30 settlements of urban status c) 33 districts
14. Turkmen S.S.R.	5 regions a) 15 cities b) 68 settlements of urban status c) 34 districts
15. Estonian S.S.R.	a) 6 cities b) 15 settlements of urban status c) 15 districts

U.S.S.R. = Union of Soviet Socialist Republics
R.S.F.S.R = Russian Soviet Federated Socialist Republic
S.S.R. = Soviet Socialist Republic
A.S.S.R. = Autonomous Soviet Socialist Republic

avtonomnaya oblast' = autonomous region
avtonomnyi (natsional'nyi) okrug = autonomous (national) district
oblast' = region
krai = territory
posëlok gorodskogo tipa = settlement of urban status
raion = district

Major connections to and within the Soviet Union

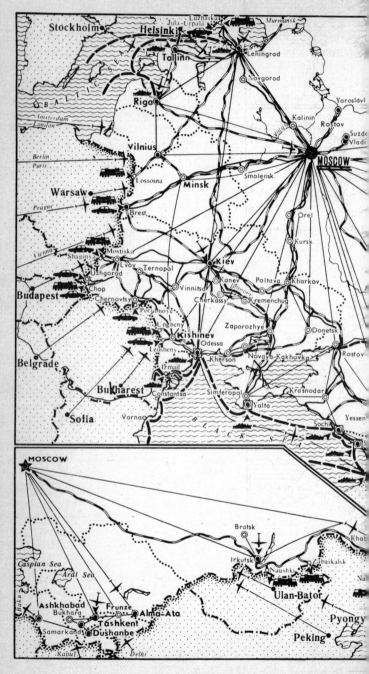

	Intourist - serviced cities and towns
	Cities frequented by tourists
	Resorts
	Points of entry in the USSR
Major means of communication in the USSR	
——	Air routes
==	Train routes
►►►	Sea and river cruises
——	Car routes

INFORMATION ON THE USE OF THE GUIDEBOOK

1. Those Soviet penal institutions known to us as of early 1980–1976 camps, 273 prisons, and 85 psychiatric prisons—are indicated on the general map of the U.S.S.R. (foldout map, last page of the *Guidebook*) with a dot.

2. Camps discussed in the text are accompanied by individual maps of the republics, territories *(kraya)*, and regions *(oblasti)* with a dot; prisons and psychiatric prisons with a square.

3. The capital cities of the various administrative units of the Soviet Union are printed in upper-case letters.

4. Only in a few instances have we found it necessary to indicate railway lines and highways on the maps. For more detailed information on intercity travel, consult a Soviet tourist map or any general guide to the U.S.S.R.

5. In addition to the general map referred to above in paragraph (1), the *Guidebook* also contains three more maps of the Soviet Union, indicating: a) women's and children's camps; b) psychiatric prisons; and c) extermination camps (i.e., labor camps, from which prisoners rarely return—also called "death camps" in this book—*trans.*).

6. The *Guidebook* contains a few city maps indicating the names of streets and the exact location of camps, prisons, and psychiatric prisons. Also included are street directions, the numbers of public transportation lines, and stop designations.

7. As penal institutions in Moscow and Leningrad are located so far apart from one another, we found it more practical simply to indicate the proper directions on the maps by the use of arrows. A list of exact addresses, names of metro stations, and numbers of public transportation lines has been added.

8. Where it was not possible to show long street distances drawn to proper scale on the city maps, a dotted line has been used. Streets so marked are thus longer than indicated on the maps.

9. Russian designations for Soviet administrative units are used on all maps of the *Guidebook: oblast'* (region); *krai* (territory); A.S.S.R. (Autonomous Soviet Socialist Republic); and S.S.R. (Soviet Socialist Republic).

10. The maps are not alphabetically arranged, but according to our estimate of the number of expected visits to and the degree of interest in the areas in question.

11. The photographs in the *Guidebook* will also assist you in finding the camps, prisons and psychiatric prisons. In some cases (as in Moscow, Odessa, and Minsk), we shall indicate where the photographs were taken from. Photographs of poor quality were replaced by faithfully drawn pen-and-ink reproductions.

12. We wish to caution the reader that the authorities from time to time change the location, address, etc. of the camps, prisons, and psychiatric prisons. The Soviet government will thus continue its attempts to conceal from the West its inhuman brutality and its hostility to religion.

List of cities in which there are Intourist offices

(cities having camps or prisons discussed in this *Guidebook* are marked with a plus sign):

R.S.F.S.R.
+ Moscow
  Borisoglebsk
+ (Murmansk Region)
+ Bratsk
+ Irkutsk
+ Ivanovo
+ Kalinin
+ Kazan'
+ Khabarovsk
+ Khvalynsk
+ Krasnodar
+ Kursk
+ Leningrad
+ Murmansk
+ Novgorod
+ Novosibirsk
+ Ordzhonikidze
+ Orël
+ Petrozavodsk
+ Pskov
  Pyatigorsk
+ Rostov-on-Don
+ Smolensk
+ Sotchi

+ Stavropol'
  Suzdal'
  Togliatti
+ Ul'yanovsk
+ Vladimir
+ Volgograd
+ Yaroslavl'

BELORUSSIAN S.S.R.
+ Minsk
+ Brest

UZBEK S.S.R.
+ Tashkent
+ Bukhara
+ Samarkand

Ukrainian S.S.R.
+ Kiev
+ Cherkassy
+ Chernovtsy
  Kanev
+ Khar'kov
+ Kherson
+ Kremenchug
+ L'vov
+ Odessa
+ Poltava
+ Simferopol'
+ Uzhgorod

TADZHIK S.S.R.
+ Dushanbe
+ Yalta
+ Zaporozh'e

MOLDAVIAN S.S.R.
+ Kishinev
+ Bel'tsy

TURKMEN .S.S.R.
+ Ashkhabad

KAZAKH S.S.R.
+ Alma-Ata
+ Chimkent

GEORGIAN S.S.R.
+ Tbilisi
  Bakuriani
  Batumi
  Borzhomi
  Gori
  Kutaisi
  Sukhumi
  Tskhaltubo

AZERBAIDZHAN S.S.R.
+ Baku
  Bil'gyakh
  Khudat
+ Kuba
  Sumgait

ARMENIAN S.S.R.
+ Erevan

LATVIAN S.S.R.
+ Riga

LITHUANIAN S.S.R.
+ Vilnius

ESTONIAN S.S.R.
+ Tallin

KIRGHIZ S.S.R.
+ Frunze

SPECIAL PURPOSE
PRISONS AND CAMPS

We do not claim that our map of women's and children's camps in the Soviet Union is complete. On the contrary, we are convinced that the number of such camps is significantly higher. Nevertheless, the tourist has been provided with a long list of specific itineraries to choose from. Those interested in learning about these islands of broken destinies need only refer to the addresses and directions provided here.

14

WOMEN'S AND CHILDREN'S CAMPS

One glance at the map will show you, for example, how to get to the children's camps in *Kalinin* and *Volkhov*. Both cities lie on the train route from Moscow to Leningrad.

In *Ul'yanovka*, a suburb of Leningrad (see map of Leningrad), you can visit a camp for those women permitted to retain custody of their infant children while serving out their sentences. In *Leningrad* itself, you will find a special women's prison on Arsenal'naya Street.

Soviet authorities deny that there are children in the camps. Here you see imprisoned youths in a camp in Orël, Oktyabr'skaya Street. (See section on Orël City). The placard on the left reads, "Honest work: the road home to the family".
Compare it to the slogan displayed in Nazi concentration camps, "Work shall set you free" (Arbeit macht frei!). (photo 1976).

A camp for 3000 children and youths in *Orël*, 350 kilometers south of Moscow, can be reached by taking the trolley bus no. 3 to the stop marked "Khimchistka" (see special map of Orël).

Similar camps can be found in the city of *Riga* (Latvia) and in the Belorussian cities of *Minsk* and *Gomel'*.

You can also visit camps for women with infants in *Khar'kov, Kremenchug,* and *Kherson* (all in the Ukraine); *Bendery* (Moldavia); and Odessa on the Black Sea.

Children's camps and camps for women with children are also located in southern Russia – in *Maikop, Ol'ginskaya, Labinsk, Ust'-Labinsk* (all in Krasnodar Territory), and Rostov.

In the Urals, children's camps can be found in *Verkhotur'e, Alatyr',* and *Kopychilitsy;* and women's camps in *Dobrye Vody, Nizhnii Tagil,* and *Zuevka.*

We know of three children's camps and two camps for women with children in *Azerbaidzhan* (see map of Azerbaidzhan S.S.R.) Similar camps are also indicated on the maps of Siberia, Altai, Kazakhstan, Tadzhikistan, and Uzbekistan. Wherever your tour leads you, you will find these camps. You need only consult the map.

As you can see, most of the women's and children's camps indicated on the map are to be found in central Russia and in the Ukraine. On the other hand, however, we have received little eyewitness testimony on camps in Siberia and the Soviet Far East, where, we suspect, a large number of such facilities are in operation.

In *Novosibirsk,* a popular tourists' destination, you will find eight camps, two of which, located within city limits, accommodate children – one on Gusinobrodskoe Highway, the other in the Zatulinskii residential area. The children from Zatulinskii are used, together with adult prisoners, in the construction of a stadium (the camps and directions on how to find them are shown on the map of Novosibirsk).

E.D., an eyewitness who has been to the camps in *Novosibirsk* for reasons connected with her work, reports that clubcarrying supervisors (officially called "educators") roaming about the camp grounds subject the young prisoners (aged 10 to 18) to merciless beatings. In addi-

Children in camp no. UZ NY 3/14 in Partizanskii, Krasnoyarsk Territory (photo 1975).

tion, the younger boys must also suffer the harassments of the older inmates – stolen food rations, sexual abuses (homosexuality is rampant), pressures to perform involuntary favors. Those who resist are beaten. Otherwise, the boys are assigned to hard labor projects – in construction, for example – or to dangerous duties in industrial plants, such as in iron foundries.

According to E.D., conditions in the intensified-regime children's camp in *Gornyi* (Toguchin District, Novosibirsk Region) are even more horrifying. The children are assigned backbreaking duties, despite the prevalence of hunger in the camp. Those who fall ill and request transfer to a hospital are beaten.

In a *Novosibirsk* women's camp situated in the vicinity of *Tolmachevo* airport, 1500 prisoners, including nursing mothers, are given physically exhausting duties in a plant in which reinforced concrete plates are manufactured.

In a camp near the *Volochaevskii* residential area, 500 women, some of them mothers imprisoned with their infants, are assigned to work in mechanics shops.

Ada Sh., an inmate at a camp for mothers with infants in *Gor'kii* until 1979, recounts that she herself was separated from her five-year old daughter. (Children are normally allowed to stay with their mothers only until the age of two.) Nursing mothers are only given 15 minutes, three times a day, to feed their babies before being forced to return to work. Ada Sh. also tells how woman prisoners, on being taken to the camp, were forced to stand in the snow with their lightly-clothed children. Many of the children fell ill and died for lack of medical attention.

Tourists visiting the sea health resort of *Odessa* are not likely to be aware of the penal institutions in the area, including two children's camps, a children's prison, and two camps for women with children (see map of Odessa).

Our research center has completed a special investigation on penal institutions for children and for women with children. Copies of the findings are available on request.

LIST OF WOMEN'S AND CHILDREN'S PRISONS IN THE SOVIET UNION

1. KANDALAKSHA, Murmansk Region — women and children
2. ARKHANGEL'SK, Arkhangel'sk Region — women and children
3. VOLKHOV, Leningrad Region — women and children
4. RIGA, Latvian S.S.R. — women and children
5. UL'YANOVKA, Leningrad Region — women and children
6. VILNIUS, Lithuanian S.S.R. — (2)-children (1); on Lukishkii Square, — women with children (1)
7. BOBRUISK, Belorussian S.S.R. — women and children
8. MINSK, Belorussian S.S.R. — women and children
9. GOMEL', Belorussian S.S.R. — (2)-children
10. DROGOBYCH, Ukrainian S.S.R. — women and children
11. UZHGOROD, Ukrainian S.S.R. — women and children
12. BENDERY, Moldavian S.S.R. — (2)-women with children
13. SARNY, Rovno Region, Ukrainian S.S.R. — women and children
14. MANEVICHI, Volyn' Region, Ukrainian S.S.R. — children
15. RAIKOVICHI, Khmel'nitskii Region, Ukrainian S.S.R. — women with children
16. DUBOSSARY, Moldavian S.S.R. — women with children
17. LIPKANY, Moldavian S.S.R. — women with children
18. RUSSKOE, Moldavian S.S.R. — women with children
19. ODESSA, Ukrainian S.S.R. — (5)-children (3); women with children (2)
20. KHERSON, Ukrainian S.S.R. — children
21. KREMENCHUG, Ukrainian S.S.R. — (2)-children (1); women with children (1)
22. KHMEL'NITSKII, Ukrainian S.S.R. — women with children
23. ROVEN'KI, Voroshilovgrad Region, Ukrainian S.S.R. — women with children
24. BAKHMACH, Ukrainian S.S.R. — women with children
25. DZERZHINSK, Ukrainian S.S.R. — women with children
26. KHAR'KOV, Ukrainian S.S.R. — children
27. CHERNIGOV, Ukrainian S.S.R. — children
28. SMOLENSK, Smolensk Region — women with children
29. KALININ, Kalinin Region — women with children
30. KOCHMAS, Komi A.S.S.R. — women with children
31. VOLOGDA, Vologda Region — women with children
32. PETROVSKOE, Voroshilovgrad Region, Ukrainian S.S.R. — women with children
33. ORËL, Orël Region — children
34. VALUIKI, Belgorod Region — children
35. NOVYI OSKOL, Belgorod Region — children
36. RYBINSK, Yaroslavl' Region — women with children
37. GOR'KII, Gor'kii Region — women with children
38. KANDEL', Ul'yanovsk Region — women and children
39. VESËLOE, Volgograd Region — women
40. VOLGOGRAD, Volgograd Region — women with children
41. TUL'CHIN, Ukrainian S.S.R. — women with children

42. OVRUCH,
    Ukrainian S.S.R. — women with children
43. ARABATSKAYA STRELKA,
    Crimean Region, Ukrainian S.S.R. — children
44. MAIKOP, Krasnodar Territory — women with children
45. LABINSK, Krasnodar Territory — children
46. UST'-LABINSKAYA,
    Krasnodar Territory — children
47. OL'GINSKAYA, Krasnodar Territory — women with children
48. MARDAKYAN, Azerbaidzhan S.S.R. — children
49. ZAKATALY, Azerbaidzhan S.S.R. — children
50. CHËRNYI GOROD (suburb of Baku),
    Azerbaidzhan S.S.R. — children
51. BAKU, Azerbaidzhan S.S.R. — (2)-children (1); women with
    children (1)
52. BUGUL'MA, Tatar A.S.S.R. — women with children
53. KAZAN', Tatar A.S.S.R. — children
54. UL'YANOVSK, Ul'yanovsk Region — women
55. BOGDANOVICH, Sverdlovsk Region — children
56. ALATYR', Chuvash A.S.S.R. — women with children
57. POT'MA, Mordovian A.S.S.R. — women with children
58. BARASHEVO, Mordovian A.S.S.R. — women with children
59. KIROV, Kirov Region — women with children
60. ZUEVKA, Kirov Region — women and children
61. DOBRYE VODY, Perm' Region — women and children
62. VERKHOTUR'E, Sverdlovsk Region — women with children
63. TOBOL'SK, Tyumen' Region — children
64. NIZHNII TAGIL, Sverdlovsk Region — children
65. KOPYCHILITSY, Perm' Region — women with children
66. ANZHERO-SUDZHENSK,
    Kemerovo Region — women with children
67. SUSLOVO, Kemerovo Region — (2) – women with children
68. PAVLODAR, Kazakh S.S.R. — women with children
69. ACHINSK, Krasnoyarsk Territory — children
70. GORNAYA SHORIYA,
    Kemerovo Region — women with children
71. DZHAMBUL-2, Kazakh S.S.R. — (2) – women with children
72. NIKOLAEVKA, Alma-Ata Region,
    Kazakh S.S.R. — women and children
73. TASHKENT, Uzbek S.S.R. — (3) – children (1); women and
    children (2)
74. NAVOI, Bukhara Region, Uzbek S.S.R. — children
75. URGA, Uzbek S.S.R. — children
76. ZING ATA, Uzbek S.S.R. — women and children
77. CHAMAL'GAN, Kazakh S.S.R. — women and children
78. DUSHANBE, Tadzhik S.S.R. — women and children
79. PARTIZANSKOE,
    Krasnoyarsk Territory — women and children
80. NOVOALTAISK, Altai Territory — women and children
81. ABAKAN, Krasnoyarsk Territory — children
82. BARNAUL, Altai Territory — women and children
83. NOVOKUZNETSK, Kemerovo Region — women and children

84. KEMEROVO, Kemerovo Region	– women and children
85. UST'-KUT, Irkutsk Region	– women and children
86. VYDRINO, Buryat A.S.S.R.	– women and children
87. TOMSK, Tomsk Region	– (3) – children (1); women and children (2)
88. NOVOSIBIRSK, Novosibirsk Region	– (3) – children (2); women with children (1)
89. VIKHOREVKA, Irkutsk Region	– women with children
90. KUZ'MIKHA, Irkutsk Region	– women (invalids)
91. SLYUDYANKA, Irkutsk Region	– women
92. ULAN-UDE, Buryat A.S.S.R.	– women with children
93. SHIKOTAN, Kuril Islands	– women with children
94. VERSHINO, Primorsk Territory	– women with children
95. MOSCOW	– (2) – children
96. DNEPRODZERZHINSK, Dnepropetrovsk Region, Ukrainian S.S.R.	– women with children
97. KOROSTEN', Zhitomir Region, Ukrainian S.S.R.	– children
98. MOSHKOVO, Novosibirsk Region	– (3) – women
99. CHEREPANOVO, Novosibirsk Region	– (3) – women

TOTAL: 119 camps and prisons for women and children[1]

[1] Those place names listed without the name of a Soviet Socialist Republic (S.S.R.) are located in the Russian Soviet Federated Socialist Republic (R.S.F.S.R.) – *trans.*

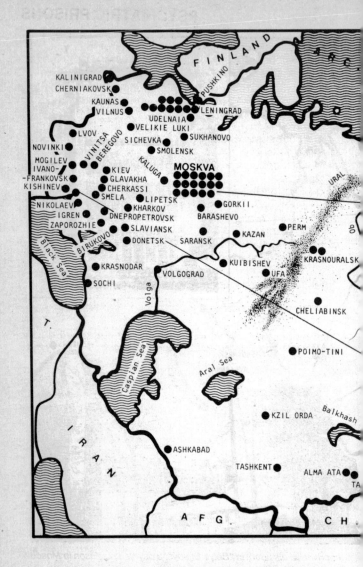

PSYCHIATRIC HOSPITALS AND SPECIAL PSYCHIATRIC PRISONS IN THE SOVIET UNION MOSCOW

1. The *Serbskii* Institute of Forensic Psychiatry, *Kropotkinskii Prospekt* 23 (metro station "Kropotkinskaya").

2. Psychiatric Hospital No. 14, Bekhterev Street 15.

Imprisoned dissident in "Belye Stolby", a psychiatric prison in Moscow (photo 1975).

(The proper English term is, of course, "mental hospital" A literal translation of the Russian *psikhbol'nitsa* (psychiatric hospital), however, has been used throughout the *Guidebook. – trans.*) Citizens who anger officialdom by demanding justice from the Procuracy or from the Presidium of the Supreme Soviet of the U.S.S.R. are often brought here. A special ward was opened in 1976. Aleksander *Argentov* is a prisoner here.

23

3. Psychiatric Hospital No. 7, *Institutskii Lane 5* (medical superintendent: Rubashov). Healthy people are imprisoned here for political reasons. Valentin *Ivanov,* for example, was brought here for having staged a one-man march demonstration to the Bol'shoi Theater with a placard reading, "I want to leave the U.S.S.R.", in 1978. Rubashov's diagnosis of Ivanov: "Misjudgment of the surrounding reality." Citizens petitioning the Presidium of the Supreme Soviet of the U.S.S.R. for a redress of grievances are often brought to this psychiatric prison for "examination".

4. Psychiatric Hospital No. 5, *Stolbovaya* (suburb of Moscow, located on the train route to Kursk). Vladimir *Avramenko* is one of a number of healthy political prisoners confined to this clinic. His crime: participating in anti-Soviet conversations.

5. The *Gannushkin* Psychiatric Hospital. Houses a special ward for political prisoners.

6. Psychiatric Hospital No. 15. Houses a ward for political prisoners.

7. Psychiatric Hospital No. 1 *("Kashchenko"). Zagorodnoe Highway 2.* Staff physicians: Morkovkin (medical superintendent), Belikov, Mazurskii, and Bel'skaya. Aleksei Popov, one of the hospital attendants at the "Kashchenko", is known among the patients for his sadism. One ward has been set aside for prisoners arrested by the K.G.B.

8. Psychiatric Hospital No. 3, *Matrosskaya Tishina 20.* Vasilii *Zhigalkin,* who was arrested for attempting to visit the American embassy, is one of the dissidents confined here. Prisoners here are kept in a separate ward under the sole jurisdiction of the K.G.B.

9. *Krasnopresnenskii* District Out-Patients Clinic for Psychiatric Diseases. Healthy prisoners here are confined together with mentally ill patients.

10. Out-Patients Clinic for Psychiatric Diseases No. 8 (medical superintendent: Volkov). Political prisoners are held here.

11. Psychiatric Hospital No. 13, *Lyublino,* Podmos-

kov'e (suburb of Moscow). Political prisoners are confined here.

12. The *Meshcherskii* Psychiatric Hospital. Contains wards for political prisoners.

13. Special Psychiatric Reception Center No. 2 of the Ministry of Interior, *Novoslobodskaya* Street 45, building no. 4. A reception center for dissidents sent here from the K.G.B.

14. Special Psychiatric Prison IZ-48/1. Housed in the *Matrosskaya Tishina* Prison, Matrosskaya Tishina Street.

15. Out-Patients Clinic for Psychiatric Diseases No. 13, *Moskva-Sevastopol'skii* Throughway 26–28. Accommodates four wards. Medical superintendent: Svishchev, tel. 1202255. One of the political prisoners here, Gavriil *Yan'kov,* a miner, was arrested for attempting to establish an independent labor union.

16. The Central Hospital for Clinical Psychiatry of the Moscow Region, *Moscow, Eighth of March Street 1* (ulitsa vos'mogo marta 1). Among the political prisoners confined here is Yurii *Valov.* His family's address: Sportivnaya Street 20/4, Tuchkovo, Ruza District, Moscow Region.

Psychiatric ward of the Odessa Region hospital in "Slobodka", Odessa city (see map of Odessa city)

PSYCHIATRIC PRISONS IN LENINGRAD

1. Psychiatric Hospital No. 5 *("Skvortsov-Stepanov"), Lebedev Street 39*. The Skvortsov-Stepanov Hospital serves as a prison for dissidents illegally declared *non compos mentis* by the state, including those arrested for their belief in God (such as Vladimir *Veretennikov* and Mikhail *Vorozhbit*). The medical superintendent, Ekaterina Kurakina, has repeatedly stated, "People who believe in God belong in a mental ward."

2. Psychiatric Hospital No. 6. Twenty-five people are confined to a single room in this psychiatric prison, and walks are not permitted. "Patients" are subjected to beatings by the hospital attendants. Lev *Konin*, one of the inmates here (1978), has informed us that, as a means of punishment, the prisoners are bound in a wet strait jacket and then tied to a bed. When the strait jacket dries, it compresses the body with frightful force. Two sadistic physicians here are named Tsvetkov and Bobrova.

3. The *Pryazhka* Psychiatric Hospital, *Maklin Street*. Political prisoners held here in secret captivity are confined to this hospital's special wards. The "Pryazhka" may be reached by bus nos. 2 and 100 from the center of the city.

4. Psychiatric Hospital no. 3. Vladimir *Borisov,* a well-known dissident and former inmate of this psychiatric prison, held hunger strikes here together with Viktor *Fainberg*. Known physicians: Popova, Isakov, Tobak, and Zhivotovskaya.

5. The *Vyborg* District Out-Patients Clinic for Psychiatric and Neurological Diseases. People known for their anti-Communist views are held here.

6. Out-Patients Clinic for Psychiatric Diseases on the Obvodnii Canal (tram nos. 10 and 19, but no. 50 from Moscow Station). Political prisoners are brought here by the K.G.B. for "examination".

7. Psychiatric Hospital No. 1 *("Kashchenko")*, Gatchina District. Special wards for political prisoners are maintained here.

8. Psychiatric Prison, *Lebedev Street* (part of the Kresty Prison complex). Notorious for its brutal conditions of confinement.

9. Psychiatric Hospital, *Pushkino,* Leningrad Region. Normal people arrested for political reasons are confined here together with insane inmates.

10. Psychiatric Hospital, *Udel'naya,* Leningrad Region. Special K.G.B. wards are maintained here. Public transportation: bus no. 75 to Ozerki stop; tram nos. 20, 21, or 28; or the electric train from the Finland Station.

*

PSYCHIATRIC PRISONS IN OTHER REGIONS

1. The Psychiatric Hospital of *Slavyansk,* Donetsk Region (Ukrainian S.S.R.). Viktor *Borovskii,* who was declared insane and confined here for holding a lecture on the works of Aleksandr Solzhenitsyn, has described maintenance system of the hospital as catastrophic and compared conditions to those of a prison, despite the fact that this facility is rated as "ordinary". (Soviet penal institutions are placed into various categories of severity: ordinary, intensified, hard, and strict or special regime etc. – *trans.*) Borovskii writes, "The hospital attendants are constantly drunk. They beat anyone that they happen to get a hold of. They rouse up the inmates in the middle of the night, taunt them, and make them dance." The names of these jailer attendants are Yurii Slepets and Arkadii Zhuravskii.

2. Psychiatric Hospital No. 15, *Khar'kov,* Khar'kov Region, (Ukrainian S.S.R.). Political prisoners are concealed here in special wards.

3. The Scientific Research Institute of Psychiatry, *Khar'kov.* Normal human beings who happen to think differently, are imprisoned here in this nest of arbitrary violence. Medical superintendent: Sosin. Staff physicians: Gritsenko, En', and the chief psychiatrist for the Khar'kov Region, Nikitin.

4. The Psychiatric Hospital of *Krasnoyarsk* (Krasnoyarsk Territory), *Kurchatov Street 14.* A psychiatric prison. Medical superintendent: Chistyakova.

5. The Psychiatric Hospital of *Poimo-Tiny,* Krasnoyarsk Territory. The medical superintendent of this psychiatric prison, Odezhkin, once declared to one of his "patients", the dissident Yurii *Belov,* "As long as the Voice of America defends your cause, you are a menace to society – and that means that legally you are not accountable for your own actions".

6. The Special Psychiatric Prison of *Sychëvka,* Smolensk Region (Facility No. YaO-100/5). One of the most terrifying psychiatric prisons in the Soviet Union. In an open letter smuggled out of the facility, the imprisoned dissident, Iosif *Terelya,* describes the inhuman punishments meted out to the inmates. Staff member, Al'bert Zelënov, physician.

7. The Psychiatric Hospital ("ordinary" regime) of *Beregovo, Transcarpathian* Region (Ukrainian S.S.R.). A psychiatric prison for political prisoners. Members of the staff: Irina Romanovich (medical superintendent), and the physicians Kirichuk (deputy medical superintendent) and Roman Bondar'.

8. The Special Psychiatric Hospital-Prison (in Russian, *spetspsikhbol'nitsa-tyur'ma*. The official name of these institutions, however, is *spetsbol'nitsa* (special psychiatric hospital). The word *tyur'ma* [prison] has been added in a number of cases by the author to indicate the prison-like conditions that reign in these facilities. — *trans*.) of *Dnepropetrovsk,* Dnepropetrovsk Region, (Ukrainian S.S.R.), located on the grounds of Prison No. 1. Leonid Plyushch, an Ukrainian dissident now living in the West, is a former inmate of this facility. The radio operator of the Soviet tanker *Tuapse,* Ivankov, who lived for a time in the West is confined here.

9. The Special Psychiatric Hospital of *Kazan'* (Tatar A.S.S.R.), Ershov Street 49, official address: ul. Ershova No. 49, p/ya UE 148/st. 6. Staff members: Col. Sveshnikov (prison superintendent), Valitov (medical superintendent), Major Saifulin (deputy prison superintendent). Many normal people are imprisoned here for their belief in God or, as in the case of N. *Plakhotnyuk,* who was arrested for distributing the proscribed journal *Ukrainskii Vestnik,* for their support of national liberation movements.

10. The psychiatric hospital ("ordinary" regime) in *Kaluga,* Kaluga Region. Normal people are concealed here among the insane. Vladimir *Rozhdestvenskii,* for example, has been incarcerated here since 1977 for having written leaflets advocating the introduction of democracy to the Soviet Union.

11. The psychiatric hospital in *Burashevo, Kalinin* Region. Political prisoners are confined here.

12. The psychiatric hospital ("ordinary" regime) in *Ovsyanka, Krasnoyarsk* Territory. Political prisoners are confined here.

13. The psychiatric hospital in *Mogilev,* Mogilev Region (Belorussian S.S.R.). Among the political prisoners jailed here for their religious beliefs is Mikhail *Kukobaka,* who was arrested for hanging an icon over his bed in the labor commune where he worked and for explaining the meaning of the Universal Declaration of Human Rights to his fellow workers. Kukobaka's "attending" physician: Nadezhda Drabkina.

14. The psychiatric hospital in *Krasnodar,* Krasnodar Territory, *Krasin Street 1.* Mikhail *Zhikharev,* one of the political prisoners here, was arrested for having demanded a just distribution of wages and bonuses in the factory where he worked. "Attending" physicians of the hospital: Ol'shevskaya and Anna Nichko.

15. The Special Psychiatric Hospital-Prison of *Chernyakhovsk, Kaliningrad* Region. Address: p/ya OM-216/st.2. General Pëtr *Grigorenko* has provided the world with information about this brutal political prison (see accompanying photograph).

16. The psychiatric hospital ("ordinary" regime) in *L'vov,* L'vov Region (Ukrainian S.S.R.), *Kul'tparkovaya Street 95.* Zinovii *Krasivskii,* an advocate of an independent Ukraine, is one of the dissidents imprisoned among the insane inmates.

17. The special psychiatric hospital-prison in *Alma-Ata,* Kazakh S.S.R. A place of confinement for political prisoners arrested for their belief in God and legally declared non-accountable for their actions.

18. The special psychiatric hospital-prison in *Smolensk,* Smolensk Region. Political prisoners are held here. Medical superintendent: Vyacheslav Bobrov.

19. The special psychiatric hospital-prison in *Talgar, Alma Ata* Region (Kazakh S.S.R.), Facility No. LA-155/7. Many political prisoners are confined here.

20. The psychiatric hospital ("ordinary" regime) in *Lipetsk, Voronezh* Region. Contains special wards for political prisoners.

21. The special psychiatric reception center in *Kiev-Darnitsa*, Ukrainian S.S.R. Houses wards for political prisoners.

22. The *Pavlov* Psychiatric Hospital ("ordinary" regime), *Kiev*. Efim *Pargamanik* has been confined here since 1977 for having persistently applied for emigration to Israel (Ward 22).

23. The special psychiatric hospital-prison (p/ya UYa-64/PB) in *Tashkent, Uzbek* S.S.R. Several wards for political prisoners. Inmates include those arrested for their belief in God.

24. The Out-Patients Clinic for Psychiatric and Neurological Diseases of *Velikie Luki, Pskov* Region. Contains wards for political prisoners.

25. The psychiatric hospital ("ordinary" regime) in *Sukhanovo, Pskov* Region. Political prisoners are confined here.

26. The Out-Patients Clinic for Psychiatric Diseases of *Sochi, Krasnodar* Territory. Many political prisoners are held here. Medical superintendent: N. Belyaeva; her address: Chaikovskaya Street 3, App. 61, Sochi. Belyaeva once declared to Mikhail *Zhikharev*, a dissident, "We are giving you treatment because you are against the Soviet state".

27. The psychiatric hospital ("ordinary" regime) in *Smela, Cherkassy* Region (Ukrainian S.S.R.). Separate wards are maintained here for political prisoners, including the Ukrainian Nikita *Plakhotnyuk*, an advocate of Ukrainian independence. His "doctors" say, "He is here because he is against the Soviet state". The fact that this is the only explanation to be heard in both *Smela* and *Sochi* only shows that instructions emanate from a single source – the K.G.B.

28. The psychiatric hospital ("ordinary" regime) in *Zaporozh'e*, Zaporozh'e Region (Ukrainian S.S.R.). Dissidents are known to be imprisoned here.

29. Psychiatric Hospital No. 2, *Chelyabinsk*, Chelyabinsk Region (Urals). Political prisoners are held in this psychiatric prison.

30. The psychiatric hospital ("ordinary" regime) in *Biryukovo*, Voroshilovgrad Region (Ukrainian S.S.R.). Wards for normal people persecuted by the K.G.B. are maintained here.

31. The Republican Psychiatric Hospital in *Novinki, Minsk* Region (Belorussian S.S.R.). Normal people are imprisoned together with mentally ill patients. Lidiya *Valendo*, for example, was imprisoned here for having applied for waiver of her Soviet citizenship and for emigration to the free world. The diagnosis of her attending physician, Nikolaenko: "Normal people do not emigrate from the Soviet Union."

32. The psychiatric hospital ("ordinary" regime) in *Kaliningrad*, Kaliningrad Region, *Aleksandr Nevskii Street 78-A*. A psychiatric prison for political prisoners.

33. The Republican Psychiatric Hospital in *Ufa*, Bashkir A.S.S.R. Special wards are maintained here for political prisoners.

34. The Republican Psychiatric Hospital in *Naujoji Vilnia* (New Vilnius), near Vilnius, Lithuanian S.S.R. Many dissidents, all healthy people, are imprisoned here.

29

35. The special psychiatric hospital-prison in *Kemerovo*, Kemerovo Region. Normal political prisoners are confined here with insane inmates. Prisoners from the surrounding camps who revolt against the harsh regimen there are placed in a special section of the hospital.

36. Psychiatric Hospital No. 1 ("ordinary" regime), *Donetsk*, Donetsk Region (Ukrainian S.S.R.). Special wards for political prisoners are maintained here.

37. The psychiatric hospital ("ordinary" regime) in *Nikolaev*, (Ukrainian S.S.R.). A prison for dissidents where the sadist physician Mariya Nikulina is notorious.

38. The special psychiatric hospital-prison in *Blagoveschensk*, Amur Region. Opened in 1972, known for the sadistic punishment meted out to political prisoners.

39. The special psychiatric hospital-prison in *Kzyl-Orda*, Kazakh S.S.R. Political prisoners are incarcerated here with mentally ill patients.

40. The special psychiatric hospital-prison in *Perm'*, Perm Region (Urals). Special wards for political prisoners are maintained here.

41. The psychiatric hospital ("ordinary" regime) in *Alekseevka* (60 kilometers from Alma-Ata) *Alma-Ata* Region (Kazakh S.S.R.). Soviet citizens of German origins in Kazakhstan who apply for emigration to the Federal Republic of Germany are sent here.

42. The psychiatric hospital in *Vinnitsa*, Vinnitsa Region, (Ukrainian S.S.R.), on *Pirogov Street*. The Ukrainian poet Iosif *Terelya* is imprisoned here in 38v.

43. The *Mogilëv* Region Psychiatric Hospital (Belorussian S.S.R.). Kurovkin was imprisoned here for discussing questions of democracy and human rights with workers. Ward superintendent: Myl'nikov; deputy medical superintendent: Kasperov.

44. The Psychiatric Clinic of the Medical Institute in *Kuibyshev*, Kuibyshev Region. Wards for "processing" political prisoners are maintained here.

45. The *Cherkassy* Region Psychiatric Hospital. The Ukrainian nationalist, N. *Plakhotnyuk*, is imprisoned here.

46. The psychiatric hospital in *Kaunas*, Lithuanian S.S.R., *Kuzmos* Street. Arvidas *Chekhanavichyus*, an advocate of Lithuanian independence, has been imprisoned here for six years. His mother, Prane Vasilyauskene, lives in Kaunas; tel. 61706.

47. The Republican Psychiatric Hospital in *Saransk*, Mordovian A.S.S.R., *Lesnaya Street 2*. The K.G.B. maintains special wards here for political prisoners.

48. The psychiatric institution in *Komsomol'skii*, near *Gor'kii*, Gor'kii Region (accommodating 16 wards). One of the political prisoners confined here is Mikhail *Sergeev*.

49. The Psychiatric Hospital of *Glavakha*, *Kiev* Region, (Ukrainian S.S.R.), p/b No. 18. Inmates here confined for their belief in God.

50. The City Psychiatric Hospital of *Kishinev*, Moldavian S.S.R. Special wards are maintained here for those imprisoned, among other things, for their belief in God.

51. The Psychiatric Hospital of *Ivano-Frankovsk*, Ivano-Frankovsk Region (Ukrainian S.S.R.). Vasilii *Sichko*, a Ukrainian arrested for having participated in a Ukrainian nationalist meeting, is imprisoned here.

52. The psychiatric hospital ("ordinary" regime) in *Vilnius*, Lithuanian S.S.R. Normal people are sent to the special wards here by the K.G.B. for "examination" and often remain as long as one to one and a half years.

53. The psychiatric hospital in *Beregovo*, Transcarpathian Region, Ukrainian S.S.R. Normal people arrested for participating in the Ukrainian independence movement and declared legally incapable of accounting for their actions are imprisoned here.

54. The Volgograd Region Psychiatric Hospital in *Volgograd*. The K.G.B. secretly maintains political prisoners in a special section here.

55. The Republican Psychiatric Hospital in *Ashkhabad*, Turkmen S.S.R. Political prisoners, declared "insane" for their belief in God, are confined in a special section.

EXTERMINATION CAMPS

This particularly horrifying map denotes those camps in the U.S.S.R. where prisoners, forced to work under dangerously unhealthy conditions for the Soviet war machine, face a virtually certain death.

These camps may be divided into three groups:
1. camps that almost no one ever comes out of alive again (the prisoners work in uranium mines and uranium enrichment plants);

2. camps where the lives and health of prisoners are exposed to dangerous work in the arms industry or in the armed services (the prisoners perform high-risk duties in military nuclear plants or clean the nozzles of atomic-powered submarines);

3. camps where prisoners are used for dangerously unhealthy jobs that lead to work disability and fatal illness (the prisoners operate glass-polishing machines, cleave mica, or work with lacquer enamels without ventilation).

EXTERMINATION CAMPS

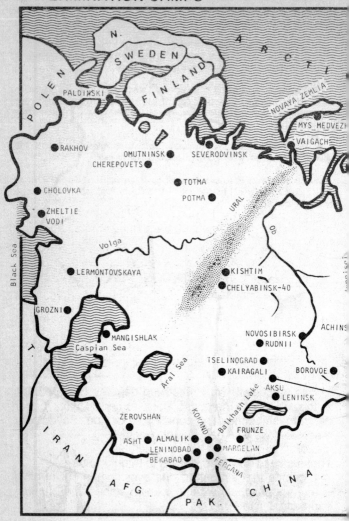

Here follows a list of these camps[1]:

1) *Paldiski* Bay, Estonian S.S.R. – cleaning of the nozzles of atomic-powered submarines;

2) *Severodvinsk*, Arkhangel'sk Region – cleaning of the nozzles of atomic-powered submarines;

3) *Omutninsk*, Kirov Region – uranium mining; the entire work area is exposed to radiation;

[1]Those place names listed without the name of a Soviet Socialist Republic (S.S.R.) are located in the Russian Soviet Federated Socialist Republic (R.S.F.S.R.) – *trans.*

4) *Tot'ma,* Vologda Region – underground uranium mining, uranium enrichment facility;

5) *Cherepovets,* Vologda Region – open-pit uranium mining, uranium enrichment facility; an extensive around the mine is exposed to radiation;

6) *Cholovka,* Zhitomir Region, Ukrainian S.S.R. – underground uranium mining;

7) *Zhëltye Vody,* Dnepropetrovsk Region, Ukrainian S.S.R. – underground uranium mining;

8) *Lermontov,* Stavropol' Territory – underground uranium mining;

9) vicinity of *Rakhov,* Transcarpathian Region (restricted military district) – open-pit uranium mining; the surrounding area is exposed to radiation;

10) *Groznyi,* Chechen-Ingusch A.S.S.R. – underground uranium mining, uranium enrichment facility;

11) *Mangyshlak* peninsula (Caspian Sea), Kazakh S.S.R. – uranium mining, uranium enrichment facility; work on nuclear reactor;

12) *Aksu,* Kazakh S.S.R. – uranium mining, uranium enrichment facility; the entire region is exposed to a high-level of radiation;

13) *Tselinograd,* Kazakh S.S.R. – open-pit uranium mining; the entire work area is exposed to radiation;

14) *Borovoe,* Kazakh S.S.R. – open-pit uranium mining; the work area is exposed to radiation; although a large health resort is located in this very vicinity, the government has characteristically refrained from warning holiday guests against the dangerous radiation;

15) *Karagaily,* Kazakh S.S.R. – open-pit and underground uranium mining;

16) *Al'malyk,* Kazakh S.S.R. – underground uranium mining;

17) *Rudnyi,* Kazakh S.S.R. – uranium mining, uranium enrichment facility;

18) *Achinsk,* Krasnoyarsk Territory – open-pit uranium mining, uranium enrichment facility in the "Glinozemnyi" plant;

19) *Leninsk,* Uzbek S.S.R. – underground uranium mining, uranium enrichment facility;

20) *Fergana,* Uzbek S.S.R. – underground uranium mining, uranium enrichment facility;

21) *Margelan,* Uzbek S.S.R. – underground uranium mining, uranium enrichment facility;

22) *Kokand,* Uzbek S.S.R. – underground uranium mining;

23) *Leninabad,* Tadzhik S.S.R. – underground uranium mining, uranium enrichment facility; the high level of radiation in the area constitutes a serious health hazard;

24) *Sovetabad,* Tadzhik S.S.R. – underground uranium mining;

25) *Bekabad.* Tadzhik S.S.R. – underground uranium mining, uranium enrichment facility;

26) *Asht,* Tadzhik S.S.R. – underground uranium mining; area exposed to high-level radiation;

27) *Zeravshan,* Tadzhik S.S.R. – underground uranium mining, uranium enrichment facility;

28) *Frunze,* Kirgiz S.S.R. – underground uranium mining, uranium enrichment facility;

29) *Chelyabinsk-40,* Chelyabinsk Region – work in a nuclear warhead plant;

30) *Kyshtym,* Chelyabinsk Region – mining and enrichment of uranium for further use in the nuclear warhead plant in Chelyabinsk-40;

31) *Novosibirsk* (northern settlement), Novosibirsk Region – work in the "Khimkontsentrat" and "Khimapparat" plants for the production of nuclear warheads;

32) *Oimyakon,* Yakutsk A.S.S.R. – underground uranium mining;

33) *Slyudyanka,* Irkutsk Region – mica-cleaving (women's camp);

34) "Dubrovlag" (Pot'ma), Mordovian A.S.S.R. – glass-grinding without ventilation;

35) *Vaigach* Island (Arktic Ocean) – uranium mining, uranium enrichment facility;

36) Cape Medvezhii, *Novaya Zemlya* – uranium mining, uranium enrichment facility;

37) *Tar'ya* Bay, Kamchatka Region – cleaning of the nozzles of atomic-powered submarines;

38) *Rakushka* Bay, Primorsk Territory – cleaning of the nozzles of atomic-powered submarines;

39) *Ol'ga* Bay, Primorsk Territory – uranium enrichment facility;

40) *Kavalerovo,* Primorsk Territory – open-pit uranium mining; danger zone containing deadly radiation;

41) *Shamor* Bay, Primorsk Territory – uranium mining, uranium enrichment facility; zone of deadly radioactivity.

Our research center has conducted a special investigation of the death camps in the Soviet Union. Unfortunately, we were not able to include all our findings in the notes to the map. Those interested, however, may receive additional information on request.

REGIONAL
PRISONS AND CAMPS

MOSCOW REGION

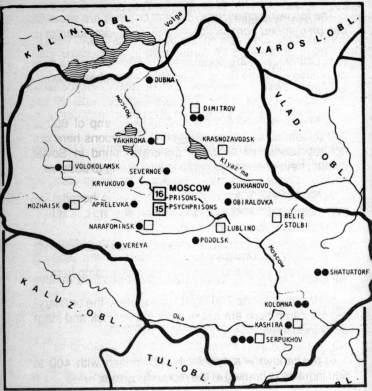

MOSCOW REGION (area: 47000 sq. km.; pop.: 12,9)

The cities of the Moscow Region are saturated with camps and prisons. Thirty-one penal facilities are located in the city of Moscow alone, while another 18 camps and ten prisons can be found on the remaining territory of the region.

The following cities, where penal facilities are situated, can be reached from Moscow by electric commuter train:

1. *Obiralovka* – the approximately 1000 prisoners from an ordinary-regime camp[1] here work in mechanics workshops;

2. *Kryukovo* – here there is a model camp of 600 to 700 prisoners, including foreigners. Conditions here are not representative of those generally found in Soviet camps; nevertheless the camp is interesting to observe;

3. *Stolbovaya* – location of a psychiatric hospital or, for all practical purposes, a psychiatric prison;

4. *Severnoe,* a village 46 kilometers north of Moscow on the way to *Dmitrov* – 1500 prisoners are working in the military sphere in an ordinary-regime camp here;

5. *Aprelevka* – the 700 to 800 prisoners in the ordinary-regime camp here are put to work in the brick and slag-block industries;

6. *Sukhanovo* – a special K.G.B. prison with 400 to 500 inmates is housed in the monastery here;

7. *Lyublino* – no camps here; there is, however, a prison here for 500 to 600 inmates. Recalcitrant prisoners are transferred to this stricter facility from the camps as a punitive measure.

8. Podol'sk – strict-regime camp for 1200 prisoners who are assigned to construction work in the military sector; ordnance proving grounds are also located here.

[1]See translator's note, p. 27.

Other cities in the Moscow Region, where penal facilities are located, include:

1. *Mozhaisk* – a city famous for its role in the heroic defense of Moscow against Hitler's invading forces in World War II, it is now the site of an intensified-regime camp for 1500 prisoners assigned to work in the reinforced concrete production industry. Inmates caught breaking the rules of the camp are often transferred to the city prison. The prison accommodates 1000 to 1200 occupants;

2. *Volokalamsk* (north of Mozhaisk) – site of an ordinary-regime camp where 1000 prisoners are assigned to construction work. Volokalamsk also accommodates a jail that, in addition to its normal function as a local penal facility, is also used to alleviate overcrowding in Moscow's eleven city prisons...

3. *Naro-Fominsk* – here there is a camp for 800 to 900 prisoners (used in construction work) and a prison for 500 to 600 inmates. Those who violate camp rules risk being transferred to the prison in this city. *Mendelevich* suffered this fate as a punishment for wearing a yarmulke and for observance of religious practices;

4. *Yakhroma* (north of Moscow on the road to *Dubna*) – ordinary-regime camp for approximately 1000 prisoners assigned to construction work and to road building and repair. Site of a remand prison for 800 inmates;

5. *Dubna* – ordinary-regime camp for 500 to 600 prisoners assigned to construction in housing and in the industrial field;

6. *Dmitrov* – ordinary-regime camp for 500 to 600 prisoners who do construction work; strict-regime camp for 600 to 800 prisoners used in the production of building-stones; prison for 700 to 800 prisoners;

7. *Krasnozavodsk* – ordinary-regime camp for 1000 prisoners in industrial construction;

8. *Noginsk* – strict-regime camp of approximately 1500 prisoners assigned to construction and repair work at

any of the several military institutes or ordnance proving grounds (restricted area) in the region;

9. *Shaturtorf* – two strict-regime camps, each with 600 prisoners used in the production of peat;

10. *Kolomna* – ordinary-regime camp for 600 to 700 prisoners used in construction; strict-regime camp for 500 to 600 prisoners who work in mechanical engineering plants under noxious conditions;

11. *Kashira* – ordinary-regime camp for 1200 prisoners used in construction work; remand prison for 600 to 700 inmates;

12. *Serpukhov* – remand prison for 1000 inmates; three ordinary-regime camps, each with 1000 to 1100 prisoners assigned to construction work in the housing and military sectors.

An ambulance of the Soviet Red Cross brings dissidents to the Kashchenko Psychiatric Hospital (Moscow), where there is a prison ward.

MOSCOW CITY

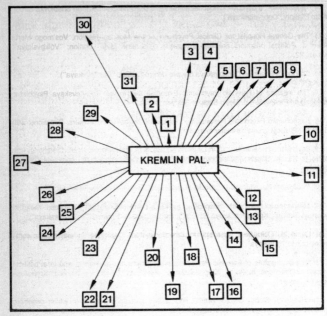

KREMLIN PAL.

Schematic plan of the penal facilities in Moscow. See list below.

Moscow city
Schematic plan of camps, prisons, and psychiatric prisons in Moscow

1. *"Lubyanka",* central K.G.B. prison on Dzerzhinskii Square (Metro Station: "Dzerzhinskii Square").

2. *"Metro"* Prison on Mir Prospect, behind the Botanical Gardens (Metro Station: "Prospect Mira").

3., 4., 5. Kazan' Station, Severnyi (Northern) Station, and Leningrad Station. In the basements of all three stations, there are underground prisons (Metro Station: "Komsomol'skaya").

6. *Gannushkin* Psychiatric Hospital. In reality, a psychiatric prison. Directions: to Metro Station "Sokolniki" or bus no. 173 to the stop marked "Sokolniki".

7., 8., 9. *Matrosskaya Tishina* Prison; psychiatric prison no. IZ-48/1 (also called "Matrosskaya Tishina"); psychiatric hospital no. 3 (in fact, a psychiatric prison). All three are located on Matrosskaya Tishina Street (nos. 4–20). Metro Station: "Izmailovskaya" and "Preobrazhenskaya".

10. Psychiatric Hospital No. 5, *"Belye Stolby"* (in fact, a psychiatric prison). Directions: electric commuter train to Kursk Station (Metro Station: "Kurskaya").

11. Ukrainian K.G.B. prison at Sukhanov Station. May be reached from Kursk Station (Directions: "Kurskaya").

12. *"Lefortovo",* special K.G.B. prison. Directions: to Metro Station "Baumanskaya" and then with the tram to stop marked "Energeticheskaya Street".

40

13. Out-Patients Clinic for Psychiatric Diseases No. 13. Political prisoners are held in special cells in Ward No. 4. Moskva-Sevastopol'skii Throughway 26–28. Tel.: 1202255.

14. *"Shablovka"*, a psychiatric hospital (in reality, a psychiatric prison), on Shablovka Street. Metro Station: "Dobryninskaya".

15. The Central Hospital for Clinical Psychiatry of the Moscow Region, Vos'mogo Marta Street 1. Political prisoners are kept in special cells here. Metro Station: "Volkovskaya"; bus no. 22.

16. Children's Prison on Danilovskaya Square (Metro Station: "Danilovskaya").

17. The Institute of Forensic Psychiatric Expertise (known as Solov'evskaya Psychiatric Hospital) on Pavlov Street. Metro Station: "Oktyabr'skaya".

18. *Kashchenko* Psychiatric Hospital; special section for political prisoners. Directions: with metro to "Profsoyuznaya", transfer to tram no. 14 or 23.

19. Psychiatric Hospital No. 13 in Lyublino (in reality, a psychiatric prison). Directions: with metro to Kazan' Station ("Komsomol'skaya Square"); then with electric commuter train to Lyublino.

20. Psychiatric Hospital No. 14, special cells for dissidents; Bekhterev Street 15.

21. *Meshcherskii* Psychiatric Hospital (in reality, a psychiatric prison). Directions: metro to Severnyi Station ("Komsomol'skaya Square"); then with electric train to "Meshcherskaya".

22. Camp at "Obiralovka" train station. Directions: from Kursk Station with electric commuter train to "Kurskaya".

23. *Serbskii* Institute of Forensic Psychiatry, where there are specialists who treat political prisoners. Directions: metro to "Kropotkinskaya", then with bus to stop marked "Kropotkinskaya Prospekt".

24. Institute of Blood. On the twelfth floor, there is a special ward in which prisoners are used as guinea pigs for medical experiments. Directions: metro to "Kutuzovskaya".

25. Krasnopresnenskii District Out-Patients Clinic for Psychiatric Diseases, where there are specialists who treat political prisoners. Directions: metro to "Krasnopresnenskaya".

26. *Krasnaya Presnya* Prison (transit prison). Directions: metro to "Krasnopresnenskaya".

27. Special prison for army officers in Pokrovsko-Streshnevo district. Directions: metro to "Sokol"; then with bus no. 88 or 176 or with trolley bus no. 12 or 70 to "Pokrovskoe-Streshnevo".

28. *Butyrka* Prison, stands opposite the Savelovskii Station. Directions: metro to "Novo-slobodskaya".

29. Special Reception Room No. 2 of the Ministry of Interior. Directions: metro to "Novo-slobodskaya".

30. Camp in Kryukovo. Directions: metro to Leningrad Station (Metro Station: "Komsomol'-skaya Square"); transfer to electric commuter train and alight at Kryukov Station.

31. Psychiatric Hospital No. 12 (in reality, a psychiatric prison). Directions: metro to "Sokol", then with bus no. 66 or 68 to "Pechann'e Street".

CITY OF MOSCOW

1. On Moscow's Dzerzhinskii Square, directly across from the *Dzerzhinskaya* metro station, stand two semi-detached buildings joined together to form a single structure; here you will find the headquarters of the K.G.B. of the U.S.S.R. and the cells of its special prison, "Lubyanka" (see photograph).

The older building on the left consists of four floors, as a view from its inner courtyard will show. The rooms on the top floor of the new building on the right are blocked off from the outside world; only the guard's room on the far right has a window. Prison cells are located directly under Dzerzhinskii Square, where residents of Moscow walk every day. A prison courtyard, enclosed by a high balustrade, is maintained on the roof of the structure. Architectural adornments decorating the corners of the building complex conceal watchtowers manned by soldiers armed with machine guns.

While we have not been able to ascertain the exact capacity of the prison, we are nevertheless in a position to say that, of the 200 cells in the complex, about half

were built to accommodate four inmates each. The other half consists of solitary confinement cells.

Prisoners who are of special interest to the K.G.B. are brought to *"Lubyanka"* for confinement. Thus, *Solzhenitsyn, Powers* (the American pilot), the alleged conspirators of the so-called "doctors' plot", and *Beria,* himself a former K.G.B. head, have all been inmates here.

2. Not far from the center of the city, next to the *Savelovskii* train station, you will find the *"Butyrka",* one of the largest prisons in Moscow.

In 1957, Chrushchëv announced the planned closing of the "Butyrka" (and the labor camps in the Soviet Union). An apartment house, however, was erected in front of the entrance to the prison instead, blocking all view of it from the street. The apartment house tenants are all employed by the K.G.B. or the Ministry of Interior. The prison remains in operation. In the drawing, you can see the double metal gates of the prison as they open up towards the façade of the apartment house. A paddy wagon is entering through the gates of the "Butyrka" with a new group of prisoners. Left of the gates is a little door to an office in the prison where the relatives of the inmates are informed by the officer on duty whether their loved ones are still alive, under investigation, or in transport. The office is open to all. We therefore recommend the tourist to visit it.

The prison block consists of no fewer than 25 large buildings with rather spacious cells for 25 or even 50 occupants. Seventy to 100 inmates, however, are in fact often locked up at a time in a single cell. A special building is maintained for political prisoners and, next to it, one for those sentenced to death. An aerial photograph of the entire prison complex will also expose the notorious *Pugachëv Tower* to view, where nightly executions by firing squad are carried out. Taking pictures of penal facilities is prohibited in the Soviet Union. Those who violate this law put their freedom at risk.

3. *"Lefortovo"*, one of the strictest K.G.B. prisons in the Soviet Union, is located in Moscow's *Baumanskii*

BUTYRKA PRISON

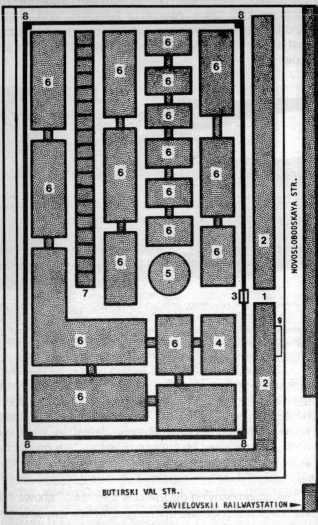

Map of Butyrka Prison in Moscow.

city district on *Aerodinamicheskaya* Street next to the
Central Aerodynamics and Hydrodynamics Institute
(ZAGI). As in the case of "Lubyanka", only political pris-
oners are confined here. Former inmates of "Lefortovo"

include such well-known figures from the dissident movement as Yurii *Orlov,* Aleksandr *Ginsburg,* and Anatolii *Shcharanskii. Solzhenitsyn* and Georgii Vins spent their last night in the Soviet Union here before being sent into exile.

A paddy wagon (voronok), with prisoners inside, waits for the gates of Butyrka Prison to open. The multi-storied apartment house on the right was built to conceal the prison from open view. Behind the gates, one can see the the fortress-like prison walls.

The photograph of 'Lefortovo" shows a series of gloomy, four-story buildings connected together by a corridor. One building is used for administrative purposes, while another six serve as areas of detention. Interrogations, accompanied by the use of torture, are conducted in the administration building.

The accompanying diagram of "Lefortovo" shows that the prison buildings are, from an overhead view, arranged in the shape of a fan. The inside walls of the buildings are lined with suspension ladders and with the doors leading to the prison cells. The empty space between the floor landings is closed off by a net at every level. There had in the past been some instances of prisoners who, exhausted by the endless interrogations and otherwise driven to utter despair, committed suicide by throwing themselves into the stairwell. As in the case of the Butyrka prison, anyone can visit the information office at the "Lefortovo", introduce himself to the relatives of political prisoners, and talk with them.

4. The *Serbskii Institute* of Forensic Psychiatry is in fact a psychiatric prison where political dissidents are confined for several months following a so-called "expert examination". In the view of such "professional psychiatrists" as Snezhkovskii and Daniil Lunts, under whose guidance the torture in the "institute" is carried out, anyone who is discontented with the Soviet regime or who has attempted to escape from this "Socialist paradise" is certainly insane and must be treated. Compulsory medical treatment must also be administered to those who try to disseminate religious ideas.

The Serbskii prison, like all others in Moscow, is surrounded by a high fence; entrance is prohibited. You may, however, at least see this horrifying place from the street (Kropotkinskii Street, *Kropotkinskaya* metro station) and read the many descriptions of it by its former inmates, especially those by *Bukovskii* and *Fainberg*.

5. The basements of the Moscow train stations "Kazan'" "Severnyi" (North), and *"Leningrad"* are used as prisons for those arrested while traveling or for those awaiting transport to another penal facility. The average Muscovite is generally unaware of the existence of these prisons.
Those, however, who have passed through these dark underground chambers know them very well.

Metro station: *"Kazanskaya"* (see map).

In Soviet criminal law, separate investigating authorities and courts exist for different occupations. A soldier, for example, does not answer to the same prosecutor or judge as, say, a transport worker. Separate penal facilities are also maintained. A transport worker in Moscow found guilty of a crime may find himself in the *"Metro"* prison on *Mir Prospekt,* which is hidden, however, from street view by the Botanical Gardens. Convicted military personnel, on the other hand, are sent to the *Pokrovskoe–Streshnevo* prison on Leningradskoe Highway behind the Voenno-Vozdushnye Sily area.

Every day, thousands of prisoners are routed through Moscow, a central transit point in the Soviet penal system, for destinations in other parts of the country. The routing usually occurs at night. The inmates are taken from their temporary prisons to the trains, and then from their transit cells in the basements of Moscow's railroad stations to their final place of servitude. Five to six thousand prisoners a day await transfer in the huge transit prison, *"Presnya"*, in *Krasnaya Presnya* District. The administration authorities of the "Presnya" are known for their depravity, tyranny, and cruelty. The turnover of prisoners in this facility, moreover, is so great that lodging a complaint here is impossible.

It is a relatively easy matter to count the number of paddy wagons tearing through the gloomy gates of the "Presnya" at night with their concealed cargo. The 30 to 40 people packed into each transport are squeezed in so tightly together that they have to carry their belongings on their heads. *Solzhenitsyn* has portrayed these nocturnal journeys through Moscow with great lucidity.

Psychiatric hospitals as well as penal facilities officially designated as prisons are maintained by the authorities in Moscow to punish independently-minded or religious citizens.

Victims are also brought to the official Special Building of Psychiatric Prison IZ-48/1, *Matrosskaya Tishina* Prison, Matrosskaya Tishina Street. Treatment of the inmates in this inferno are appalling. Mentally healthy human beings are administered heavy doses of neuroleptic drugs. Recalcitrant inmates are held bound for hours or even days in a wet strait jacket. Once the strait jacket dries, the victim's body becomes compressed as if in a vice. Prisoners, moreover, are beaten by so-called hospital attendants, who in fact are criminals, and subjected to electric shocks at the slightest provocation. Evidence of all these terrifying methods has long been known to the entire world; the Soviet government, however, continues to practice them.

Kropotkinskaya Square and Surrounding Area

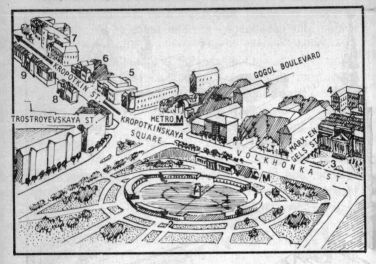

1. Kropotkinskaya Metro Station; 2. Moskva Swimming Pool; 3. Pushkin Art Museum; Karl Marx and Friedrich Engels Museum; 5. Soviet Peace Committee; 6. Aleksandr Pushkin Museum; 7. Natural Science Club; 8. Lev Tol'stoi Museum; 9. Academy of Art of the U.S.S.R. The arrow on Kropotkin Street (upper left) points in the direction of the Serbskii Institute.

Mentally sound but politically uncomfortable citizens are victim to the same practices in special wards of ordinary psychiatric hospitals in Moscow. These hospitals, however, are in fact disguised psychiatric prisons. A list of these facilities, their addresses, and directions on how to find them follows:

1. The *Kashchenko* Psychiatric Hospital, Zagorodnoe Highway 2 (f. 23). The hospital is located only a few blocks' walk from the metro station along Donskaya Street.

2. Psychiatric Hospital No. 14, *Bekhterev* Street 15 is

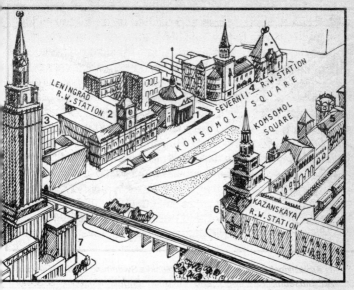

1. Komsomol'skaya Metro Station; 2. Leningrad Station; 3. International Post Office; 4. Yaroslavl' Station (Northern or Severnyi Station); 5. Main Club Building of the Railroad Workers; 6. Kazan' Station; 7. Hotel "Leningradskaya".

notorious as a reception center for citizens who persist in demanding their rights in the offices of the Procuracy or the Presidium of the Supreme Soviet of the U.S.S.R. The complaints tend to cease, however, after these people have been exposed here to a "cure".

A similar facility, Psychiatric Hospital No. 7 on *Institutskii* Lane 9, has served as a "medical institution" for those, for example, who have attempted to establish a council of Soviet labor unions independent of party control. Supporters of the free labor movement in the Soviet Union continued unintimidated to fight for their cause to this day, despite the ever-present threat of imprisonment in a psychiatric prison. Here is the report of one such labor rightist who fell victim to the state's arbitrariness:

"...Afterwards, I was approached by an official, whom I had not met before and who refused to identify himself, in the reception room of the Presidium of the Supreme Soviet of the U.S.S.R. Following a short conversation with him and a repetition of that which I had already explained to other officials, I was asked into the adjoining room. Not anticipating anything sinister, I consented. After having entered the room (at the end of a corridor), I was requested to wait. The official then went out. Immediately upon his departure, four men dressed in white uniforms entered the room and ordered me to follow them. I refused and said that I was healthy, upon which they grabbed me, threw a mask over my face, and carried me through an inner door and out onto the street, where an ambulance with a red cross painted on it was waiting for me. They stuffed me into the vehicle like a sack of potatoes and took me to Psychiatric Hospital No. 14, or so I was told. I soon found myself talking to the physician on duty in the presence of some other people. The physician said to them openly, 'The patient is inexplicably obsessed with his quest for justice. There are signs, furthermore, of a persecution complex'. And so, I was thrown in together with the 'loonies' for having joined the efforts of other workers to establish a labor union independent of the VTsSPS (The Central All-Union Council of Trade Unions)." – From a despatch of one of the organizers of the Soviet free-labor movement, *Klebanov.*

Another "patient" in Psychiatric Hospital No. 7, Valentin *Ivanov,* was arrested for marching to the Bol'shoi Theater with a placard reading, "I want to leave the U.S.S.R." The diagnosis of the "physicians": "Misjudgement of the surrounding reality." The diagnosis was signed by the physician Rubashëv. Have him called into the reception room when you visit the hospital, and talk to him.

3. *"Belye Stolby",* a psychiatric prison ("Kursk" railroad line to *Stolbovaya,* 15 to 20 minutes from Moscow). Healthy political prisoners are confined here together with the mentally ill. Ask to visit Vladimir *Avramenko,* a "patient" imprisoned for "anti-Soviet" views.

4. The psychiatric hospital-prison at *Matrosskaya Tishi-*

na Street 20 (As we know, this is not the only prison on this street…). Here again are dissidents held for allegedly medical reasons.

5. The *Meshcherskii* Psychiatric Prison. Here there is a special ward where normal human beings are "treated" for having criticized the CPSU dictatorship.

A very rare photograph, probably the first of its kind. A "box" or isolation cell in the K.G.B. prison "Lubyanka" in Moscow. As you can imagine, the photographer took this picture at the risk of being thrown into it himself.

6. Psychiatric Hospital No. 15. Imprisoned dissidents are forcibly "treated" in concealed special wards here.

7. Special Psychiatric Reception Center No. 2, *Novoslobodskaya Street 15,* building No. 4. This psychiatric prison falls under the jurisdiction of the Ministry of Interior and the K.G.B. Dissidents are sent here from the provinces. After having been confined here for a time, they are returned to psychiatric hospitals in their home areas.

8. Psychiatric Hospital No. 18, *Lyublino* ("Severnyi" railroad line, 10 to 15 minutes from Moscow). Politically uncomfortable people are held here in what is called a medical facility, but what in fact is a psychiatric prison.

9. In Moscow, there are several out-patient psychiatric clinics in which dissidents are held in confinement. Seen from the outside, they look quite innocuous. They serve the function of supervising public mental health. In fact, however, they have been converted into small psychiatric prisons.

We know of only two such facilities in Moscow: The *Krasnopresnenskii* District Out-Patients Clinic for Psychiatric Diseases and Out-Patient Clinic for Psychiatric Diseases No. 8.

Altogether we know of 23 penal facilities in Moscow. It is highly likely, however, that there are others that we have not yet been informed of.

THE SPECIAL K.G.B. PRISON
IN MOSCOW-LEFORTOVO

Here you can see a map and photograph of this frightful prison. The photograph, secretly taken from the roof of the neighboring building, shows what a gloomy and depressing place the "Lefortovo" is.

The prison, however, is even more horrifying from the inside. In it reigns a death-like, oppressive darkness. Pris-

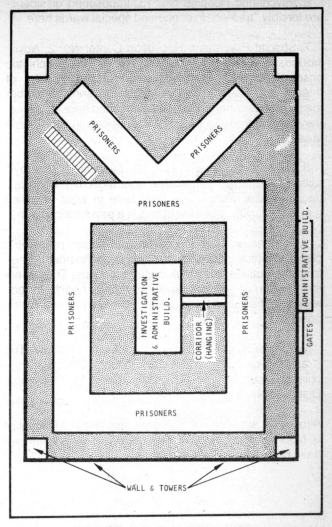

oners here are thrown into solitary confinement for the slightest provocation. The solitary confinement cells are kept at cool temperatures. The floors are covered with water. The cells lack a bed and sometimes even a bench.

Here is a report from A. Sh.: "I spent 28 days in solitary confinement cell no. 3 in the basement of Lefortovo Prison. Not having a bed, I had to stand up to my ankles in water the whole time. I was given a daily ration of 300 grams of bread, twice a day a mug of water. After a few days in a standing position, I began to fall over. Soon I found myself sitting in the water and filth on the floor of the cell."

There have also been prisoners in these cells who have never come out again. Physicians, for example, falsely accused by the state of poisoning their patients, have died here, only to be posthumously rehabilitated.

One of the bitter jokes circulating in the Soviet Union runs as follows: "According to the constitution of the U.S.S.R., every citizen has a right to a posthumous rehabilitation."

But even without these killings, the victims of the K.G.B. are sufficiently tortured here: exhausting interrogations, complete isolation, intimidation, threats of family persecution, or being placed in a room with thugs already incited to attack them. There are several methods that the K.G.B. has at its disposal to extract "voluntary confessions".

The map and photograph also show the central prison building where interrogations are held. Inmates about to be interrogated are brought here through a suspended corridor attached to the building.

An aerial view would show that the prison buildings of "Lefortovo" are arranged in the form of a fan. Their inner walls are lined with suspension ladders and cell doors. The empty spaces between landings have been spanned with nets so as to prevent desparate prisoners from committing suicide by throwing themselves into the stairwells. This has happened in the past.

Photograph of the special K.G.B. prison "Lefortovo". Solzhenitsyn spent his last night here before his expulsion from the Soviet Union. Tortures and executions by firing squad take place here. Its very name evokes fear in the Soviet Union.

The photograph was taken from above: a) on the right (foreground) is the prison building. In its deep cellars are the notorious "icy" isolation cells. Ice forms on the walls of the cells even in the summer; b) on the left is the investigative and administration building, in which the examining magistrates of the K.G.B. "work" day and night by interrogating dissidents and "enemies of the people" – that is, human beings fighting for fundamental human rights; c) as you can see, these two structures are connected by a corridor through which prisoners are led from the prison area to the examining magistrates; d) under the prison courtyard, there is another prison building. There are five four-story buildings in the Lefortovo prison complex (photo 1976).

Countless prisoners have passed through these corridors, including the American pilot, *Powers,* and dissidents such as *Solzhenitsyn* and *Bukovskii.* Innocent victims of the Soviet regime continue to languish in the countless cells of this special strict-regime K.G.B. prison. *Shcharanskii,* who was arrested and eventually sentenced to 15 years for wishing to emigrate to Israel, was imprisoned here while under investigation. He is now an inmate at a prison in *Chistopol',* Tatar A.S.S.R. (see map of and notes on Tatar A.S.S.R.).

Cell for four inmates in Lefortovo (Moscow), a special K.G.B. prison.

55

LENINGRAD CITY

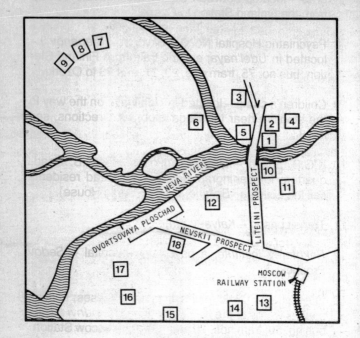

LENINGRAD
(pop.: 4 600 000)
Key to the Sketch of the City

1. *"Kresty"* - *Arsenal'naya* Quay. Tram no. 30 to Arsenal'-naya Quay.

2. Special Psychiatric Prison – Akademik *Lebedev Street* 2. Tram no. 30 to Arsenal'naya stop.

3. Psychiatric Hospital No. 5; here there is a special ward under the control of the K.G.B. – Akademik *Lebedev Street 39*. Tram no. 30 to Akademik Lebedev Street.

4. Women's prison – *Arsenal'naya Street*. Bus no. 107; tram nos. 3, 8, 19, and 38.

5. Hotel Leningrad.

6. Out-Patients Clinic for Psychiatric and Neurological Diseases; houses special wards of the K.G.B. – *Komsomol Street,* Vyborgskii District.

7. Men's camp; farm work, vegetable deliveries to Leningrad – located between Ozerki and Shuvalovo; train from the Finland Station to Ozerki.

8. Psychiatric Hospital No. 3 ("Skvortsov-Stepanov") – located in Udel'naya; electric train from Finland Station, bus no. 75, tram nos. 20, 21, and 23 to Ozerki.

9. Children's camp – located in Udel'naya on the way to the stadium near the Bega Club; for directions, see no. 8.

10. K.G.B. prison – Liteinyi Prospekt, in K.G.B. Headquarters for Leningrad Region; Leningrad residents call the building "Bol'shoi Dom" (the Big House).

11. Transit prison – Kalyaev Street.

12. Bekhterev Institute, a psychiatric hospital – Sedov Prospekt.

13. Out-Patients Clinic for Psychiatric Diseases; houses special wards of the K.G.B. – on the Obvodnyi Canal; bus no. 50, tram nos. 10 and 19 from Moscow Station.

14. Psychiatric Hospital No. 1 ("Kashchenko"); in reality, a psychiatric prison – from Baltic Station to Gatchina; from there on foot to Rozhdestvenskoe.

15. Psychiatric hospital in Pushkino – from Vitebsk Station to Detskoe Selo.

16. The Pavlov Hospital for Psychiatric and Neurological Diseases; contains special K.G.B. wards for dissidents – bus no. 49 to line 15 on Vasil'evskii Island.

17. Psychiatric Hospital No. 2; in reality, a psychiatric prison – located on Pryazhka River Quay 2, near Makulin Street next to the house where the poet Aleksandr Blok once lived; bus nos. 2, 49, and 100 as well as trolley bus no. 1 to Admiralteiskii Zavod stop.

18. Kazanskii Sobor – anti-religious propaganda museum.

THE KRESTY PRISON (K.G.B. PRISON AND PRISON HOSPITAL) IN LENINGRAD

A large monument of Lenin (no. 9) located near the Finland Station (no. 8) and the *Finlyandskii vokzal* metro station marks the spot where the revolutionary leader gave his first speech in Russia following his return from the West in 1917. All tourists who visit Leningrad are therefore taken to observe this historic site. From here, the tour bus usually drives along *Arsenal'naya Quay*, passing a massive stone wall on the right. The guide will announce, "This is a cardboard factory, which produces boxes for the famous Skorokhod shoe factory in Leningrad". And the guide will point to a signboard near the entrance (no. 4). He will not be lying. There are indeed cardboard factory workshops behind the wall on Arsenal'naya Quay. What he will neglect to say, however, is that the workers at the factory are also prisoners of the infamous *Kresty* Prison located behind the same wall. The official name and mailing address of the prison is: *Sledstvennyi Izolyator 45/1.*

Over 10000 prisoners are kept in this huge prison. Half of them have already been tried and convicted; the rest are still under investigation. The convicted prisoners are confined in the building marked no. 7 on our map; those under investigation are held in no. 6. Building no. 3 used to serve as a women's prison within Kresty; now it houses a psychiatric prison hospital. The separate entrance on Akademik *Lebedev Street* is marked no. 14 on the map.

Prison vans sometimes enter through the prison gates (no. 5). Those patient enough to wait for one may photograph a van transporting prisoners through the gates.

Visitors may also enter the small prison courtyard through the entrance marked no. 11 and meet the crowds of people, waiting to leave a parcel for an imprisoned relative. Entrance to the yard is absolutely free. You can talk to these unfortunate people and learn about the terrible fate of the prisoners. You may, moreover, offer to help them; if their need of your proffered assistance is stronger than their fear of it, they will accept it. Request an audience with the prison commander, Colonel Smirnov, and ask him about the treatment of political prisoners here, the punishment cells in which the inmates are tortured, and the beatings to which they are subjected.

A scientific laboratory is maintained in building no. 7 by the Soviet Navy (OKB 16). Known as a "sharaga" (very similar to the one described by *Solzhenitsyn* in his brilliant novel, *The First Circle),* the laboratory is manned by imprisoned scientists assigned to conduct military research.

Cell windows are sealed off with wooden boards or "muzzles", as the prisoners call them. Each cell of twelve square meters was built to accommodate no more than two prisoners; eight people are now confined to a single unit.

The observant visitor will note that, of the windows facing Akademik Lebedev Street, only one, made obvious by its size and its clean glass pane, has not been "muzzled". This window belongs to the cell in which *Lenin* was once imprisoned. One can see the extent to which prison conditions have deteriorated. Lenin had the cell all to himself; he could see the sky and enjoy sunlight through his large window. Prisoners today, however, are packed into crowded cells and rarely get to see the light of day. Such was the experience of Eduard Kuznetsov, a political prisoner in today's Russia and hero of the first Leningrad trial of 1970, as an inmate in cell no. 242.

The Kresty Prison is connected to the *Bol'shoi Dom* (the Big House) on the other side of the Neva River by an underground corridor. Here you will find the Leningrad headquarters of the K.G.B. and four of its prison buildings. This dreadful building complex, located between Liteinyi Prospekt and Kalyaev Street, will be on your left as you cross the bridge over the Neva (no. 12).

59

The address of the K.G.B. prison is *Liteinyi Prospekt 4.*

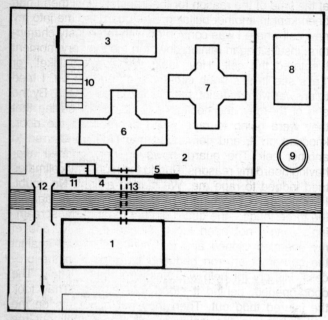

Map of the Kresty and K.G.B. prisons

1. K.G.B. administration building and prison.
2. *Kresty* Prison.
3. Psychiatric prison hospital.
4. Signboard "Kartonazhnaya fabrika" (Cardboard factory) over the entrance to Kresty Prison.
5. Prison van entrance to Kresty Prison.
6. Pre-trial detention building (accommodating approximately 5000 inmates).
7. Convicted prisoners building (accommodating approximately 5000 inmates).
8. Finland (train) Station.
9. Lenin Monument.
10. Prisoners' courtyards.
11. Entrance to the yard where parcels for prisoners are accepted.
12. Bridge on Liteinyi Prospekt over the Neva River.
13. Underground corridor under the Neva River linking the K.G.B. building with Kresty Prison.

Here are some excerpts from the testimonies of a few former inmates of these three prisons.

1. "I was transferred to cell no. 404, second floor, fourth building. I had refused to talk to my investigator during the pre-trial investigation period. I was not aware at the time of the reason for the transfer. Until then I had been kept in another building. The guard led me into my new cell where I was confronted with three lusty characters. Insults began raining down on me the very moment I entered the cell. 'Hey, look! We've got a kike!', or 'Let's see if he's been circumcised', and so on. I tried to answer with restraint, but the 'jokes' continued. By the end of the day, the hooligans were openly saying that they were going to rape me. I approached the door, knocked on it, and demanded that I be transferred to another cell. The guard, however, only grinned after having heard my reasons. During the night, my cellmates tried indeed to rape me. We started a fight. No doubt, I would have been unable to defend myself against the three thugs – the guard did not react to my screaming – had I not been lucky. During the fight, one of my enemies slipped and fell, hitting his head against the corner of an iron bed and cracking it in the process. His cry for help was answered immediately. The door opened; behind it stood four guards. They took the injured thug out. Then they put handcuffs on me and led me to the isolation cell. There they put me into a strait jacket and threw me onto the floor. There was no bed in the cell. It was damp and cold. Soon afterwards, I heard a howling sound, like that of a malfunctioning waterpipe. The sound, which continued for three days, gave me a headache and even hallucinations. I was then summoned to the investigator and was given a false, self-incriminating statement to sign. I refused, whereupon I was told that I was going to be tried for gangsterism for having crippled my cellmate. My version of the story made the investigator laugh. (His name was Morozov, an investigator in the city procurator's office.) In his attempt to get me to sign a self-incriminating statement, he ordered me thrown into the isolation cell three times for seven days at a time. Once he had me put into a 'slit' for 24 hours. (A 'slit' is a kind of closet, 70 x 70 centimeters, in which it is impossible to sit or move.) I was given no food or water. I was not even allowed to go to the toilet; I had to let the urine run down

61

my legs. After the torture was over, I was made to clean the 'slit'." – From the testimony of Z. *Nisan* on his imprisonment in Kresty in 1978.

2. Here is a description of the K.G.B. prison:

"When I was walked from Kresty through the underground corridor to the K.G.B. prison, I immediately realized that I was in another place. The corridors here were wide, the guards were wearing K.G.B. uniforms, and there was carpeting on the floors (to enable the guards to approach the cell doors quietly and peep through the peepholes). After having been shown to my cell, I soon discovered that my new cellmates and I were being listened to by microphone and even observed by camera. We decided to test this by staging a conversation of how we would use a knife we pretended to have to attack the guard. We spoke as if we had hidden it in one of the mattresses. About ten or 15 minutes later, a group of guards burst in and handcuffed us. They cut the mattresses open but, of course, found nothing… We laughed." – From the testimony of K. *Zalman,* 1975.

3. The prison hospital and psychiatric hospital.

"In the K.G.B. prison, the investigator constantly repeated, 'Only the mentally ill would turn against the Soviet state. The fact that you made anti-Soviet placards and leaflets is a sign of your insanity.' I did not want to talk with the investigator at all for fear of blabbing something out. So, for keeping silent, I was told that I was insane. On the morning of October 8, 1976, I was taken out of my cell and informed that I was to undergo psychiatric examination in a psychiatric hospital. And so, I was searched; my belongings were returned. And then I was packed into a Red Cross van and driven over the bridge on Liteinyi Prospekt to the psychiatric prison hospital on Akademik Lebedev Street.

New arrivals at the camp. An escort guard orders the prisoners out of the paddy wagon (voronok). Imagine what persuaded the photographer to risk so much in secretly taking this picture.

"The reception procedure there was a mixture of what you experience in a hospital and in a prison. You are given a shower, searched, and put into a course robe. Then you are taken to a ward cell, where you see a mixture of mentally ill and absolutely healthy people. There were sex maniacs there, for example, as well as religious people, such as nuns. One woman there was given a psychiatric examination because she had applied for an exit permit from the Soviet Union; another because she had tried to commit suicide. There I came to the realization that, in the U.S.S.R., making an anti-Soviet placard, praying to God, trying to leave the country, or not wanting to live at all – all meant the same thing. You were insane! There were 18 beds in our ward. Because we were a 'quiet' section, we were allowed to go out of the ward during the day. The corridor, as a result, was always overcrowded. Only at night were we locked in.

"The next morning, I was taken for treatment instead of to an examination. I was to be given injections, but I refused. Force was used; the orderlies twisted my arms. I continued to resist, explaining that I was not sick but was brought here for examination only! They succeeded, however, in giving me a few injections after all. I lost consciousness... I came to in bed." – From the testimony of J. V., 1976.

LENINGRAD REGION

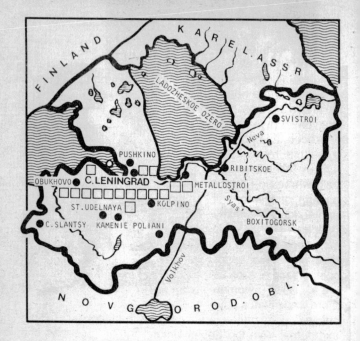

LENINGRAD REGION

In Leningrad itself, considerable time is needed to locate all the penal facilities in the city — eleven psychiatric prisons and psychiatric hospitals (which contain special K.G.B. wards), three prisons, and four camps. In Leningrad Region, we know of at least another ten camps, though we suspect that there are more.

In *Svir'stroi,* to the north, there is a strict-regime camp where 500 to 600 inmates are assigned to road construction and repair. The name of the camp commander is Captain Maksimov.

In *Rybitskoe,* there is an ordinary-regime camp for approximately 500 invalid prisoners assigned to farm work. Camp commander is Captain Nesterov.

Camps are also found in the outlying areas of Leningrad Region, such as on the road to *Kolpino* as well as in Kolpino itself (two ordinary-regime camps for 1000 prisoners each). Prisoners there are given work in machine

Freedom of religion – "Soviet style": one of 200 000 destroyed churches in the Soviet Union.

repair shops and are used in the Kolpino naval construction factory for the loading and unloading of shipments. The approximately 500 prisoners in the camp in *Pushkino* are used in both road repair and farm work. Camp commander is Major Eremeev.

At the camp in *Metallostroi,* 700 to 800 inmates are put to work in the production of hardware items, such as locks, springs, and bedsprings, for the Leningrad Region. Camp commander is Captain Khvostov.

In a strict-regime camp in *Obukhovo,* approximately 1000 inmates are used in military construction.

In a strict-regime camp in *Slantsy,* some 800 prisoners are used in shale-mining. Camp commander is Captain Trubkin.

In *Kamennye Polyany,* there is a special-regime camp for 500 to 600 prisoners who are put to work in quarries.

In an intensified-regime camp in *Boksitogorsk,* some 1000 prisoners are used in aluminum bauxite mining and industrial construction.

In the Slantsy and Boksitogorsk camps, many of the prisoners were arrested for religious reasons.

In *Ul'yanovka,* located 50 kilometers from Leningrad, there is a women's camp for 1200 inmates; in *Volkhov,* 100 kilometers from Leningrad, you will find another for 1500 inmates. Women with infant children are also held here. The prisoners are used as seamstresses. (See special map of women's and children's camps.)

When you visit Leningrad, do not forget to visit that miracle of architecture, the *Cathedral of Our Lady of Kazan'.*

Instead of worshiping crowds, you will see there a signboard reading, *"Center of Anti-Religious Propaganda" and "There is no God!"*

Now take a look at the receipt for a fine levied against those punished for "belief in God", and consider the extent to which "freedom of religion" exists in the Soviet Union.

BELORUSSIAN S.S.R.
(area: 207600 sq. km.; pop.: 9600000)

We know of altogether 33 penal facilities in Belorussia, all of which are indicated on our map.

Two of them may be found in *Polotsk* and *Novopolotsk,* which lie on the road from Moscow to Vitebsk. In *Polotsk,* there is a men's intensified-regime camp (designated as facility no. UZh-15/10-1) of 1000 prisoners assigned to construction work and to loading and unloading duties. In an ordinary-regime camp in *Novopolotsk* (designated as facility no. UZh-15/10) approximately 1000 inmates are used in the woodworking industry and road construction.

You will be told that these camps are for ordinary criminals, but request a meeting with Mikhail *Kukobaka,* Pëtr *Ragoz,* and Ivan *Lepen',* all of whom were imprisoned for their religious beliefs. These inmates will be able to testify to the fact that there are political prisoners among the ordinary offenders in the camps.

In *Vitebsk,* we know of a large prison with some 3000 inmates and a camp of 1500 prisoners used in industrial construction.

In *Orsha,* further to the south, you will be able to observe subunits A, E, V, and Zh of camp no. UZh-15/12 as well as camp no. UZh-15/6-V. In these five ordinary-regime camps, all located within city limits, some 8000 prisoners work in industrial construction, road construction and repair, galvanized tableware production, and farming. (Peasants from this region have been flocking to the city to escape the hardships of farm life here.)

In *Gor'kii,* even further to the south, about 1000 prisoners at camp no. UZh-15/9 manufacture spare metal parts for use in the local industry. The plant in which they work may be reached by bus no. 3 from the center of the city.

On your arrival in *Mogilev,* you will be able to visit a prison for 2500 to 3000 inmates and two camps. In

Women-and-children's camp in Minsk (Opanskaya Street). Photograph taken from a train bridge. See map of Minsk (photo 1978).

camp no. UZh-15/5, 1500 prisoners are assigned to work in the *Lovsanovyi* industrial complex (bus no. 14 from the center of the city), while the 600 prisoners of camp no. UZh-15 are engaged in the manufacture of metal tableware.

You may be interested in visiting two children's camps in *Bobruisk.* One of the camps, located on *Bakharev*

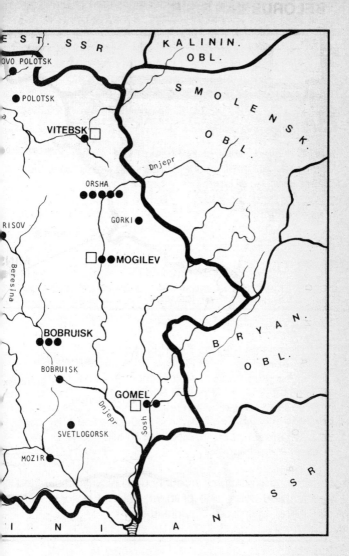

Street, where 1000 children manufacture furniture and packaging containers (boxes), may be reached from the center of the city by bus no. 20. The other camp (bus no. 6) holds 600 to 800 children who are put to work in a mechanics shop. Among these children are those who were forcibly taken from their parents to be "re-educated". Because the parents practiced their religion, they were regarded as a "bad" influence on their children. In Bobruisk, 1500 male prisoners work in a reinforced concrete construction plant under intensified-regime conditions (bus no. 2 from the center of the city). Bus no. 11 will take you to the rubber tire plant, where about 1 000 prisoners from camp no. UZh-15/2 are engaged. The conditions under which they work represent a health hazard. It is not atypical that the English, Italian, and West German engineering specialists employed at the camp have remained silent on the working conditions there.

In *Soligorsk,* west of Bobruisk, more than 2 000 prisoners are assigned to the construction of a potassium chloride industrial plant.

In *Svetlogorsk,* south of Bobruisk, approximately 1 500 prisoners are assigned the construction of a chemical industrial plant.

Prisons in which those arrested for political or religious reasons are jailed together with common offenders may be found in *Grodno* (2 000 inmates), *Brest* (1 000 inmates), *Pinsk* (800 inmates), and *Gomel'* (2 000 inmates).

Men's camps may be found in *Molodechno,* 127 kilometers from Minsk; in *Glubokoe,* capital of Glubokoe District, located north of Molodechno; in *Borisov,* 65 kilometers by train from Minsk; in *Baranovichi,* 145 kilometers by train from Minsk; in *Ivatsevichi,* 55 kilometers by train from Baranovichi; in *Volkovysk,* 50 kilometers by train from Ivatsevichi; and in *Mozyr',* 130 kilometers by train or by road from Gomel'.

Camps are scattered throughout all of Belorussia, and in each and every one of them, political prisoners are concealed among ordinary offenders.

MINSK, BELORUSSIAN S.S.R.
pop.: 1 300 000

Foreign tourists here are usually quartered in the special Intourist hotel, The Minsk, which looks out onto *Lenin* Prospekt. From the rear windows of the upper floors of the hotel, you can see the gloomy walls and

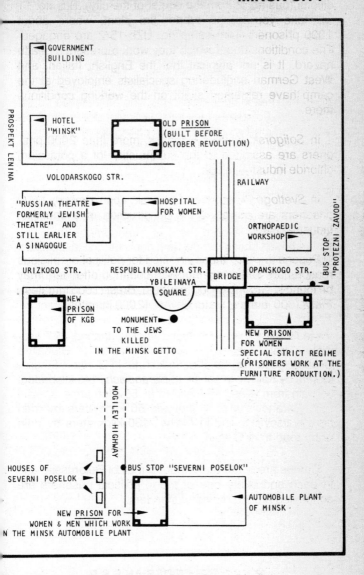

buildings of the so-called "Old Prison", located on *Volodarskii Street*. Three thousand prisoners languish there in stench, cramp living conditions, and hunger. You will be told that this is a prison for criminals. Do not believe it. The facility includes a special building for 500 to 600 political prisoners.

But this is only the beginning. Walk from The Minsk along Lenin Prospekt until you get to Volodarskii Street and cross it. On the next corner, on Uritskii Street, you will see the large building of the special K.G.B. prison, which also contains the offices of the Belorussian K.G.B. It is sometimes called the "inner prison". More than 1000 prisoners from all over Belorussia are incarcerated here. Inmates include dissidents who have called for the introduction of democracy into the Soviet Union, students who attempted to post notices calling for the independence of Belorussia and its separation from the U.S.S.R., as well as members of various religious groups, such as Baptists, Jehovah's Witnesses, Seventh-day Adventists, and Pentecostals.

If you walk or drive along Uritskii Street towards Yubileinaya Square, where there is a monument dedicated to the Jewish ghetto victims, and continue on Respublikanskaya Street, you will reach a bridge crossing the railroad tracks. From the bridge, you will see on the right, next to the railroad tracks, a huge camp prison where more than 3000 female prisoners work in a furniture factory. The name of the bus stop is *"Proteznyi zavod"* (orthopedic plant).

On the map of the Belorussian S.S.R., you will see a pen-and-ink drawing of the camp as seen from the bridge.

A large strict-regime camp prison for women is located on the right-hand side of the highway to *Mogilev* near the Minsk city line as you drive away from the Belorussian capital. On the left, you will see the houses of the Northern Settlement *(Severnyi Pocëlok,* which is also the name of the bus stop). Next to the women's facility, there is a camp for male prisoners assigned to work in an automobile plant.

*

UKRAINIAN S.S.R.
(area: 603700 sq. km.; pop.: approx. 50000000)

In examining this large map, the reader must bear in mind that the Ukraine is made up of 25 regions, an area of more than 600000 square kilometers, and a population of nearly 50000000 inhabitants (1979). Altogether, we know of 126 camps, 42 prisons, and 17 psychiatric prisons in the Ukraine.

Unfortunately, however, we are not in a position to provide the reader with an exact description of all the camps, prisons, and psychiatric prisons in the Ukraine, which has thus far unsuccessfully, but heroically struggled to achieve independence from the Soviet Union. In order, therefore, to present as complete a picture to the reader as possible, we have added a few special maps of a number of Ukrainian cities and regions in our *Guidebook* (*L'vov* city and region, *Chernovtsy, Odessa* city and region, *Zhitomir* Region, *Rakhov* and vicinity, and Kiev).

Women's and children's facilities, psychiatric prisons, and death camps located in the Ukraine have been listed in separate sections of this book.

And now, let us begin our journey. Most of the penal facilities shown on our map are easily accessible by all modes of transportation. For precise information on train or airplane arrivals, consult any Soviet timetable.

We should like at the outset to make special reference to the death camps, where prisoners are assigned to work in uranium mines. Facilities of this kind may be found in *Cholovka,* Zhitomir Region; *Zhëltye Vody,* Dnepropetrovsk Region; and *Rakhov* (near the Rumanian border), Transcaucasian Region. The prisoners confined in these camps were sentenced to hard labor – but not to death. By working in the uranium mines, however, they become exposed to deadly radiation. The production of uranium is an urgently necessary part of the Soviet leadership's armament program. Detailed information of these facilities may be found on the special map of the death camps.

Women's and children's camps in the Ukraine, which are indicated on the general map of the Soviet Union, may be found in *Drogobych, Uzhgorod, Odessa, Kremenchug, Khmel'nitskii, Bakhmach, Dneprodzerzhinsk, Ovruch, Roven'ki, Khar'kov, Chernigov,* and *Kherson.*

Children's camps (ages 14 to 18 years) may be found in *Odessa, Sarny, Bakhmach, Manevichi, Strelka* (Crimea), *Korosten', Drogobych, Roven'ki, Khar'kov,*

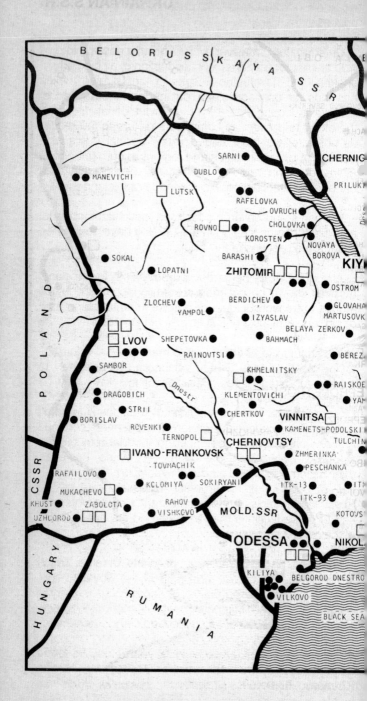

UKRAINIAN S.S.R.

...AYA OBL.

...OVGOROD SEVERSKI

...ACH

K U R S K A Y A   O B L.

VOR. OBL.

BELGOR. OBL.

SHOSTKA

SUMI

EREKRESTOVKA

KOTLOVO

...TOLOVO-SUKHODOLKA

SUHODOLKA

KURIANSK

SEVERODONETSK

POLTAVA

KREMENCHUG

...NA

...CHI

...ROVARI

...RISPOL

KHARKOV

DIKANEVKA

KRASNI LUG

ITK-13

PETROVSKOE

PEREVALSK

ITU 60

VOROSHILOVOGRAD

LENINSKOE

KRASNI KUT

...GANCHA

PRIVOLNOE

SLAVYANSK

MAKEEVKA

MOKROTOVO

...RKASSY

ST.PRIVOLNOE

DZHERZHINSK

Sahara

KRASNODON

...EPROPETROSK

DONETSK

...ADNII POSELOK

...EPRODZERZHINSK

ZAPOROZHYE

VOLNYANSK

KULGESH

P.SITNIKOVO

ANTRATSIT

ZHELTIE VODI

...ROVOGRAD

VOLNOVAKHA

SHAKHTERSK

ROVENKI

...VOI ROG

NIZHNII DONBASS

...ZBRUEVKA

...GRIGORIEVKA

DARIEVKA

OSIPIENKO

MOLOCHANSK

...ERSON

BERDNIANSK

MELITOPOL

ZHDANOV

R O S T O V   O B L.

...DZHANKOI

...PATORIA

...

AZOV SEA

SIMFEROPOL

SARABUS

FEODOSIA

KERCH

SEVASTOPOL

Chernigov, Kremenchug, and *Petrovskoe* (Voroshilovgrad Region).

Since we have already included information on the psychiatric prisons of the Soviet Union in a separate section of the *Guidebook,* we shall limit ourselves here to listing the locations in the Ukraine where mentally healthy human beings have been "sentenced to insanity": *Slavyansk* (Donetsk Region), *Khar'kov* (two facilities), *Beregovo* (Transcaucasian Region), *Dnepropetrovsk* (two facilities), *L'vov, Kiev, Smela* (Cherkassy Region), *Zaporozh'e, Biryukovo* (Voroshilovgrad Region), *Donetsk, Nikolaev, Vinnitsa, Cherkassy, Glavakha* (Kiev Region), and *Ivano-Frankovsk.*

We should especially like to recommend a visit to *Kiev, Odessa, L'vov,* and *Chernovtsy.* For detailed information, see the special maps of these cities.

Other cities where you may find penal facilities include:

1. *Dnepropetrovsk* – a) The Igren' Special Psychiatric Prison (Directions: electric train to Igren'); b) special psychiatric hospital-prison, *Chicherin Street 101* (no. 308/RB-9).

2. On the map of *Chernovtsy,* you will see a prison, on the grounds of which there is a concentration camp for 1000 prisoners. Request permission from the administration to visit it.

3. In the *Uzhgorod* city prison, in which there are approximately 1100 inmates, is a special section for political prisoners and another for women. Ukrainian freedom fighters and religious prisoners are among those confined here.

4. The prisoners of three camps in *Kherson* are assigned to work in a shipyard, in which warships are constructed. Many of the prisoners were arrested for practicing their religion.

5. If you should take the train or drive from Zhitomir north to Korosten', make a stopover in *Novaya Borovaya* and *Cholovka* and visit the camps there. The prisoners

in these facilities are condemned through their assigned work in the uranium mines to die a slow death.

6. Up to 1000 prisoners are held in camp ITK-3, a large facility in *Kulgechi* (east of Zaporozh'e in Donetsk Region). Terminally diseased prisoners are brought here not to be given medical care (there is no hospital in the area), but to die. Many of the prisoners, both Christians and Jews (such as those who sought to emigrate to Israel, including the brothers Arkadii and Leonid *Weinman),* are confined here.

7. In *Shepetovka,* located in Volyn' Region southwest of Zhitomir, approximately 1500 prisoners are confined. In 1968, an uprising here took place as a result of the systematic beatings. The guards shot into the crowds of prisoners, who in their protests demanded justice. Ten people were killed; others saw their sentences extended and were sent to the uranium mines.

8. About 1000 prisoners in *Darievka,* a village in Kherson Region (on the Black Sea), are subjected to the arbitrariness of the authorities and their trained, red armband-sporting criminals, the prisoner-group leaders of the camp. In 1971, desperate prisoners at the camp went on strike only to be fired on by the guards in their watchtowers. There were casualties. More than 50 prisoners were tried and despatched to unknown destinations.

9. About 800 prisoners in camp no. 86/8 in *Simferopol'* (Crimea), which is located on the road to Feodosiya, are assigned to especially exhausting work in a quarry.

10. On the south to Ismail from Odessa, or down the Danube, you may stop off in *Vilkovo* ("the Venice of Odessa") and visit four camps on nearby islands in the river. See the notes on Odessa Region for details.

11. Two thousand prisoners in a camp in *Irpen',* a suburb of *Kiev* accessible from the Ukrainian capital by electric train, are assigned to the metallurgical industry or are put to work in the production of radio component parts. The camp is located in the immediate vicinity of a convalescent home for Ukrainian writers.

The children of Pavel Ritikov who in 1975 was sentenced to five years imprisonment for his belief in God. His mother's address: Podgornaya Street 30, Krasnodon, Ukrainian S.S.R., U.S.S.R. Ritikov was arrested again in 1980.

ZHITOMIR CITY AND REGION
(city – pop.: 250000)
(region – area: 29900 sq. km.; pop.: 1700000)

1. Pre-trial detention prison of Zhitomir (400 cells in which 2000 inmates are confined.

2. Pre-trial detention jail, *Kommunisticheskaya Street 3* (20 cells in which about 300 prisoners are confined).

3. K.G.B. Prison of Zhitomir.

4. *Berdichev* – camp for 2000 prisoners assigned to construction work.

5. *Novograd-Volynskii* – camp for disabled prisoners; most of the 600 to 700 prisoners here are suffering from tuberculosis and are unable to work.

6. *Novaya Borovaya* (on the train route between Zhitomir and Korosten') – camp about two kilometers from the train station for approximately 2000 prisoners assigned to uranium mining.

ZHITOMIR REGION

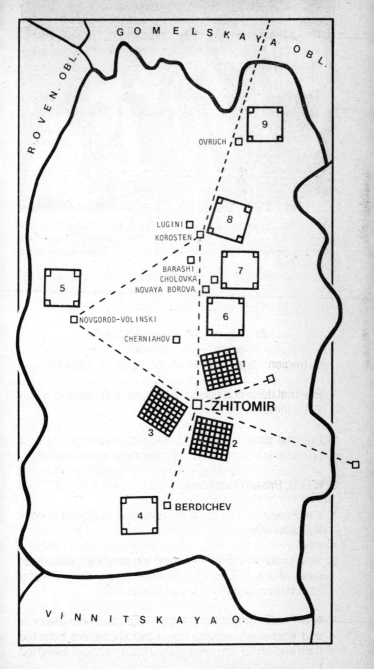

7. *Cholovka*—camp for approximately 2000 prisoners assigned to work in a uranium quarry.

8. *Korosten'*— camp for approximately 2000 prisoners assigned to work in the production of furniture and electrical appliances.

9. *Ovruch* – women's camp for approximately 800 to 1000 prisoners assigned to work in a textile factory.

*

L'VOV REGION
(part of Region no. 9 on the foldout map)
(area: 21800 sq.km.; pop.: 2500000)

In L'vov Region, we know of eleven camps, two prisons, and one psychiatric prison hospital, the latter of which contains ordinary-regime cells.

1. *L'vov* city, capital of the region, *Chapaev Street 20* (see special map of L'vov) – Ministry of Interior pre-trial detention prison for 1000 to 1200 inmates; labor camp of up to 500 prisoners assigned to construction work in the city; strictly guarded special prison for 300 inmates.

2. *L'vov, Mir Street 1* – K.G.B. prison of up to 500 political prisoners.

3. *L'vov, Kul'tparkovaya Street 95* – psychiatric hospital houses special wards administered by the K.G.B. and having up to 100 political prisoners.

4. *L'vov, Stryiskaya Street* – camp no. VL-316/48, a forced-labor facility, in which approximately 2000 prisoners are assigned to the manufacture of motorized farm equipment.

5. *L'vov, Shevchenko Street,* official address: Box 30, Camp No. VL-316/30 – more than 1500 prisoners in this forced-labor facility are assigned to the furniture industry.

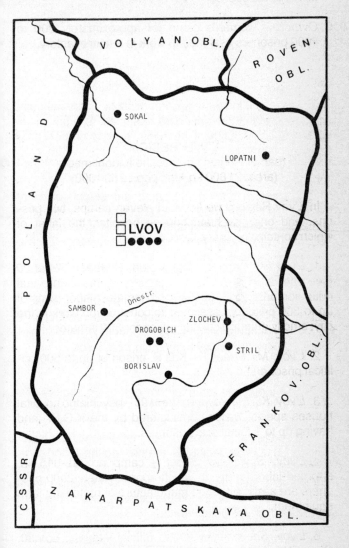

6. *L'vov* – camp no. GSP-5, no. VI-5/48-2 has approximately 1000 prisoners assigned to work at construction sites in the city; many of the prisoners here were arrested for their belief in God.

Altogether there are two prisons, one psychiatric hospital (prison), and four camps in L'vov with a combined population of 7000 prisoners.

There are another seven camps located in smaller cities in L'vov Region:

1. *Sokal'*, 76 kilometers north of L'vov – special camp of more than 3000 prisoners assigned to work in the metallurgical industry. Directions: by car or train from L'vov.

2. *Lopatin*, in the northern part of the region – ordinary-regime camp for 1500 to 1800 prisoners assigned to various construction projects. Directions: train northwest to Busk or to Brody; then, from either location, 55 kilometers by car to the camp.

3. *Zolochev*, east of L'vov – ordinary-regime camp of 1000 to 1200 prisoners assigned to the production of steel-frame constructions and hardware items. Directions: 155 kilometers by train or car from L'vov.

4. *Drogobych*, in the southern part of the region – two camps (ITK no. 1 and ITK no. 2) of 1500 prisoners each assigned to construction work. Camp commander of one of the facilities, a forced-labor settlement, is Captain Lupen. The other facility is a strict-regime labor camp. Directions: 129 kilometers by train south from L'vov via Truskavets. (ITK: Ispravitel'no-trudovaya koloniya – Corrective labor colony; this is the official name of the penal camps in the U.S.S.R. – *trans.)*

5. *Borislav*, 139 kilometers south of L'vov – ordinary-regime camp of 1200 prisoners assigned to construction work.

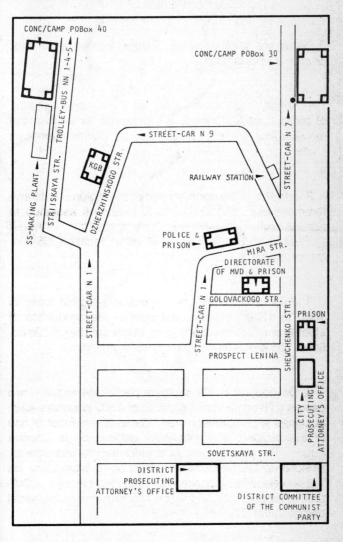

6. *Stryi* – forced-labor camp of 500 prisoners assigned to machine workshops.

Thus, to our knowledge, the total number of prisoners in L'vov Region is 16000.

ODESSA REGION

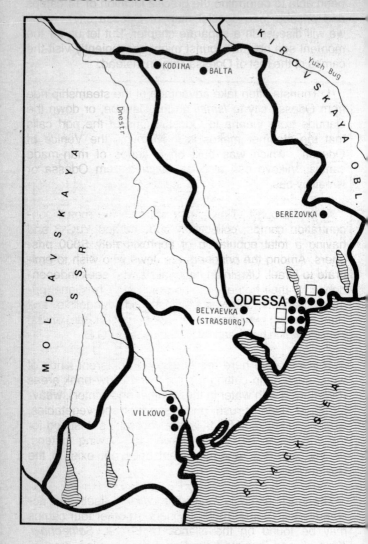

ODESSA REGION
(area: 33 000 sq. km.; pop.: 2 400 000)

The K.G.B. apparently feels that 20 concentration camps and three prisons are adequate for such a populous region. This is a rather "modest" figure, however, when compared to the number of penal facilities in the Novosibirsk or Sverdlovsk regions, or in Krasnoyarsk Territory.

Alone within the boundaries of Odessa city, we have been able to determine the precise location of 14 camps and prisons (see special map of Odessa city), which we will discuss in a separate chapter. But let us for the moment see how the tourist might conveniently visit the camps of the rest of Odessa Region instead.

1. Tourists often take advantage of the steamship ride from Odessa city to *Ismail* on the Danube, or down the Danube from Vienna to Odessa. One of the port calls that the steamer makes is in *Vilkovo,* "the Venice of Odessa", which was built on a series of man-made canals. Vilkovo can also be reached from Odessa or Ismail by bus.

In and around Vilkovo, you will find five men's concentration camps, collectively code-named YuG-3 and having a total population of approximately 5000 prisoners. Among the prisoners are Jews who wish to emigrate to Israel, Ukrainian nationalists who seek independence for their homeland, and practicing Christians (primarily Baptists, Jehovah's Witnesses, Evangelists, and Pentecostals) who refuse to be a part of the official church, which has been infiltrated by the K.G.B.

The prisoners here are engaged in different kinds of work, such as in cutting rush in marshy low-bank areas (overflowed with water in the summer and winter), weaving mats made of rush, packaging fruit and vegetables, working in sovkhoz fields where vegetables destined for the cannery in Ismail are grown, and sewing mittens. As you can see, unemployment does not exist in the Soviet Union.

The main camp is located in *Vilkovo* itself and accommodates some 3000 prisoners. Another four camps may be found on the islands of *Ermak, Solnechnyi, Kislitskii,* and *Zmeinyi* in the Danube. (There is a Zmeinyi island in the Black Sea. – *trans.)* About 500 prisoners are confined in each of these camps.

This is the true "beauty" of the Danube and Black Sea islands, and of the "Soviet Venice". V.M., a former political prisoner in Vilkovo, tells of the modern steamships that, with their gay music and their tourists from Vienna, used to sail past his camp. He recounts how he and his fellow prisoners had observed these vessels with anguish and disgust while having to suffer both hunger and the tyranny of the guards.

2. West of Odessa lies *Belyaevka* (Strasburg), site of a men's camp for 2000 to 2500 prisoners assigned to construct roads, military airfields, and other military objects. Belyaevka is easily accessible from Odessa by train or bus.

3. In a men's camp in *Berezovka,* northeast of Belyaevka, 2000 prisoners are assigned to construction projects, such as laying train tracks (to Belyaevka and to Odessa). Berezovka may be reached from Odessa by train or bus.

4. In *Balta,* north of Berezovka, 500 to 600 prisoners of a men's camp are sent to do farm work in the nearby sovkhozes. The city may be reached from Odessa by train or bus.

5. Approximately 300 prisoners from the men's camp in *Kodyma* in the north of the region perform farm work in the nearby sovkhozes. The city is accessible from Odessa by train or bus.

The local leadership has thus found a reliable source of slave labor to take the place of peasants who left the village to escape its poverty.

*

ODESSA CITY
(pop.: 1 050 000)

Odessa was given the title of "heroic city" for its role in the war. This is the first thing an Intourist guide will tell you. He will also take you on an obligatory tour of the war monument, the *Pushkin* monument, the *Primorskii* Boulevard, and the *Arcadia* and its beaches.

ODESSA CITY

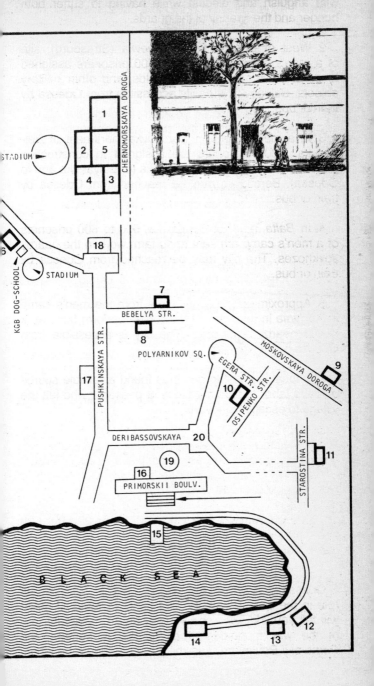

87

The guide, however, will not tell you how to find the concentration camps, prisons, and psychiatric prisons of the city. He will not explain how you might visit the camps for women and their infants or the children's labor camps. But you will find these camps on the accompanying map. We know of 14 such frightful places in the heroic city.

Your guide will refuse to take you to the camps. You will therefore have to go yourself by taking the tram or trolley bus indicated on the map. Ask someone to point out the stop where you wish to get off, or take a taxi. Simply tell the driver the address, and you will soon see places concealed from the view of tourists visiting the Soviet Union — places where political and religious prisoners are kept confined among ordinary criminals.

The authorities are particularly interested in placing political prisoners in camps designed for common offenders so as to hide them from the view of world opinion. Do not forget your camera or movie camera. We will be delighted to receive any photographs that you may take of these penal facilities.

As a tourist, you will be quartered in an Intourist hotel, that is, either in *The Odessa* (no. 16) on *Primorskii* Boulevard or in *The Krasnaya* (no. 17) on *Pushkinskaya* Street. We will therefore give you directions on how best to reach the penal facilities in the city from these two locations.

1. We can most easily begin our tour by first visiting the penal complex on *Chernomorskaya Road,* consisting of a women's camp, a children's camp, and a camp for adolescents (14 to 18 years of age).

Take the tram no. 3, 10, 13, 14, 29, or 29a from the train station (no. 18) to the stop marked *"Pravoslavnoe kladbishche"* (Orthodox cemetery), located on the right. On the opposite side of the street, you will see a large, gloomy prison building. There are camps that stand to the left and right of the building that can also be seen from the side streets.

An immense and dismal structure. This is the K.G.B. headquarters in Odessa, Odessa Region on the Black Sea, Ukrainian S.S.R. Located in the center of the city on Bebel' Street, the prison is made up of several buildings (photo 1976).

Simply approach the complex without making any inquiries and take photographs of it, as if you were interested in the cemetery and its monuments instead. You may even enter the administration offices of the complex and request permission to see the camps, which is not prohibited by law.

2. From the Khvorostin public gardens (no. 20) at one end of Deribasovskaya Street, you can easily walk along Komitetskaya Street to Polyarnikov Street. Take a right on Veger Street and continue until you get to the corner of Osipenko Street, where you will see a large white building with windows sealed off with bricks (no. 10, see photograph). Approximately 2000 inmates in this women's camp prison, in effect, a textile factory, are assigned to sewing bed linen and military uniforms.

Visit them! You would be risking nothing more than a refusal, but word of your arrival would reach the unfortunate prisoners and give them moral support. Many of the inmates in this "blind", windowless building are religious women who were arrested for having taught their children to believe in God. The children were taken away from their mothers to be "re-educated".

3. If you should like to visit those children who have been taken away from their parents, you need only walk to *Primorskii Boulevard,* where you will find the Potemkin Steps. Descend the steps and enter the harbor area. Then take a launch across the bay to *Dofinovka,* site of a special home for children whose parents are serving prison or camp sentences. The "specialness" of this home is evinced by its barbed-wire fence and watch-posts.

From the Potemkin Steps, you can also take the tram no. 7 or bus no. 146 to *Dofinovka* via *Luzanovka.*

4. The same transportation lines will also take you to the *"Tsentrolit"* factory and to a factory for reinforced concrete products. At each of these locations you will find a men's camp of more than 1000 prisoners. Prisoners built both of these factories and are now assigned to work in them.

5. Take the tram no. 130 from the Khvorostin public gardens (no. 20) to *"Slobodka"* on *Starostin Street,* where you will find the Odessa Region hospital. Political and religious prisoners are maintained by the K.G.B. in the hospital's special ward for the mentally ill (no. 11). The physicians there have often said, "Today, only madmen believe in God."

6. The special psychiatric hospital-prison of the K.G.B. in Odessa, however, is even more frightening. Located on *Moskovskaya Road,* it can be reached by tram no. 104, 117, 118, 128, or 132. The dissidents here are "cured" of their sanity in their prison cells through the administration of drugs that dull the mind.

7. Walk along Pushkinskaya Street from the hotel Krasnaya (no. 17), take a right on Bebel' Street, and continue for a few blocks; you will soon find the large

building of the Ministry of Interior on the right. The Department of Visas and Registration (O.V.I.R.: Otdel viz i registratsii), where you can see a line of Jews waiting to apply for emigration from the Soviet Union, and a pretrial detention prison are also located here.

Further along Bebel' Street on the left stands a large gray, gloomy building with columns, in which the K.G.B. offices for the Odessa Region and a special K.G.B. prison are housed.

Reiza P. has described the frightful months of investigation that she spent in this death-like building.

8. The special children's prison (no. 6) on *Proletarskii* Boulevard 33A may be reached eigher on foot or by tram from the train station (no. 18), located on Tomas and Pushkinskaya streets.

As you can see, children are well represented in Odessa: a special home, two camps, and even a prison. Keep this in mind the next time you visit a typical children's home. Next to the children's prison you will find the Dynamo Stadium and a special K.G.B. watchdog training school. The barking of the dogs reminds both the residents of the area and the imprisoned children of the kind of country in which they live and of what is hidden behind the façade of their "happy lives".

*

CHERNOVTSY
(pop.: 220000)

On *Sovetskaya Square* in the old city of *Chernovtsy* (formerly Czernowitz) stands a large prison concealed from the eyes of the tourist by a huge plywood billboard, on which numerous Soviet slogans appear. The vertical dimensions of the billboard correspond to the full height of a four-story building. On the other side of the billboard, you will note that the windows of the facility are opaque so that the prison bars on the inside cannot

CHERNOVTSY CITY

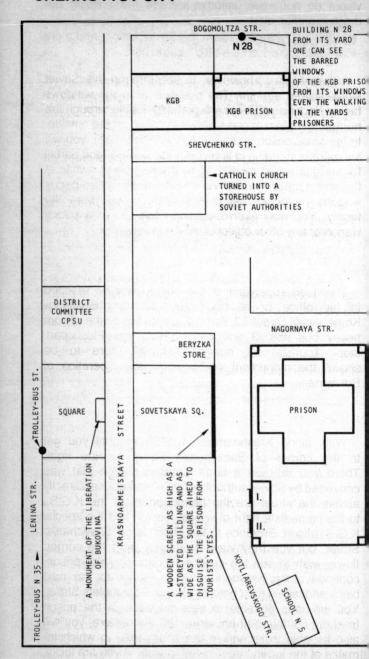

BOGOMOLTZA STR.

N 28

BUILDING N 28
FROM ITS YARD
ONE CAN SEE
THE BARRED
WINDOWS
OF THE KGB PRISON
FROM ITS WINDOWS
EVEN THE WALKING
IN THE YARDS
PRISONERS

KGB

KGB PRISON

SHEVCHENKO STR.

← CATHOLIK CHURCH
TURNED INTO A
STOREHOUSE BY
SOVIET AUTHORITIES

DISTRICT
COMMITTEE
CPSU

NAGORNAYA STR.

BERYZKA
STORE

PRISON

SQUARE

SOVETSKAYA SQ.

I.

II.

A WOODEN SCREEN AS HIGH AS A
4-STOREYED BUILDING AND AS
WIDE AS THE SQUARE AIMED TO
DISGUISE THE PRISON FROM
TOURISTS'EYES.

KRASNOARMEISKAYA STREET

TROLLEY-BUS STR.

LENINA STR.

TROLLEY-BUS N 35

A MONUMENT OF THE LIBERATION
OF BUKOVINA

KOTLIAREVSKOGO STR.

SCHOOL N 5

92

be seen from the street. Prison employees and supervisors do not wear uniforms outside the building but dress in civilian attire.

It is quite easy, however, to see through this Soviet smokescreen attempt. The prison bars in the windows facing Nagornaya Street are perfectly visible through the normal, transparent glass panes installed on the outside. In the small prison courtyard (no. I on the map), you will see people standing in line waiting to leave a food parcel for an imprisoned relative. If you were to wait awhile at the prison gates (no. II), you would eventually see paddy wagons *(voronoki)* taking prisoners to and from the facility. You may even take a photograph of a paddy wagon or any other object of similar interest.

The head supervisor of the prison may be reached in his office or at his home address: Bogdano-Khmel'nitskii Street 52, Apt. 14. Directions to the prison: trolley bus nos. 3 and 5 to Sovetskaya Ploshchad' stop. Tourists are normally brought here to be shown the monument dedicated to the Liberation of Bukovina.

Walk along Krasnoarmeiskaya Street until you get to the corner of Shevchenko Street on the right. There you will see a large Catholic church that was converted by Soviet authorities into a storehouse. Directly across the street are the headquarters of the K.G.B., to the immediate right of which you will find the special K.G.B. prison. Entrance to the prison is on *Shevchenko* Street, but you may view the facility from the corner. If you wish to see the iron-bar windows of the prison, continue along Krasnoarmeiskaya Street to the next block and take a right onto Akademik Bogomolets Street. You will thus be able to see the back of the prison from the courtyard of house no. 28. From here, you will also be able to recognize the courtyards, in which inmates of the facility are allowed to walk. If you are lucky, you will even have the chance to observe how the inmates move about the prison yards. You should be able to take interesting photographs from this position.

The prison across from Sovetskaya Square is shaped in the form of a cross. In it, there are 94 cells constructed to hold 500 prisoners, though the facility is usually filled well beyond its normal capacity. The special K.G.B. prison was built to hold 200 to 300 prisoners.

A. Feldman, a Jewish activist, serving his sentence in a camp for ordinary offenders in the Ukraine. His crime: his attempt to get an exit visa for Israel.

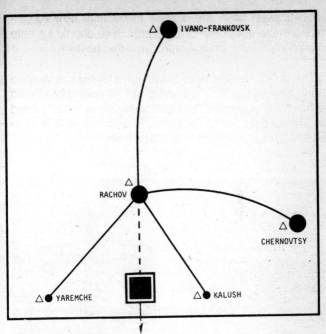

a) Death camp in Rakhov

b) A Baptist family in the Soviet Union in the midst of the ruins of its destroyed house. A common prayer meeting had taken place here without official permission, which is practically impossible to get. Courageous people mounted a sign over the ruins of the house: "Hated without cause". (Photo 1977).

95

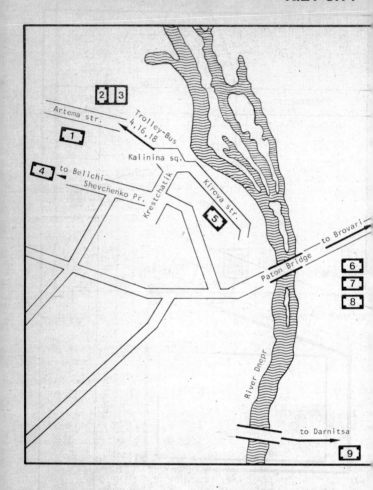

KIEV

*From the central bus terminal at **Kalinin Square** (at one end of Kreshchatnik Street) you may take trolley bus no. 4, 16, or 18 to **Lukyanovskii Rynok** stop to visit the well-known **Lukyanovskii** Prison. Among those confined here with ordinary criminals are civil rightists, religious people, and nationalists struggling for an independent Ukraine.*

A walk in the opposite direction (on the other side of Kalinin Square) along Kirov Street will take you to the "Dom Ofitserov" (House of Officers). There, opposite the Yunyi Zrytel' Theater, is a building housing the K.G.B. headquarters for the entire Ukraine and a special K.G.B. prison.

*Across the Dnepr River is **Darnitskii** District (Darnitsa), a part of Kiev. There are eight penal facilities in the city today. In Tsarist times, there was only one.*

LUKYANOVSKAYA PRISON

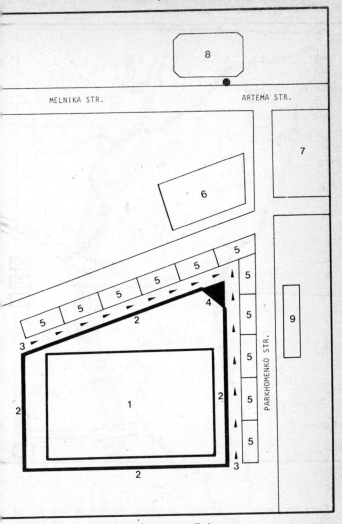

Lukyanovskaya Prison

Directions: Trolley bus nos. 4, 16, and 18 from the central terminal at Kalinin Square to the bus stop marked "Samolëtnyi zavod" (Airplane plant; no. 8 on the map). Continue on foot along Parkhomenko Street, past Lukyanovskii Market (no. 7) on the left and a public park (no. 6) on the right. On the first corner, you will see a seven and eight-story apartment house (no. 5), which was built expressly for the purpose of screening the Lukyanovskaya Prison building (no. 1) off from general view. The prison gates and entrance are located directly on the corner (no. 4). The entire prison is surrounded by a stone wall (no. 2), and around the wall itself extends a corridor guarded by watchdogs.

MOLDAVIAN S.S.R.

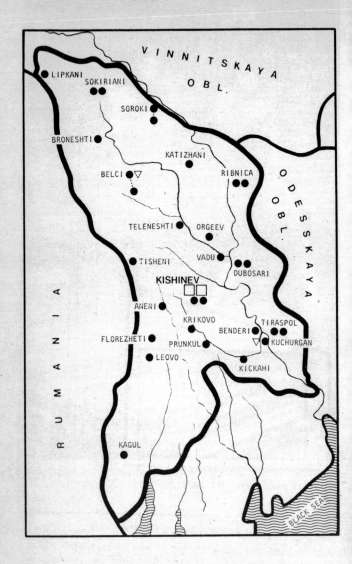

MOLDAVIAN S.S.R.

(area: 33 700 sq.km.; pop.: 3 980 000)

We know of 28 forced-labor camps (including two children's camps), one prison, and two psychiatric prisons in Moldavia.

Imprisoned women unloading asbestos plates from a freight train wagon in a camp in Bendery, Moldavian S.S.R. (photo 1977).

1. Three of these penal facilities may be found in *Kishinev,* the capital of Moldavia: a prison for 1200 to 1500 inmates on *Kuznechnaya Street;* a psychiatric hospital in which healthy people, including those arrested for supporting Moldavian independence, are confined

with the mentally ill; and a camp for 1800 to 2000 prisoners assigned to construction work within the city.

2. In *Sokiriany,* in northern Moldavia, there are two camps: an ordinary-regime camp of 800 to 900 prisoners used in construction work and in machine repair shops, and a strict-regime camp of 500 to 600 prisoners assigned to stone quarries.

3. In *Soroki,* 140 kilometers by car or train from Kishinev, approximately 1000 prisoners from an ordinary-regime camp are used in the construction industry and in metal workshops in which hardware items are manufactured for local industry. In a strict-regime camp located south of Soroki, 600 to 700 prisoners are assigned to work in the superphosphates industry.

4. In *Broneshti,* site of a rather large strict-regime camp, up to 6000 prisoners, many of whom were arrested for practicing their religion, are put to work in lime pits under conditions hazardous to health. Broneshti may be reached by car or train from Kishinev.

5. In *Bel'tsy,* 100 kilometers by car or train from Kishinev, up to 800 prisoners from a strict-regime camp are assigned to a stone quarry. Another 500 prisoners from an ordinary-regime camp located west of the city are used in construction work.

6. In *Kotyuzhany,* 140 kilometers by car or train from Kishinev via Orgeev and Rezina, healthy inmates are confined in the special wards of a psychiatric hospital under prison-like conditions.

7. In *Teleneshti,* 50 kilometers by car from Kishinev via Kalarash and 83 kilometers by train, 900 to 1000 prisoners in an ordinary-regime camp are assigned to construction work.

8. In *Vadu*, 18 kilometers north of Kishinev on the road to Dubossary, up to 600 prisoners in an ordinary-regime camp are assigned to construction work.

9. In *Rybnitsa*, 99 kilometers by car or train from Kishinev, you will find two camps: a strict-regime camp of 700 to 800 prisoners assigned to work in a quarry; an ordinary-regime camp of 1500 to 1600 prisoners assigned to work in the construction industry. Rybnitsa is also connected to Dubossary by steamship traffic on the Dnestr River.

10. In *Dubossary*, 36 kilometers by car or train from Kishinev, some 1500 children in an ordinary-regime camp are put to work in the production of containers for canned goods. Another 800 to 1000 prisoners in a strict-regime camp here are assigned to work in a quarry.

11. In *Orgeev*, 46 kilometers by car or train from Kishinev, up to 1000 prisoners from an ordinary-regime camp are assigned to irrigation and farm work.

12. In *Tisheni*, 42 kilometers by car or train from Kishinev, 800 to 900 prisoners from an especially harsh strict-regime camp are put to work in a quarry.

13. Up to 1000 prisoners in a strict-regime camp in *Kitsany*, 42 kilometers by car or by train from Kishinev, are engaged in the mining of marble.

14. In *Aneni*, 60 kilometers from Kishinev, about 800 prisoners in an ordinary-regime camp are used in construction and farm work.

15. In *Kuchurgan*, 85 kilometers by train from Kishinev, up to 1500 prisoners in an ordinary-regime camp are assigned to work on the construction of a hydroelectric power plant or are being used in the development of an irrigation project.

16. Two ordinary-regime camps, each with 1500 prisoners, are found in *Tiraspol'*, 80 kilometers by car or by train from Kishinev. The administration of the camps, however, is located in the southernmost part of the city. Inmates at one camp are used to manufacture packaging containers; the prisoners at the other facility are assigned to construction work.

17. In *Bendery*, 80 kilometers by train from Kishinev, 500 to 600 prisoners in an ordinary-regime camp are used to construct apartment houses within the city itself or are assigned to road construction.

18. In *Krikovo*, 30 kilometers by car or by train from Kishinev, 2000 prisoners from a large strict-regime camp are sent to work in quarries. Jews who have applied for emigration to Israel or members of other denominations arrested for practicing their faith are among the inmates at this camp.

19. In *Prunkul*, 45 kilometers from Kishinev and accessible by car, 500 to 600 prisoners in a strict-regime camp work at a stone quarry.

20. In *Leovo*, 104 kilometers by train or car from Kishinev via Kotovsk, 1200 to 1500 prisoners from an ordinary-regime camp are being used in the construction of a cannery and winery.

21. In *Lipkany*, 120 kilometers by train or car from Kishinev, 800 to 1000 prisoners in a children's ordinary-regime camp are used to produce packaging containers.

22. In *Kagul*, 180 kilometers by train from Kishinev, 1800 to 2000 prisoners in an ordinary-regime camp are engaged in construction work.

L.B., a former prisoner of the Moldavian camp system, reports on his experiences in the camp in *Krikovo*.

"We were brought to this strict-regime camp in 1975. There were a number of Jewish prisoners like myself here. We were arrested on various false charges after having received our visas to Israel. Our first day at the camp began with the confiscation of our books and personal belongings. Those who showed any resistance were immediately beaten up and thrown into an isolation cell. The very next day, having already been exhausted by the prison conditions and by undernourishment, we were sent straight to the quarry. Work norms were not individually set but determined, rather, by the performance average of the entire brigade. The prisoners were thereby motivated to keep an eye on each other in case anyone stopped working. No one, after all, wanted to have his rations reduced, be thrown into the isolation cell, or forfeit the privilege of receiving a visit or a package (a privilege that was granted only once a year, but even so...).

The guards often beat the prisoners up. Once, in 1976, two prisoners escaped from the camp. The guards, however, discovered them hiding in a haystack, and stabbed them to death with their bayonets. The guards later boasted of their deed.

The prisoners at this camp were worked to exhaustion. But there were those – the religious prisoners – whose visual presence was a source of strength for the others. There were many of them. They prayed openly and maintained an image of unbroken serenity even when they were thrown into the isolation cell or denied their privileges. Two such men were Boris *Plyuta,* a Pentecostal, and Semen *Korzhanets,* a Baptist. Their courage proved to be of enormous help to us.

MORDOVIAN A.S.S.R.

(area: 26200 sq. km.; pop.: 1100100)

The history of the Mordovian camps and their origins in the years immediately following the Revolution of 1917 have largely been forgotten. Prisoners in those days were used to construct a highway – and later a special railroad – from Pot'ma to Temnikov. No Soviet map will show these paths of travel; officially, they do not exist. Along this *"Dubrovlag"* route, as it is called, you will find a chain of labor camps and nothing else. We have therefore added a map of the area to the *Guidebook*. Until recently, most of the camps of the "Dubrovlag" were populated with political prisoners, but these people are now being transferred to camps in the Perm' Region (see separate map) in the Urals. Yet political prisoners may still be found in *Sosnovka, Lesnoi* (camp no. 19; commander: Captain Kiselev; K.G.B. commissioner: Captain Boroda), and *Barashevo*. Foreigners are imprisoned here as well.

104

Mordovian camps: the way from the camp to the work area. Mordovian A.S.S.R., east of Moscow, west of the Kuibyshev Reservoir on the Volga River (photo 1976).

We know today of eight camps and one prison on the "Dubrovlag" route. Seven of them are strict-regime camps; the facility in Sosnovka is a special strict-regime camp (in effect, a prison). The prisoners here, whose number at each of these camps varies between 500 and 2500, are used in logging, lumber processing, furniture manufacturing, machine plant work, the production of radio housings, souvenir manufacturing for export (cuckoo clocks), and the production of steering wheels and chassis for automobiles.

In *Barashevo,* you will find a camp hospital and a women's camp.

In *Ruzaevka,* there is a transit prison for 1500 inmates and an ordinary-regime camp of approximately 1200 prisoners who have been put to work in a woodworking plant.

In *Saransk,* you will find a pre-trial investigation prison, a special K.G.B. prison, and an ordinary-regime camp for about 600 inmates assigned to work in local industry.

Whole generations of prisoners have passed through the "Dubrovlag" camps, including thousands of foreigners, many of whom were abducted and brought into the Soviet Union.

Prisoners at the special strict-regime camp no. 1 are dressed in striped, numbered uniforms and confined in cells. The work to which they are assigned here involves the grinding of glass on carborundum disks in unventilated shops. Many of them, as a result, fall ill with silicosis.

Many of the inmates in the "Dubrovlag" camps are serving their sentences for practicing their religious beliefs. Inmates found to possess texts of the Holy Scriptures, crosses, or – in the case of Jews – yarmulkes are forcibly dispossessed of them, bound at the wrists, and then thrown into the isolation cell.

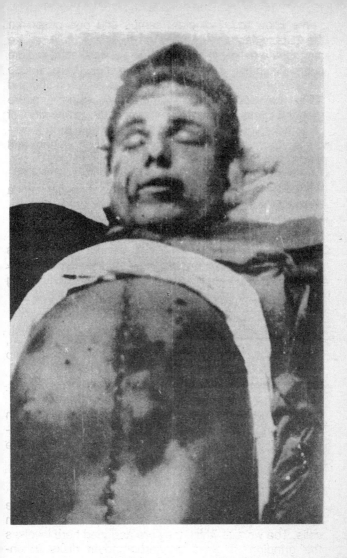

At age 20, Ivan Moiseev was forcefully inducted into the Soviet Army. As a Christian, he considered military service irreconcilable with his religious convictions.

Shortly after his induction, his parents were informed that he had died of an illness. The parents received the body in a soldered lead coffin in July 1972. On opening the coffin, the parents discovered six knife wounds in their son's chest, the real cause of death apparently. This is how the K.G.B. made short work of a young man unwilling to disavow his religious convictions.

Ivan Moiseev's parents live in Volontirovka, Suvorov Region, Moldavian S.S.R., southwest U.S.S.R. (capital: Kishinev).

In 1960, an uprising and strike took place at the Mordovian camps. In contrast, however, to the uprisings in *Kingir, Noril'sk,* or on the *Vorkuta* River, where the rebelling inmates were shot by firing squads, the strike was ended "peacefully". The "instigators" were punished with an extention of their terms of imprisonment.

Cemetery of unmarked graves along the Pot'ma railway (Moscow–Kuibyshev line), in Barashevo, Mordovian A.S.S.R., east of Moscow (capital: Saransk). This line was built by prisoners. Those who died in the process were buried alongside the railroad tracks. All there is left to see are wooden stakes with the numbers of the buried prisoners painted on them (photo 1976).

ORËL REGION
(area: 24 700 sq. km.; pop.: 931 000)

In the separate notes to the map of Orël city, which is located 500 kilometers south of Moscow, we have included the addresses of the special psychiatric prison for dissidents, the K.G.B. prison, a pre-trial investigation prison, and a children's camp. We shall therefore only refer in this section to those camps in Orël Region sited outside of the capital city.

In *Bolkhov,* 80 kilometers north of Orël, approximately 2 000 prisoners in a strict-regime camp are used in construction work. Captain Efimov is the commander of the camp. The K.G.B. commander here is Captain Novoselov.

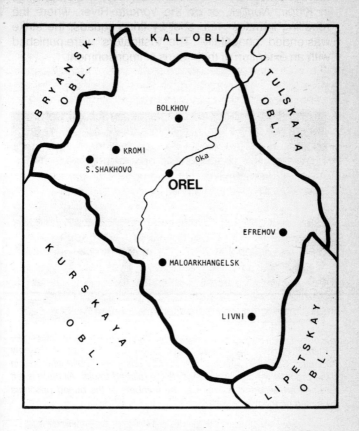

In *Kromy,* 40 kilometers south of Orël, 500 to 600 prisoners from an ordinary-regime camp, designated as facility no. 22/3, assemble farm machines in machine shops. The commander of the camp is Captain Sarygin.

In *Maloarkhangel'sk,* 80 kilometers southeast of Orël, some 1000 camp prisoners are used in the construction of military equipment.

In *Efremov,* 160 kilometers east of Orël, 1500 prisoners from a strict-regime camp, designated as facility no. 22/6, manufacture reinforced concrete plates.

In *Livny,* 150 kilometers southeast of Orël, 800 to 900 prisoners from camp no. 22/7 are used in a lumber mill. The commander of the camp is named Captain Potapov.

We do not have any information in our possession on the possible brutal treatment of prisoners in the camps of this region. Eyewitness reports, however, can testify to the brutality exercised in the special psychiatric prison in Orël city. The hospital attendants there quietly pick out criminals from the camps to steal and to "keep order" for them. The slightest disobedience on the part of the prisoners will get them a real thrashing, a spell in the strait jacket, or the electric shock treatment. The attendants rob the prisoners not only of provisions sent to them by their families, but also of their prison rations. The weak are raped and turned into homosexuals.

There is no point in making complaints. The physicians and guards only laugh and answer, "Just keep quiet, and no one will punish you." Among the mentally healthy here are those who were arrested for religious reasons. The hospital attendants persecute them and prevent them from praying or from talking with each other. The prison and the psychiatric prison are located at *Razgradskaya Street* 3 and 2.

Demand a visit with the prisoners, and loudly inform the authorities there that you are aware of all these humiliations!

Overhead view of a psychiatric prison in Orël, 347 kilometers south of Moscow. Prisoners are walking in the courtyard (photo 1976).

ORËL CITY

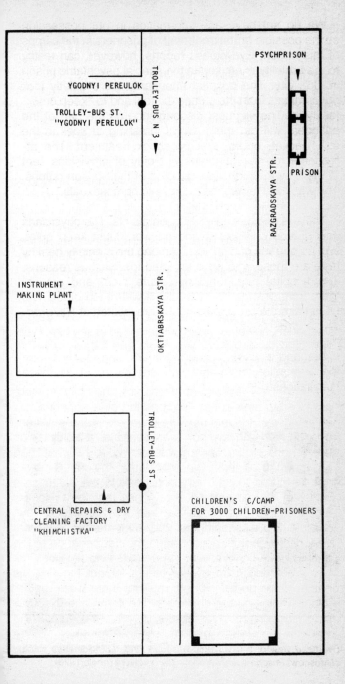

111

ORËL CITY
(pop.: 300000)

Trolley bus no. 3, which drives past the tool factory, will take you directly to a children's camp. Catch the trolley bus at the stop marked *"Yagodnyi Pereulok"* and get off at *Khimchistka* stop in front of the dry-cleaning factory. You will see the large factory building with the sign "Kombinat bytovogo obsluzhivaniya" on it on your right. Across the street on your left, you will see the watchtowers of the children's camp in which approximately 3000 prisoners are held.

We quote an excerpt from the eyewitness testimony of Elena K., whose 14-year-old son was imprisoned in this camp after the family had applied for emigration to Israel. The boy had knocked over a newspaper stand with his bicycle, was arrested and charged with hooliganism, and sentenced to two years' forced labor. The youth was apparently given such a long sentence so as to prevent the family from leaving the Soviet Union.

"I have often gone to the camp to visit my son Sergei. Very often, however, I was not permitted to see him. I was told that he would behave badly and fail, as a result, to fulfill his normal work quota.

"After a few lessons in mechanics, the children were assigned to their duties, such as the assembly of a few appliances or the manufacture of vegetable cans. Whenever a visit with my son was possible, a soldier was posted in the room. My son was allowed to eat what I had brought him all right, but only during the visit. He was not permitted to take anything back to the camp area with him. My son would always say that the prisoners did not have enough to eat and that he was always hungry. He also said that the work quotas were set very high – that is, according to the performance of the entire brigade. Anyone in the brigade who did not work well was beaten up by the others for not meeting his share of the quota. He told me that there were regular criminals among the children in the camp and that they exercised control over all the others. They forced the younger inmates to perform services for them. Those who refused were beaten. The older boys often mishandled the younger ones and sexually assaulted them.

The 'tutors' – that is, guardians – wandered about the place in a drunken state instead of attempting to put a stop to the abuses on the part of the thugs. On the contrary, the thugs were appointed as brigade leaders and told to push the others to fulfill their work quotas.

"My son often broke into tears and complained about the exhausting work, about the thugs and about his always being hungry. I cried with him because I could not help him. All the objections that we had raised in court had no effect."

Tourists are not prohibited from requesting permission from the camp administration to see the facility and talk to the children.

*

LITHUANIAN S.S.R.
(area: 65 200 sq. km.; pop.: 3 400 000)

In Lithuania, an independent country until its occupation by the Soviet Union in 1939, the tourist can visit eleven concentration camps and seven prisons. There were only two prisons in independent Lithuania. We have no knowledge of any camps.

Four prisons and three concentration camps – one of them for children – may be found in the capital city of *Vilnius*. In *Lukiškés* Prison (in Russian: *Lukishki*), women are confined with their infant children. See the special map of Vilnius for details on how to find the penal facilities of the city.

In *Panevežys,* northwest of Vilnius, you can visit a large women- and- children's camp. More than 2000 women prisoners there work in a sewing factory (army uniforms, tank covers, cartridge pouches).

LITHUANIAN S.S.R.

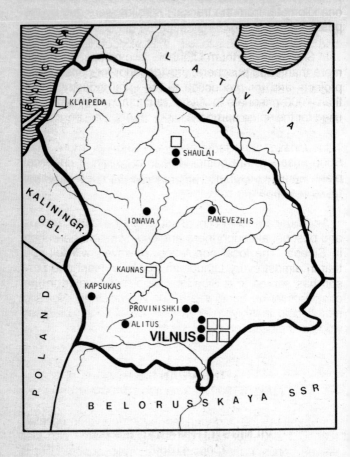

If you take the train or drive for 60 kilometers from Vilnius in the direction of Kaunas, you will see *Provinishki* (Lithuanian name: Pravieniškes) on the right-hand side. Along the railroad tracks is a zone guarded by soldiers and watchtowers, where prisoners unload lumber transported here for processing at the furniture factory or the woodworking plant. These two enormous and profitable plants are manned by prisoners from two large camps located about one kilometer from the railroad tracks. Some 3 000 inmates work themselves to exhaustion in the production of upholstered furniture, elegant yachts, and carved hunting rifle butts (see map of these two camps).

On approaching Provinishki, the tourist will be able to spot atomic rocket warheads above the trees about one kilometer from the tracks. The silos were dug by the prisoners.

In *Šiauliai,* in northern Lithuania, two camps, each with more than 1500 prisoners, provide labor for construction projects and for production in the local industry. More than 1000 prisoners in *Alytus* in southern Lithuania are used for the same purposes.

In *Jonava,* 30 kilometers from Kaunas, more than 5000 prisoners are being used to construct a chemical plant. Female prisoners have been assigned to auxiliary tasks in a separate zone there.

As you can see, Lithuania is covered with camps and prisons, although there are fewer of them here than in Siberia. The local population, however, will tell you that in almost every Lithuanian family, at least one person has served in a Siberian camp, participated in the construction of mine shafts in *Vorkuta* and *Noril'sk,* mined gold in *Kolyma* or coal in Kazakhstan, or sawn wood in the taiga forests of *Krasnoyarsk* or *Irkutsk.*

*

VILNIUS (LITHUANIAN S.S.R.)
(pop.: 410 000)

One of the most beautiful areas in Vilnius is *Gediminas* Square (16), to which we refer as a point of reference. Walking away from Gediminas Square along Lenin Prospekt, you will see on your right a public garden and a monument (Lenin Square). In front of the square is a conservatory (10) and next to it, a very similar building (2) in which the K.G.B. maintains a special penal facility for political prisoners. The same building was used by the Gestapo in World War II.

Because the architecture of the K.G.B. building strongly resembles that of the conservatory, residents of Vilnius often jokingly refer to it as the *"Dzerzhinskii*

VILNIUS CITY

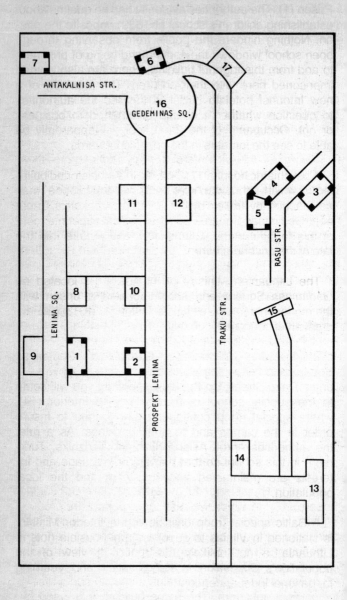

School of the Arts". (Dzerzhinskii was head of the secret police in the early years of the Soviet state.)

On the other side of the square, you will see *Lukiškés* Prison (1). The authorities evidently had no qualms about establishing children's school no. 6 (9) opposite the prison. Nothing hinders the pupils from observing through open school windows the coming and going of prisoners to and from this frightful building. There are also women imprisoned here with their children. The proximity of a new Intourist hotel to Lukiškés has led the authorities to question whether it should be opened to business or not. Occupants of the 22nd floor will apparently be able to see the inmates in the prison courtyards.

A psychiatric hospital (7), housed in a multistoried building in which Lithuanian dissidents are imprisoned, may be reached by trolley bus no. 2 from Antakalnis Street near Gediminas Square. Visit the medical superintendent of this frightful place, Glauberson, and inquire into the fate of the prisoners here.

The Lithuanian Ministry of Interior (6) is located on *Gediminas* Square and accommodates a prison with the modest name of pre-trial detention jail (KPZ: Kamery predvaritel'nogo zaklyucheniya).

By following Universitetas Street from Gediminas Square and continuing past the university (17), you will enter *Traku* Street. On the left-hand side, you will come to the special school of the Ministry of Interior (14), where special troop contingents are trained to insure order in the camps and to quell uprisings. As a rule, the authorities enroll Asians (Uzbeks, Tadzhiks, Turkmen) in this school so that barriers of language and interests are maintained between them and the local population.

A Baltic special troop division of the Interior Ministry is stationed in Vilnius to suppress any possible riots in Lithuania, a not unlikely eventuality in view of the population's opposition to Russification and yearning for national independence.

On *Lenin* Square, you will find the Supreme Court of the Lithuanian S.S.R. (8). Many trials of local dissidents have taken place in this gloomy building, among them that of *I. Schneider,* a former political prisoner and hero of the Lithuanian resistance movement. Our

Guidebook contains a picture taken during his trial. The photographer was obviously taking a serious risk.

On the right-hand side of Lenin Prospekt as you face away from Gediminas Square, you will easily find the *Café Neringa,* where young people congregate. It is also a favorite meeting place of Lithuanian dissidents. Knowing this, the K.G.B. planted its own people in the café – communist emigrés living in the Soviet Union – ostensibly to work as waiters and so on, in fact, however, to function as agents provocateurs. The agents inturn play up their foreign image for the benefit of suspected dissidents. This, however, was not enough for the K.G.B. A lodger on the second floor of the apartment house (12) across the street from the café was given notice. Soon afterwards, a wiretap and note-taking machine was installed in the apartment. Microphones were concealed in the café both at the tables and in the niches in the large room.

A children's camp (3) is located behind the train station on *Rasu* Street not far from a cemetery. Approximately 500 to 600 children between 14 and 18 years of age are put to work in the machine shop at the camp.

At the same location – behind the Holy Gates, entrance to the admirable buildings of a former Catholic monastery, which is designated on older city maps of Vilnius as an "architectural landmark" – you will find two men's camps and a "sharaga", a special scientific laboratory (4) in which imprisoned designers work.

Over the gates of the old monastery, you will find a glass box containing an electric control panel used by the camp guards to maintain security at the camp.

The "sharaga" *(Solzhenitsyn's* description of the "sharaga" in *Marfino*—near Moscow—in his *GULAG Archipelago* is worth recalling) is used to develop automatic remote control and electronic devices designed to guard restricted areas in Soviet camps and prisons and to prevent escapes. Restricted experimental areas have also been marked off within the walls of the monastery, where specialists test these devices. (Similar instruments may have already been installed at the Berlin

Wall.) The radio components factory here, in which ordinary camp prisoners are put to work, houses the "sharaga" on its top floor. For details of the camp interior, see the separate map of *Rasu* Street and the accompanying notes in our *Guidebook.*

Next to this "monastic" facility is another men's camp (5) for 500 prisoners. Theoretically, the inmates at this camp were brought here to be "treated" for alcoholism. In fact, however, they have been assigned to forced labor.

On *Maskvos* Street, you will find a transit prison. The number of prisoners in Vilnius is so large, that a special penal institution had to be constructed for their accommodation until they could be transferred to other facilities.

Lukiškés was the only prison in Vilnius before the Soviet occupation of the country. Now there are four prisons and three concentration camps here.

Not without reason do Soviet citizens display the popular proverb, "Life has gotten better, life has gotten happier!"

*

THE CAMP IN THE MONASTERY ON RASU STREET

Along the ancient Rasu Street, approximately 500 meters from the Holy Gates, which is included on every Intourist itinerary, you will find the walls of the former monastery.

Entrance to the monastery is alas prohibited, despite its official designation as an architectural landmark. The real "landmark" here is a concentration camp, which is guarded by the K.G.B.

The prisoners here are assigned to work eigher at the camp's radio factory or in its research laboratory. The laboratory, manned by 1300 prisoners, is used for planning the construction of new camps and for developing electronic security devices. Camp commander is

Colonel Lukšas, his deputy is Colonel Adomaitis. Lieutenant Colonel Novikov is head of the K.G.B. operations section.

There are five sections in the laboratory: architectural construction, sanitation engineering, planning, designing, and communications.

The laboratory is directed by Antonas Lumbas, a sadist and an anti-Semite, and by Colonel Prochukanov, the deputy interior minister of Lithuania. The laboratory "services" all the camps in the Soviet Union. It has been endowed with up-to-date equipment from the United States, West Germany, and Japan. Prisoners assigned here are worked to physical exhaustion. M.K., 1.77 meters tall, once worked in this laboratory. He recounts that his weight fell to 47 kilograms as a result of his fatiguing duties. As in Stalin's time, the prisoners here today – in 1980 – are warned that, if their work is deemed unsatisfactory, they will be sent to the logging areas or mines of Siberia. M.K. suffered this very fate; he was transferred to Arkhangel'sk Region to work in the aluminum bauxite mines (see his testimony in the section on Arkhangel'sk Region).

As indicated on the map, the camp is divided into a living and a work area. The living area of the prisoners is accommodated in the former church of the monastery, which has been converted into a barracks. The radio factory (6) and the laboratory (5) are located in the work area. Here you will also find the isolation cell (7).

The glass tower over the camp gates will lead you to the work area. Here, along the fence, are five or six rows of automatic remote controlled and electronically monitored obstacle courses, where engineers from the laboratory test the most advanced security devices developed for use in the camps or along international frontiers (Berlin Wall!).

Key to the map of the camp on Rasu Street

1. LTP – camp for the compulsory treatment of alcoholics (500 prisoners).
2. Camp for 1300 prisoners; production of radios and electronic devices – living quarters.
3. Work area of the camp.
4. Glass tower, used in conjunction with an experimental electronic device to insure the security of the restricted area; the gates to the camp are located under the tower.

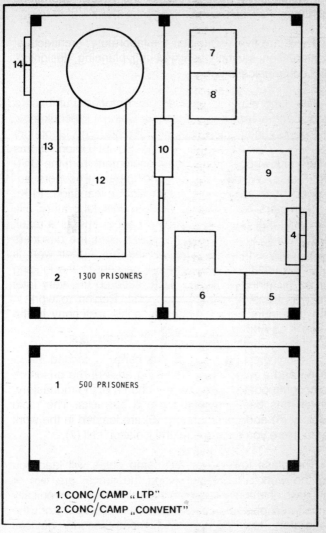

1. CONC/CAMP „LTP"
2. CONC/CAMP „CONVENT"

5. "Sharaga" – the scientific laboratory in which imprisoned construction and electronics specialists develop plans for building and maintaining the security of camps and prisons in the Soviet Union.
6. Radio and electronics factory.
7. Lockup (isolation cell).
8. Camp administration.
9. Storage area.
10. Guard house, situated between the living and work areas.
11. Gates between the living and work areas.
12. Former church of the monastery now used as living quarters by the prisoners.
13. Watchpost.
14. Gates to the camp.

Map of the camps in Provinishki (Pravieniškes), Lithuanian S.S.R., located between Vilnius and Kaunas.

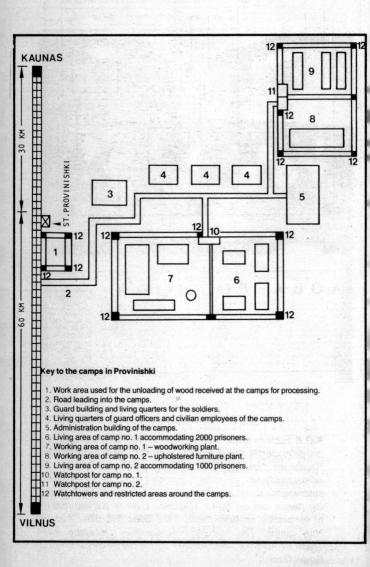

Key to the camps in Provinishki

1. Work area used for the unloading of wood received at the camps for processing.
2. Road leading into the camps.
3. Guard building and living quarters for the soldiers.
4. Living quarters of guard officers and civilian employees of the camps.
5. Administration building of the camps.
6. Living area of camp no. 1 accommodating 2000 prisoners.
7. Working area of camp no. 1 – woodworking plant.
8. Working area of camp no. 2 – upholstered furniture plant.
9. Living area of camp no. 2 accommodating 1000 prisoners.
10. Watchpost for camp no. 1.
11. Watchpost for camp no. 2.
12. Watchtowers and restricted areas around the camps.

K.G.B. sections responsible for political reeducation publish special propaganda newspapers for prisoners. Here is one of them: 'Trudovaya zhizn' (Working life). In this photograph, you can see an assembly hall, in which hundreds of prisoners in a special strict-regime camp are seated: numbers on their chests, drooping heads, striped prison uniforms. Look at the expressions of exhaustion on these faces. How does this differ from the Nazi camps? The newspaper is dated 24 December 1974. These are not Stalin camps; these are the Brezhnev camps of the Soviet Union.

123

LATVIAN S.S.R.

LATVIAN S.S.R.
(area: 63 700 sq. km.; pop.: 2 500 000)

According to eyewitness reports of former political prisoners, there were as of 1979 twelve forced-labor camps, including one children's and one women-and-children's camp, and eight prisons in Latvia.

Within *Riga* itself, there are four concentration camps.

1. No. OTs-78/7, *Krustpils Street 53,* Škirotava District. Approximately 2000 to 2300 of this men's ordinary – regime camp are used in the city and surrounding areas in construction work. Directions: electric train (Ogre line) or tram nos. 5 and 15 from the train station.

2. No. OTs-78/5, *Brasa* (suburb). Men's camp of approximately 2000 prisoners. Directions: electric train (Saulkrasti line) or trolley bus nos. 13 and 14 to Brasa stop.

3. No. OTs-78/6, *Ilgeciems* District (on the other side of the Dvina River). Women's camp of approximately 1500 prisoners. Directions: tram no. 1.

4. No. OTs-78/8, *Olaine* (suburb). Men's camp of approximately 2000 prisoners. Directions: electric train (Jelgava line).

We also know of two prisons in the Latvian capital.

1. Prison No. 21, a pre-trial investigation prison of approximately 1500 inmates. Directions: electric train to "Vagonnoe Depo" station (Škirotava District).

2. K.G.B. prison, on the corner of *Lenin* and *Engels* streets. Contains approximately 500 prisoners. Directions: bus nos. 1, 21, and 32; trolley bus nos. 4, 6, 7, and 17.

Camps and prisons located in other Latvian cities:

1. *Ventspils* – men's camp for about 800 prisoners

Sign pointing to a concentration camp near Riga, capital of the Latvian S.S.R., northwest U.S.S.R., on the Baltic Sea. Only the camp number is given: p/ya (P. O. Box) OTs-78/7 (photo 1975).

125

assigned to construction work; transit prison for about 600 inmates.

2. *Dalbuti* – prison for about 500 inmates.

3. *Jelgava* – two men's camps, each with about 1000 prisoners; prison for 1000 inmates.

4. *Valmiera* – two men's camps (an intensified-regime and a strict-regime facility), each with 1000 prisoners; prison for 500 to 600 inmates.

5. *Cesis* – children's camp for 1800 prisoners used for the manufacture of kitchen furniture and boxes.

6. *Rezekne* – men's camp for 1200 prisoners; prison for 500 inmates.

7. *Daugavpils* – men's special-regime camp for 800 to 1000 prisoners; prison no. 24 (1000 inmates).

8. *Brasa* – men's camp no. OTs-78/9 (1800 prisoners).

Those who have seen these camps and prisons have prolifically commented on the cruelty of the guards and K.G.B. personnel. Here is an excerpt of one such testimony.

Ya. R., who was a prisoner in camp no. OTs-78/7 (Riga, Krustpils Street 53), reports: "Colonel Aleksei Antonov was camp commander, though we rarely saw him. He ran the camp from his office. His low visibility, however, was compensated for every day by the cruelty of his assistants. Aleksandr Denisov, responsible for maintaining camp discipline, was a good example. A sly and malicious person, Denisov would order the prisoners thrown into the isolation cell for the slightest transgression, such as failing to remove their caps in his presence or not sitting on their own plank-beds in the barracks. Worst of all was K.G.B. Captain Elmar Zaul, head of the operations section at the camp. A real Gestapo type, his aim was to humiliate people. In his office, he had rubber hoses, boxing gloves, and even handcuffs attached to electrical wiring. All this was mere pretence, but there were times when he dropped all pre-

Начальник Главлита
Латвийской ССР

...Луцевич.. /Луцевич А.А./
3...сентября... 1974 года   г. Рига

А К Т № 8

Мы, ниже подписавшиеся ст. редактор Главлита Латвийской ССР
ЗИЛЕ В. Я. и начальник спецчасти БОГОЛАНОВА В. Л. составили настоящий акт в том, что перечисленные в нем материалы, конфискованные из бандеролей, поступивших из-за границы в *августе* месяце подлежат уничтожению:

1. E. Dunsdorfs "Latvijas vēsture" 1710-1800 g.   1300
2. Bībele   (")
3. H. damša ... nigan ... karoga, saukaivaći· sarkană   (")
4. Sēklinš   16

Всего подлежит уничтожению ... двенадцать ... наименов.
в ... ... экз.

Ст. редактор: Зиле
Начальник спецчасти: ...

Правильность произведенных записей в акте проверил
Ст. редактор: Зиле

Документы перед уничтожением сверены с записями в акте и полностью уничтожили путем сожжения.
"____" ___ 197 года

Ст. редактор:
Начальник спецчасти:

This document states that the Latvian K.G.B. has confiscated a copy of the Bible as anti-Soviet literature and that the Bible is to be burned.

tence to frighten those prisoners who refused to collaborate with the K.G.B. by informing on their fellow inmates. Those who could not be intimidated were thrown into the isolation cell. Zaul thus often beat the prisoners himself; it was not unusual to hear the cries of his victims from his office.

"One of Captain Zaul's deputies was Alfred Berziňš. He was two meters tall, drank constantly, beat the prisoners, and carried two medals on his chest – 'Outstanding Worker of the K.G.B.' and 'Outstanding Worker of the Ministry of Interior'.

"In our camp, there were about 2000 prisoners living in five barracks. Each prisoner was allotted 0.7 square

127

A truck used for transporting prisoners. An escort and the hands of a prisoner on the bars. (Camp no. OTs-78 in Riga.) Capital of Latvia, Baltic Sea coast. (Photo 1975.)

meters of 'living space'. Though our official workday lasted eight hours, we had to work longer than that in order to meet our quotas. After work, we were forced to perform 'public services' for the camp – without pay. For our basic labors, we received five to ten rubles a month after taxes.

"We were assigned to several different jobs, such as the construction of the Popov Radio Factory, a grain factory, or a bituminous concrete plant. The personnel of the lumber plant, moreover, consisted entirely of prisoners.

"There were other Jews like myself who were confined here – as political prisoners, in effect – for attempting to emigrate to Israel. A number of inmates were also imprisoned here for religious reasons or for protesting against the Soviet occupation of Latvia. I recall one Latvian, for example, who was sent here for throwing black paint on the Lenin Monument in Riga. A certain *Kovetskii* was sentenced to twelve years in this camp for attempting to emigrate to Sweden illegally. *Zhuravlev,* formerly a member of the Soviet embassy staff in Indonesia, had his teeth knocked out for describing life in foreign countries to his fellow inmates. A Tatar was beaten up for telling the other prisoners about the violent

128

resettlement of his people from their Crimean homeland. *Dudkin,* a Jew, was subjected to a beating for holding conversations on Zionism. A certain *Belinitskii* was beaten up for merely interceding on behalf of a fellow inmate in the presence of a camp supervisor, who shouted in response, 'Don't try to defend the others; worry about your own hide!'

"I repeatedly saw how prisoners at our camp were driven to despair by the arbitrariness of the authorities and the exhausting work. Many of them chose to end their lives by opening their veins.

"I also remember the exceptional humiliations to which the religious prisoners were subjected. Personnel at the camp stuffed dirty food into the mouths of Jewish or Moslem prisoners, for example, and shouted, 'Eat, you swine!' They ridiculed religious Christians through ironic reference to parables from the Bible or instigated non-believers to attack them. In making effective use of the principle, 'divide and rule', the camp authorities often incited the Russian prisoners against their fellow Latvian inmates. Captain Zaul himself once fomented a fight – indeed, a slaughter – between the Russian and Latvian prisoners; against the Jews he often incited all the other nationalities. Once, on Yom Kippur, they tried to beat us up while we were in prayer.

"Our camp was, according to prisoners who were sent to us from other penal institutions, relatively lenient – it was classified as an ordinary-regime facility. The strict, intensified, and special strict-regime camps were much worse."

*

NOVOSIBIRSK REGION
(area: 178 200 sq. km.; pop.: 2 505 000)

Novosibirsk Region may be reached from Moscow by train or airplane.

For the benefit of the tourists, the state likes to boast of Novosibirsk, with its modern buildings and its scientific community ("Akademgorodok"), as the "Capital of Siberia".

We should like to try to show you what is hidden behind the façade of this "capital".

In Novosibirsk city, you may visit four prisons – an ordinary-regime pre-trial investigation prison, two K.G.B. prisons, and a transit prison – and 15 camps, of which two are for children, one for women, and one for the seriously ill. For directions on how to find these facilities and other details, see the special map of Novosibirsk city.

Let us now cast a glance at the facilities hidden in the forests of Novosibirsk Region.

1. *Cherepanovo,* capital of the district of the same name, south of Novosibirsk. Here you may find twelve camps, of which three are for women, with a combined population of 12 000 prisoners assigned to logging or wood processing. Directions: 88 kilometers by train or car from Novosibirsk (via Berdsk).

2. *Toguchin* and *Tabulcha,* both in the easternmost part of the region. A men's strict-regime camp of 1500 prisoners may be found in each location. Directions: Tabulcha may only be reached by car; Toguchin is accessible by the train to Kemerovo.

3. *Moshkovo.* Here there are nine camps, including three facilities for women, with a total population of more than 10 000 prisoners assigned to construction, logging, and seamstress work. Directions: by car, 58 kilometers northeast of Novosibirsk.

4. *Kochenevo,* north of Novosibirsk. Approximately 2000 prisoners of a strict-regime camp here are used in logging and wood-processing (prefabricated houses, track ties, poles).

5. *Kuibyshev,* west of Novosibirsk. About 500 prisoners in an ordinary-regime camp here are used in the construction industry. At least another 3 000 inmates are confined in a notorious strict-regime transit prison here. The number of inmates at this facility fluctuates constantly, as prisoners are brought here from all over the Soviet Union for further distribution to the camps.

6. *Barabinsk,* south of Kuibyshev. Here there is a transit prison (about 2 000 prisoners) similar to that in Kuibyshev. Both cities lie on the train route between Novosibirsk and Omsk.

7. *Raisino,* south of Ubinskoe. The approximately 1000 prisoners at camp no. 91/13 (a particularly harsh strict-regime facility notorious for the savage arbitrariness of its personnel) are dressed striped prison uniforms. Directions: 360 kilometers by train from Novosibirsk to Ubinskoe.

8. *Vengerovo* District, western part of the region. Some 5000 prisoners from an especially harsh strict-regime camp here are put to work as loggers. They, too, must wear striped prison uniforms. Directions: Vengerovo city, which lies 120 kilometers west of Kuibyshev, may be reached from Novosibirsk by the train to Omsk.

9. Near *Kyshtovka,* in the extreme northwestern part of the region. We know of at least four especially harsh strict-regime camps in this area, though eyewitnesses have reported that there are others, the precise location of which, however, cannot be substantiated. These are death camps. The prisoners are sent into the pits to mine uranium ore and die only after few months of work in them. The population of these camps cannot be verified, though it is known that the number of prisoners here steadily increases. Prisoners convicted of insurrection or sentenced to death are among those who are sent here.

A review of all the known penal facilities in Novosibirsk Region will yield the following statistics: 51 concentration camps and five prisons.

A highly "developed" region...

*

NOVOSIBIRSK CITY
(pop.: 1400000)

Not without reason is Novosibirsk called the "Capital of Siberia". Fifteen concentration camps and four prisons provide sufficient grounds for calling it a "capital".

Here is a list of those locations not to be found on an Intourist itinerary.

1. Near *Tolmachevo* Airport, by way of which you are likely to enter Novosibirsk, 800 to 1000 prisoners at camp no. 91/2, a men's ordinary-regime facility, are put to work in the wood-processing industry. The inmates at this camp are usually given a maximum sentence of "only" ten years. Ask someone to show you *Tarnaya* Base. There you will see the fence and the watchtowers of the camp. Inquire into the reinforced concrete construction plant located in the same area. A women's camp, where 1500 prisoners are given "light" duties, may be found there.

2. On the way to *Akademgorodok,* which is included on all Intourist itineraries, you will find camp no. 91/3, a men's intensified-regime facility of more than 1000 prisoners. The maximum sentence meted out to the inmates here is 15 years. Ask for *Matveevka* District so that you will not lose your way. The watchtowers of the camp will serve as a benchmark.

3. In the city's *Dzerzhinskii* District is a pre-trial detention prison in which 3000 inmates are waiting for their day in court and subsequent transferral to a camp. The prison is always full, though the actual number of inmates incarcerated here varies. Twenty prisoners are confined to a cell, thus allowing 1.5 square meters per person. The cells contain double-level plank-beds; mattresses and linen are not provided. The cells are dirty and infested with lice. The prison also accommodates four death cells. Executions are carried out by firing squad.

4. You will find another prison on 1905 Street (ulitsa 1905-ogo goda) of no less than 2000 to 3000 inmates. It serves as a transit facility between Moscow and the camps in Siberia, the Far East, and the regions north of the Arctic Circle.

5. Another two prisons may be found in the building housing K.G.B. and Interior Ministry offices on *Kommunisticheskaya Street 49.* Like the other two prisons in the city, these two facilities, both of which are adminis-

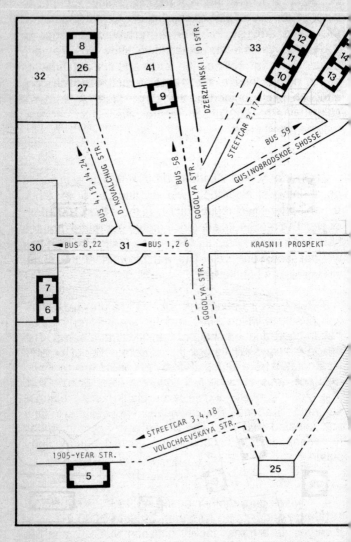

tered by the K.G.B., contain political prisoners. Charged with having violated criminal statutes, the inmates here are serving terms of imprisonment for practicing their religious faith, refusing induction into military service, or attempting to leave the country illegally.

6. On *Tankisty Street* in the southwestern part of the city, 600 to 800 prisoners in a strict-regime camp,

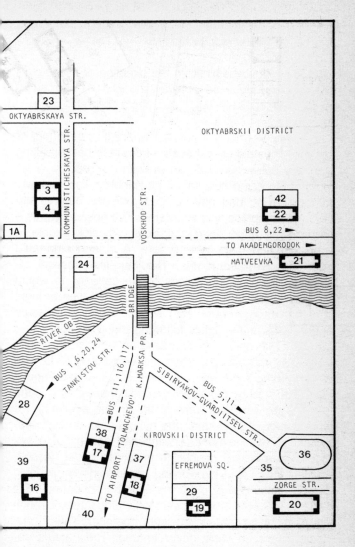

designated as no. 91/5, are assigned to work in the manufacturing of furniture and ammunition containers (in the "peace-loving" Siberian Farm Machine Construction Plant). The prisoners here are serving sentences of 15 years.

7. In *Dzerzhinskii* District in the northern part of the city, about 1000 prisoners from camp no. 91/8, a strict-

regime facility, are assigned to work in two nuclear warhead plants, innocuously designated as "Chimkontsentrat" and "Chimapparat". The high level of radioactivity emanating from the plants renders dangerous any visit to the immediate vicinity.

8. Leaving Novosibirsk (in the direction of Kemerovo) on the *Gusinobrodskoe* Highway, you will see three camps on your left: no. 91/9, no. 91/10, and a children's camp.

Camp no. 91/10 is a hospital where sick prisoners or prisoners completely exhausted from their backbreaking work are delivered. O.Z., an eyewitness, reports: "I arrived at the camp hospital on Gusinobrodskoe Highway without having had any camp experience before, and I thought the place was an inferno. The hospital wards – barracks, in effect – were packed with sick people. It was cold and damp everywhere. A stench emanated from the overfilled rooms. The thug-like hospital attendants lived off the rations of the patients, to whom the physicians in turn paid no attention. I was brought into the surgery ward, as I was suffering from acute appendicitis. Immediately following the operation, I was sent out with some other patients to work in the courtyard or in the kitchen. We were also made to tidy up the operating room and clean the surgical instruments. I was shocked by the sanitary conditions. Several of the forceps, for example, were rusted. In the evenings, we were assigned to sharpen the hypodermic needles systematically with a hone. I witnessed dozens of cases in this 'hospital' of desperate prisoners driven to self-mutilation by the brutal working conditions in the logging camps. Instances of prisoners who had chopped off a finger, swallowed a nail, or stitched a dirty thread through the flesh of an arm or leg were common. These prisoners, however, were never treated. The doctors' response was, 'You messed yourself up, now you can go rot to death for it'."

9. In the *Volochaevskii* residential area, a new housing development in Novosibirsk, you will find three camps, two of which are men's intensified-regime facilities. The prisoners here – 1000 inmates in one camp, 500 in the other – are assigned either to housing construction or

to machine workshops. About 500 prisoners in the third facility, a women's ordinary-regime camp, are put to work as seamstresses.

Prison in Novosibirsk city (capital of Novosibirsk Region; on the Ob' River, southwest Siberia). Note that the Soviet authorities have walled up the windows by half their original size. This prison was built in the days of the Tsars (photo 1977).

10. Two men's strict-regime camps are located in *Zael'tsevskii* District. The prisoners in these facilities (1500 inmates in one camp, 800 in the other) are assigned to work in stone and granite rock quarries.

11. In another part of the city, prisoners confined to a camp for adolescents (aged 16 to 18) perform auxiliary duties at the building site of a stadium in the *Zatulinskii* residential area, which is also under construction. Homosexuality is rampant in this penal facility; the youths leave it with serious psychological problems.

12. Two thousand five hundred prisoners sentenced to short terms of two or three years are brought under armed escort to the Trud engineering plant in Oktyabr'skii District to work in the arms industry. They perform dirty and hazardous auxiliary duties or are otherwise given work in lumber workshops.

13. The prisoners of a camp in *Kirovskii* District are put to work in a plant in which heavy military equipment is produced.

You will easily find your way to the camps and prisons in Novosibirsk by referring to our map, which will also provide you with information on the public transportation lines of the city.

*

PERM' REGION
(area: 160600 sq. km.; pop.: 3023000)

Perm' Region is located in the central part of the Ural Mountain Range (western slopes). Its accessibility to the rest of the Soviet Union, however, is facilitated by the navigability of the Kama River, which flows through it. The region enjoys both an abundance in forests and minerals (potassium, coal, etc.) and a highly developed mechanical engineering industry in a number of urban centers *(Perm'* city, *Kizel, Aleksandrovsk).* Continental climate predominates in the region. Temperatures during the six-month long winter fall to as low as −45° C.

The logging and timber transportation industries in Perm' Region are manned primarily by the prisoners from

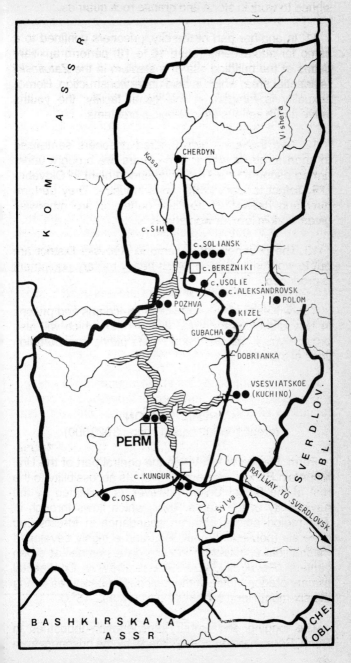

camp nos. 207 and 244. (Most of the lumber extracted from this area is destined for export.) Theoretically established as labor settlements for ordinary criminals, the camps here are also populated with a large number of political prisoners tried and convicted on trumped-up charges. These so-called secret political prisoners include those, such as the Jewish activists in the Zionist movement, fighting for their religious freedom or for the independence of their national regions (the Baltic republics, the Ukraine, the Caucasian republics, etc.). In addition, there are special political forced-labor facilities in the region known as the *Perm' Camp Complex* for Political Prisoners located in the vicinity of *Vsesvyatskaya* near *Kuchino.* The prisoners here are primarily put to work in the construction and mechanical engineering industries. Logging forced-labor camps may be found in the vicinity of *Kizel, Pozhva, Polom, Kokornya, Solikamsk, Sim, Gubakha, Cherdyn',* and *Usol'e.* Prisoners are also put to work in potassium mines near Solikamsk as well as in machine factories in *Solikamsk, Vsesvyatskaya, Berezniki, Kizel,* and *Aleksandrovsk.*

In *Osa* and *Dobryanka,* prisoners are assigned to work in the production and processing of petroleum and petroleum products. In *Aleksandrovsk,* they are put to work in a brickyard. The general administration of the camps in Perm' Region is located in *Kungur.*

The number of prisoners in the camps is not known. The smaller facilities, however, are believed to have a population of 300 to 500 and the larger ones of 1500 to 2000 prisoners.

The working conditions in the Solikamsk potassium mines constitute a serious health hazard. The death rate there is extremely high.

The facilities for the political prisoners are without exception forced-labor camps. The inmates there are exposed to systematic abuse. Kept in a state of permanent hunger, they are forced to perform hard-labor duties. Cases of merciless beatings of the prisoners by the guards are rather frequent.

We know the exact address of 24 camps and prisons in Perm' Region. In addition, we have knowledge of a group of several camps, known under the general designation, of *"Burepolom"*, located in the vicinity of *Polom*. Prisoners here are put to work in the logging industry. Because we do not know how many camps belong to this group, we have marked them as a single facility on the map.

Many well-known political prisoners have been confined in the Perm' Camp Complex: Professor Yurii *Orlov,* Anatolii *Shcharanskii,* Aleksandr *Ginsburg,* Georgii *Vins,* and many others.

1. *Perm':*   a) special isolation prison
             b) transit camp and hospital
             c) pre-trial detention prison
2. *Kungur:* a) general direction of all the camps in Perm' Region
             b) transit camp
             c) prison
3. *Osa:* strict-regime camp
4. *Vsesvyatskaya* (Kuchino): two concentration camps, nos. 389/35 and 389/36
5. *Dobryanka:* strict-regime concentration camp
6. *Gubakha:* strict-regime concentration camp
7. *Kizel:* strict-regime concentration camp
8. *Aleksandrovsk:* strict-regime concentration camp
9. *Usol'e:* strict-regime concentration camp
10. *Solikamsk:* five strict-regime concentration camps
11. *Berezniki:* a) strict-regime concentration camp
                b) prison
12. *Sim:* strict-regime concentration camp
13. *Cherdyn':* strict-regime concentration camp
14. *Polom:* camp complex (the number of camps is unknown)
15. *Pozhva:* strict-regime concentration camp

*

SVERDLOVSK REGION
(area: 194 800 sq. km.; pop.: 4 400 000)

Sverdlovsk Region is located on the east-central spurs of the Ural Mountains. Though harsh in climate, with temperatures falling to −45° or even −50°C. in the winter, the region is nevertheless endowed with an abundance of mineral wealth: ferrite, manganese, bauxite, copper, etc. Extensive logging areas, moreover, may be found

SVERDLOVSK REGION

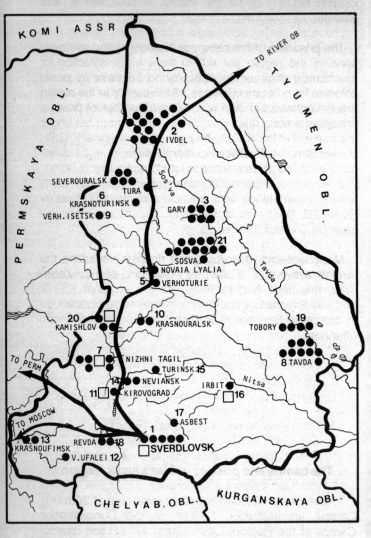

in several parts of the region, such as in *Sos'va, Tavda, Ivdel',* and *Gari,* from which large quantities of lumber are sent into export.

We know of 81 camps and five prisons in Sverdlovsk Region. The number of camps here, however, in which prisoners are assigned to the logging industry, is much higher. We are unfortunately unable to provide the reader with their exact locations.

The camps in the north provide labor primarily for the logging industry or for the mining of coal, ferrite, and bauxite.

The prisoners of the camps in the central and southern parts of the region are put to work in construction or mechanical engineering. Established primarily as penal colonies for ordinary criminals, all the camps in the region are nevertheless known to include a number of political prisoners among their inhabitants, all of whom fall under the purview of the K.G.B. Address of the regional K.G.B.: Vainer Street 4, Sverdlovsk. Responsible for legal questions involving Jews is Lieutenant-Colonel Grigorii Ivanovich Abramov. Address of the regional court that deals among other things with political questions: Malyshev Street 2B. The name of the judge specializing in political cases is *Zhalaev.*

Many well-known political civil rightists, including the Jewish activists V. *Kukui,* V. *Markman,* and L. *Zabelizhenskii,* have had to deal with the regional K.G.B. and the Sverdlovsk court. All of them were imprisoned in camps in Sverdlovsk Region together with common offenders.

*

The camps and prisons of Sverdlovsk Region

1. *Sverdlovsk* city, capital of the region (pop.: 1 300 000). Central Administration Section of the Concentration Camps of the Region: *Lenin Street 17;* section director is Colonel Dezdirëv. There are five concentration camps in the city: a) no. Ushch-349/1 in *Kirovskii* District, known as *"Kamennye palatki"* (stone tents); b) no. Ushch-349/10 in *Chkalovskii* District near the slaughter house; c) no. Ushch-349/43 in *Verkh-Isetskii* District; d) no. Ushch-349/2 near the Ivanovskoe cemetery; e) the special isolation prison *Repin Street 4.* In addition, there is a special pre-trial detention prison in the K.G.B. building at Vainer Street 4 and a pre-trial detention prison

of the Ministry of Interior for criminal offenders. In the immediate vicinity of the latter facility, you will find a transit prison in which political prisoners among others are incarcerated. Total estimated number of prisoners in the camps and prisons of Sverdlovsk city: 10000 to 11000.

2. *Ivdel'* – site of the administration of those camps that provide labor for the logging industry. We have knowledge of eleven camps that deliver wood and another three facilities from which prisoners are used for railroad repair and construction (in this case, the railroad line leading to the Ob' River). Total number of prisoners of the Ivdel' camps: over 10000.

3. *Gari* – We know of twelve camps in which approximately 8000 prisoners are assigned to work in the logging industry. The number of camps in this area, however, is in fact much higher.

4. *Novaya Lyalya* – the prisoners of the camp complex located in the outlying districts of the city are put to work in a paper factory. The number of camps within the complex is unknown. We only know that one of the camps, no. Ushch-349/41, has 1000 prisoners assigned to construction work or to auxiliary duties in the paper factory. Commander of this camp: Major Vyacheslav Mikhailovich Smirnov. Active K.G.B. agent in the camp: First Lieutenant Rakhimov. Administration supervisor: Captain Klimov.

5. Children's camps in *Verkhotur'e* (ordinary-regime facility for 500 to 700 prisoners) and *Krasnotur'insk* (strict-regime facility for 400 to 500 prisoners). The children manufacture wooden containers for finished products.

6. *Nizhnii Tagil* – ordinary-regime camp for women (no. Ushch-349/3). The 500 to 700 prisoners work in a garment factory in which camp uniforms are made.

7. *Nizhnii Tagil* – special camp (no. Ushch-349/13) in which 800 to 1000 inmates – imprisoned former members of the K.G.B., the Ministry of Interior, the courts, and the procuracies – are assigned to workshops in which locks and mattress wires are manufactured.

8. Vicinity of *Tavda* — at least ten camps, in which up to 1000 prisoners are confined, may be found here in the taiga. The prisoners are assigned to work as loggers.

9. Logging prison camps in the vicinity of *Severoural'sk, Krasnotur'insk,* and *Sos'va.* We know the precise location of only a few of these facilities (see map).

The prisoners of Sverdlovsk Region are assigned to various work installations: arms factories in which tanks are manufactured; mines where iron, asbestos, and other minerals are excavated; logging camps; quarries; and construction sites for apartment houses and industrial projects.

10. *Krasnoural'sk:* two concentration camps, no. Ushch-349/14 and Ushch-349/18
11. *Kirovgrad:* concentration camp no. Ushch-349/6 and prison
12. *Verkhnii Ufalei:* concentration camp no. Ushch-349/24
13. *Krasnoufimsk:* concentration camp no. Ushch-349/31
14. *Nev'yansk:* concentration camp no. Ushch-349/45
15. *Turinsk:* concentration camp no. Ushch-349/64
16. *Irbit:* concentration camp no. Ushch-349/71 and prison
17. *Asbest:* concentration camp no. Ushch-349/62
18. *Revda:* concentration camp no. Ushch-349/30
19. *Tabory:* concentration camp complex; we know the exact location of only four camps
20. *Kamyshlov:* concentration camp and prison
21. *Sos'va:* concentration camp complex; we know the exact location of only five camps

KAZAKH S.S.R.
(area: 2717300 sq. km.; pop.: 13700000)

Kazakhstan is one of the larger republics of the Soviet Union. The number of penal facilities here is also large. We know of 89 camps, ten prisons, and three psychiatric prisons. Nevertheless, we have reason to believe that our information on Kazakhstan is by no means complete.

146

A detailed listing of all the information we have on the penal facilities in Kazakhstan would suffice for an entire book on the subject. We shall therefore limit ourselves to the most interesting or most easily accessible population centers where these institutions may be found.

Let us begin with *Alma-Atà*, the capital of the republic. The official guide will show you a clean and verdurous city, but he will fail to include the special K.G.B. prison on

Special psychiatric prison in Talgar (20 kilometers east of Alma-Ata, on the highway from Alma-Ata to the Chinese border), Kazakh S.S.R. Here you see the forbidden zone around the building and a placard stating that it is prohibited to approach this area. The forbidden zone is guarded by troops of the Ministry of Interior (photo 1977).

your itinerary. Located in the inner courtyard of the Kazakh K.G.B. building, the special prison was designed to hold 1200 inmates. A pre-trial detention prison for 2000 inmates may also be found in the capital.

If you were to set out for the mountains from Alma-Ata – perhaps to visit the famous apple groves there – you would pass by ten camps (nos. 155/3, 155/11, 155/16, 155/17, 155/21, 155/24, and others) hidden in the valleys near the edge of town. The 6000 to 7000 prisoners confined in these facilities are taken every day to work on the construction of military installations in the mountains or to build a strategic road (in the direction of China). Ask to be taken to *Talgar.* There you may visit Psychiatric Prison No. LA-155/7, where hundreds of dissidents – ethnic Germans wishing to emigrate to Germany, religious people – languish. (See the accompanying photograph of this frightful building.)

In *Alekseevka,* about 50 kilometers from Alma-Ata, you may visit a psychiatric hospital classified as an ordinary-regime facility. In it, however, there are special wards for healthy inmates sent there on orders from the K.G.B. The majority of them are Germans who wish to emigrate from the Soviet Union. In the words of one of the psychiatrists at the hospital, "Only the insane want to leave the U.S.S.R."

A special psychiatric prison may also be found both in *Alma-Ata* itself as well as in *Kzyl-Orda.*

And now we shall provide you with the addresses of a

148

few death camps. As the *Guidebook* contains a special map of and detailed notes on all the known death camps in the Soviet Union, we will merely list those found in Kazakhstan: nos. 155/48 and 155/57 in the camp complex in *Aksu,* camp nos. 155/36 and 155/37 in *Tselinograd,* camp no. 155/69 in *Karagaily,* and one camp each in *Borovoe* and *Rudnyi.* These are special strict-regime camps. Their combined population is not known. As dying prisoners are taken away, more and more new death candidates are brought in. We can estimate, however, that there are 2000 to 2500 prisoners in each camp.

Most of the prisons in Kazakhstan have been designed as special strict-regime facilities to which camp inmates are transferred as punishment for some transgression. The prisons in *Ust'-Kamenogorsk* and *Semipalatinsk* are two such facilities. The 19th century writer, *Dostoevskii,* who was once an inmate here, wrote that the prisoners in these penal institutions were given very nourishing food and treated humanely by the escort guards. Today, however, starvation reigns in these prisons, and the administration authorities there are notorious for their cruelty and sadism.

I.Sh., an eyewitness, reports: "I spent a whole year in the prison on *Dostoevskaya Street* in *Semipalatinsk* and another year in the fortress prison in *Ust'-Kamenogorsk.* It was a nightmare. The personnel at the facilities beat the prisoners constantly. We had no energy to resist, as we were kept in a state of constant undernourishment. Nevertheless, the guards were afraid of us. They never entered our cells. Whenever they wanted to grab someone, they waited instead for a prisoner to come out of his cell on his way to his routine exercise and separated him from the others. Then they beat him savagely and threw him into the isolation cell. Prisoners returned from the lockup all covered with bruises."

It is interesting to note that former Soviet Premier G.M. *Malenkov* was sent to *Ust'-Kamenogorsk* following his ouster from power to assume direction of a hydroelectric power plant. He has thus never been a victim of the penal system for which he, Stalin, and other Soviet leaders are responsible.

More than 2000 inmates are confined in the special

section of a large transit prison in *Petropavlovsk*. The prison is dirty and pervaded by a stench. Communicable diseases are rampant here.

In *Ural'sk*, 1200 inmates are confined in a special prison known for its cruel and arbitrary regimen. Major Medvedev, the prison commander here, has a favorite saying, "Ural'sk is as far from Moscow as from the moon!"

Prisoners at the camps in Kazakhstan are assigned the most diverse kinds of duties – from construction work to work in mines and factories.

Prisoners, for example, in the camps in northeastern Kazakhstan (*Leninskii, Zyryanovsk, Oktyabr'sk, Ust'-Kamenogorsk, Zharma,* and *Karaul*) are put to work in lead mines. Despite the fact that the work is hazardous, the Communist state refuses to provide its slaves with a special diet or protective clothing.

At a camp near *Dzhezkazgan*, Karaganda Region, 1500 prisoners are assigned to work in copper mines under extremely hazardous conditions. A special prison for unruly inmates is located in the same area.

Dzhezkazgan was the scene of a camp uprising in 1953 at a time when there were more than 10 000 prisoners there. Driven to despair by the harsh regimen of the facility complex, the prisoners proclaimed a strike to demand humane treatment by the authorities, remuneration for their labor, and the right to correspond with, receive packages from, and occasionally meet with their relatives.

The alarmed local authorities attempted to calm the prisoners and promised to meet their demands. As might have been expected, however, the prisoners were deceived and their leaders arrested, whereupon the strike flared up again. This time, Moscow intervened. Special units of the M.V.D. (the Russian initials for Ministry of Interior; in this case, a former name of the K.G.B.), tanks, airplanes, mortars, and killers armed to the teeth were despatched to storm the unarmed prisoners. Among the insurgent camps was a women's facility, most of the 500 prisoners of which were Ukrainians arrested for participating in the anti-Communist national liberation struggle. The women of the camp took position between the tanks and the men they sought to defend. Yet the tanks rolled on. Think about these heroines when you visit Dzhezkazgan.

Women-and-children's camps may be found in *Chamal'gan* and *Nikolaevka* (such facilities are discussed in a separate section of the book).

Prisoners are employed in the extensive building activities in the military sphere in Kazakhstan. More than 6000 prisoners, for example, are participating in the construction of the secret city of *Stepnogorsk,* where three

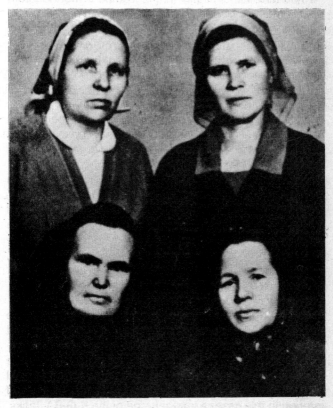

The sons of these Christian mothers in Taldy-Kurgan, 210 kilometers east of Alma-Ata, Kazakh S.S.R. in Central Asia, are in prison. Beginning in the upper left-hand corner going clockwise: Nadezhda Ivanovna Batulko, Naberezhnaya Street 92; Aleksandra Arsent'evna Pavlov, Mayakovskii Street 2a; Nadezhda Timofeevna Batulko, Gagarin Street 57; Frida Karlovna Kasper, Michurin Street 29. Remember them in your prayers!

camps are located. One thousand eight hundred prisoners from another camp are assigned to the construction of secret military installations near *Karsakpai, Nikol'-skii, Prorva, Karatobe, Aksai,* and *Aral'sk.*

On the *Mangyshlak* peninsula (see special map), you will find camps that provide work gangs for uranium enrichment plants and military construction projects.

More than 2000 prisoners from camp p/ya 154/53-D are assigned to work in an open-pit coal mine.

We do not have enough space to list all the camps in Kazakhstan of which we have knowledge. These penal facilities, however, are indicated on our map by a dot, behind each of which you will find the human face of prisoners confined to a camp, prison, or psychiatric prison.

It is interesting to note that uprisings have not only taken place in the camps. In 1960, for example, workers of the Metallurgical Industrial Plant and other installations in *Temirtau,* 35 kilometers northwest of Karaganda, staged hunger riots. They demanded bread from the authorities, and received bullets instead. The uprising was quashed in a sea of blood. Hundreds of workers, as a result, ended up in the camps.

*

MANGYSHLAK PENINSULA

The Mangyshlak Peninsula is a salt desert jutting out into the Caspian Sea. It may be reached by ship from *Gur'ev* at the mouth of the Ural River, which empties into the Caspian Sea, or over land through the Mërtvyi Kultuk desert.

There you will find uranium mines, two uranium enrichment plants (nos. 1 and 2 on the map), a nuclear power plant (A), and a cool-water plant (no. 3) in the immediate vicinity of the power plant. In addition, there is a large complex of concentration camps on the peninsula. The prisoners here are assigned to hard labor in the uranium mines and the enrichment plants. Because the camp area is a strictly guarded off-limits zone, we were not able to determine the number of facilities here.

P.M., formerly employed as an engineer on Mangyshlak, provided us with a map of the area and with information on the camp complex. He reports having seen hundreds of prisoner teams every morning on his way to work from the port of *Erilaev* being escorted to their duty areas. Each team consisted of 200 prisoners. Civilians at the complex are

MANGYSHLAK PENINSULA

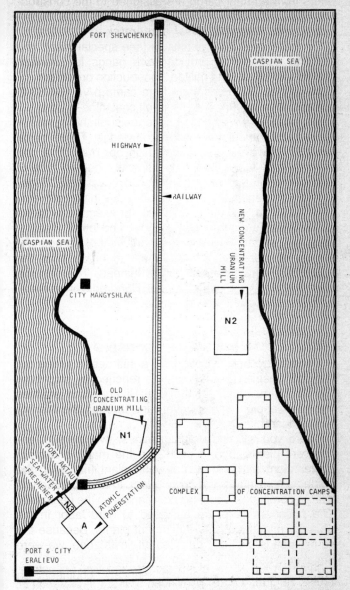

employed in management positions or as watchmen.

The director of the entire complex on the peninsula is Grigoryan, a "Hero of Socialist Labor", whose answer to the suggestion that a few trees be planted on Mangyshlak was, "The best decorations here are the watchtowers and barbed-wire fences".

IRKUTSK REGION

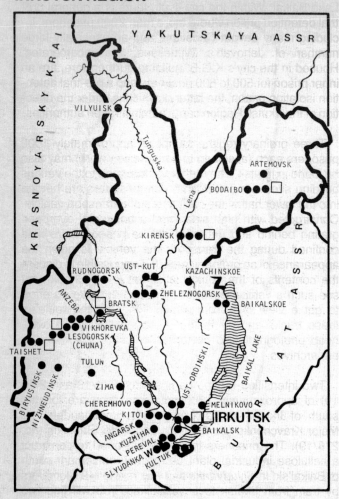

IRKUTSK REGION
(area: 767 900 sq. km.; pop.: 2 300 000)

Although we know of 48 camps and five prisons in Irkutsk Region, we are convinced that our information is incomplete. There are a large number of camps in the taiga, the locations of which we cannot pinpoint. In *Biryusinsk,* for example, we can provide precise information on only one camp. Yet according to *Bolonkin*, a political prisoner, there are altogether 25 camps in the vicinity. We do not, however, have their exact addresses.

The capital of the region is *Irkutsk* city, located near Lake Baikal. Within the city itself, there is a general pre-trial detention prison where more than 2000 prisoners, including many devout Christians and an especially large number of Jehovah's Witnesses, are incarcerated. Housed in the city's K.G.B. building, furthermore, are an inner prison for 500 to 600 prisoners and a pre-trial detention isolation prison, the latter of which is under the direction of the Irkutsk Region camp administration authorities.

Three ordinary-regime camps of approximately 1000 prisoners each (assigned to construction work) may also be found in Irkutsk. The method of transport to the various building sites is most original. The prisoners are herded into the lower half of the cargo area of a transport vehicle. Constructed with high sides and a horizontal overhead grating behind and under which the prisoners are held confined during the transport, the vehicle is given the appearance of an ordinary truck. It is impossible to discern the contents of the vehicle at street level. Should you see such a vehicle escorted by a guard, make an effort to get a view of it from above. Find out the route of these trucks and try to find a way of taking an overhead photograph. Do not forget to send us a copy for our archives.

Two intensified-regime camps (nos. 278/18 and 278/19) of approximately 1200 prisoners each are located south of Irkutsk in *Baikal'sk*. Camp commanders are Major Kravchenko (no. 278/18) and Major Sapelkin (no. 278/19). The prisoners there are assigned to construct a cellulose industrial plant and a new settlement south of Baikal'sk. In *Slyudyanka* and *Kuz'mikha* (40 kilometers by train from Irkutsk to Lake Baikal), you will find two women's camps in which the prisoners maintain the custody of those of their children two years of age or less. The 1500 women in the strict-regime camp in Slyudyanka are assigned to sew prison uniforms. A men's strict-regime camp located in the same city has 1600 prisoners who are put to work in the mica mines nearby.

In an ordinary-regime camp in *Kuz'mikha,* 700 to 800 women made invalid through forced-labor duties in other penal facilities must nevertheless continue working. Here they are assigned to cleave mica by hand for the electronics and arms industries. A similar camp (no. 04) for male invalids assigned to the same dangerous work is located in *Mel'nikovo,* near Irkutsk.

A men's special strict-regime camp of 1500 to 1600 prisoners put to work in marble quarries may be found in *Pereval* near Slyudyanka. The men there must wear striped, numbered prison uniforms.

The 1000 to 1200 prisoners in a strict-regime camp in *Kultuk* work in construction in the military sphere.

In *Angarsk,* about 50 kilometers northwest of Irkutsk, the prisoners of two intensified-regime camps completed the first phase in the construction of a synthetic gasoline plant and have now begun the second. Approximately 2000 prisoners are confined in each camp.

In *Cheremkhovo,* 140 kilometers from Irkutsk, you will find another two strict-regime camps, in each of which 1500 to 2000 prisoners are confined. They are assigned to construct minepits or to work in coal mines.

The administration of the *"Kitoilag"* camp complex is located in *Kitoi.* The complex consists of at least three strict-regime facilities of 800 prisoners each and provides labor for the logging industry and for a wood-processing plant. How many additional camps belong to the "Kitoilag" complex is known only to the K.G.B. and the Ministry of Interior.

In both *Vilyuisk* (accessible only by airplane) and *Bodaibo* (accessible by train from Taishet in the south), you will find a strict-regime camp of 1000 to 1200 prisoners put to work in gold mines.

There is also a prison for 800 to 1000 inmates in *Bodaibo.* In *Kirensk,* southwest of Bodaibo, there are three strict-regime camps of 800 to 1000 prisoners each who are assigned to logging or to wood-processing. There is also an isolation prison of up to 500 inmates in the same city known for its brutal regimen. Many of the prisoners in *Bodaibo, Kirensk,* and *Kitoi* are Christians (Baptists, Pentecostals).

In *Kazachinskoe,* there is a camp that provides labor for the logging industry. We do not have precise data about this facility.

Two strict-regime camps of 800 to 900 prisoners each are located in *Ust'-Kut.* The prisoners are assigned to the logging industry.

Three strict-regime camps may be found in *Zhelezno-gorsk.* One facility provides the labor of 1000 prisoners for the logging industry; the others assign 2000 prisoners each to work in the wood-processing industry (track

(See page 172 *for the original photograph.*)

ties, prefabricated houses, commercial lumber).

In *Bratsk,* we know of at least one ordinary-regime camp (we believe that there are others) for 1500 prisoners assigned to work in industrial construction within the city. You will also find a prison for 600 to 700 prisoners here.

In the taiga, 35 to 40 kilometers from *Anzeba,* there are three strict-regime camps of 600 to 800 prisoners each assigned to logging or to producing commercial lumber.

In *Rudnogorsk,* north of Bratsk, there are three special strict-regime camps of 500 to 700 prisoners each assigned to work in the mines.

This ends our list of camps located in one of the "most famous" areas of the Soviet Union, the *"Ozerlag".*

Should you travel by train from Taishet to Bratsk, you will notice wooden stakes with numbers along the railroad embankment. These are graves. Both the railroad here and the cities and towns in the area were built by prisoners. This is building socialism.

STATION OF TAISHET CITY

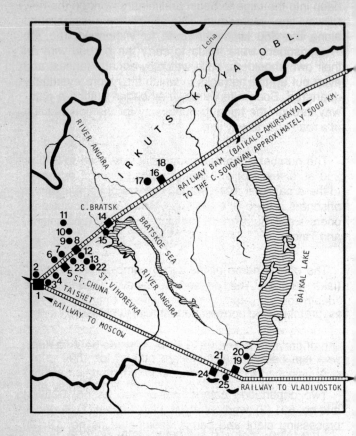

THE TAISHET-BRATSK AND BAIKAL-AMUR
RAILWAY LINES

In Irkutsk Region, along the Moscow-Vladivostok rail-way line, you will find the small train station of *Taishet* city (no. 1 on the map of Taishet). Probings for the construction of a railway embankment towards the north-ern tip of Lake *Baikal* and the *Bodaibo* gold mines (no. 16) were taken as early as 1941. The basic work, however, was not initiated until after 1945. It was then that trainloads of prisoners, including prisoners of war, began to arrive in Taishet on their way to the camps. Most of the prisoners of war were Germans, but there were also Spaniards, Belgians, Hungarians, and Ruma-nians who accompanied them. Altogether, more than 100 000 prisoners were brought to this area.

Formations of prisoners had already been marched deep into the taiga to begin preliminary work on the new railway line. More than 100 camps were established along the 350 kilometer route to *Vikhorevka* (no. 8). The prisoners were made to carry the barbed wire on their own shoulders, build watchtowers and fences, and even put up the barracks in which they were eventually quartered. Soon afterwards, they began cutting a pathway through the taiga to make way for the construction of a road and railway line.

The number of camps eventually increased to 300 or 350 as a result of the uninterrupted inflow of prisoners to the area. After 1946, large numbers of Japanese war prisoners arrived at the camps. Among the Soviet prisoners were Russians, Ukrainians, Jews, Belorussians, and Tatars.

The official name of the camp complex is *"Ozerlag"* (lake camps). The prisoners, however, called it the "death route", referring to the railroad they were building. Having died of hunger and backbreaking work, the prisoners were buried along the railroad tracks in a long line of graves marked with wooden stakes bearing numbers rather than the victims' names.

Two deportation camps, designated as no. 025 (3) and no. 601 (2), were established in *Taishet* (1). A wood-processing plant and camp, designated as no. 19 (7), as well as deportation camp no. 04 (6) may be found near *Chuna* (5). In *Vikhorevka* (no. 8), you will find a camp hospital (13) for the prisoners of the penal facilities located along the entire length of the railroad, a prison (22), and several camps (nos. 9, 10, 11, and 12). A number of camps were established near what are now the city of Bratsk hydroelectric power plant. (Only camp no. 15 on the map continues to exist.) Apart from the city jail, there is also a special "Ozerlag" prison (20) and a camp (21) in Irkutsk (19). Several thousands of prisoners have been brought to the vicinity of *Bodaibo* (16), yet we know of only two camps (17 and 18) in the area. Prisoners at a camp (4) located between Taishet and Chuna are assigned to the production of bricks, whereas track ties are made at a camp (23) situated between Chuna and Vikhorevka.

The accompanying map indicates those penal facilities known to us as of 1978. In 1960 and 1961, several camps in this vicinity were disbanded, the prisoners of these facilities having been transferred to other parts of the country. Most of the political prisoners were taken to the Mordovian camps (*Pot'ma*, "*Dubrovlag*"; see the section on the Mordovian A.S.S.R. in this book), whereas the majority of the ordinary offenders were transferred to the vicinity of *Bodaibo* (16). There they continued construction of the railroad to *Sovetskaya Gavan'* on the Pacific coast. This part of the railway line was named BAM, the abbreviation for "Baikal-Amur Line".

In 1955, the surviving ten percent (9000 to 10000 people) of the German prisoners of war originally brought to the "Ozerlag" complex were released and returned home. The remaining non-Soviet prisoners were transferred to the "Dubrovlag" complex or to other, unknown destinations.

Camp no. 025 (no. 3 on the map) in *Taishet* lies directly on the railway line past which passenger trains from Moscow regularly travel on their way to Vladivostok. The barbed wiring and the watchposts are explained to train occupants with a large sign on the camp fence reading, "*Neftebaza*" (Oil facility).

The inmates of Prison No. 410 (12) in *Vikhorevka* (8) languish under frightfully arbitrary and unbearably severe conditions. Here is an eyewitness report from a former political prisoner, who spent about a year in this facility:

"It was daytime when we arrived in *Vikhorevka,* a small settlement not far from the Bratsk hydroelectric power plant. When I saw the prison building from the outside, I was surprised to see how gloomy a place could be made to be. This squat, gray one-story concrete building, located on the perimeter of the settlement, was surrounded by an old, gray wooden fence and an off-limits zone with watchtowers. The walls, floors, and ceilings of the prison were cast with cement and iron bars into a cold block. This indestructible reinforced-concrete vault was built in the wintertime. Thus, in order to make the concrete harden as quickly as possible, salt had been added to it. The result, however, was that the floors, walls, and ceiling were constantly wet. With a creak of the door and a squeak of the hinges, I was locked into my cell of 15 square meters. I was 'at home'. Directly opposite the door was a window under which stood a large plank bed for eight persons. It was made of thick wooden blocks held together by iron clamps that were spaced some 30 to 40 centimeters apart from one another. Ice glimmered in the indentations in the floor. The window was also covered with a thick layer of ice. Drops of water clinged to the ceiling; water trickled down the walls.

"A single oven, positioned between two cells, was used for heating. Yet, because it was placed behind iron bars, we could not even warm ourselves up on it. We received two billets of firewood a day – about a quarter of a log – for use in the oven. The oven was only moderately warm and naturally could not, as a result, heat the cells. Our bodies were the only source of heat in these reinforced-concrete cubicles. Light could hardly penetrate the ice layering on the ironbar windows. Over the door, there was a light bulb of not more than 25 watts. The yellow gleam could hardly illuminate the cell."

The Bratsk hydroelectric power plant was constructed by prisoners who gave it the name of "Bratsk Cemetery". The plant is now shown to foreign tourists who have no idea that it and the city itself were built by prisoners whose unmarked graves now lie under the sidewalks of Bratsk. Bratsk may be reached by train from Taishet.

Key to map of *Taishet*:

1. Taishet; site of the "Ozernyi" administration.

2. Deportation camp no. 601 (one kilometer from Taishet), for 1500 to 2000 prisoners. Next to the camp on the

right is a prison for 300 to 500 inmates. Camp address: Zhkh-358/601.

3. Deportation camp no. 025, located directly on the main railway line. For 1500 to 2000 prisoners. Address: Zhkh-385/025.

4. Camp no. 014 for 800 to 900 prisoners assigned to a brickyard. Address: Zhkh-385/014.

5. *Chuna;* on the Taishet-Bratsk railway line.

6. Special camp for disabled prisoners, no. 04, two kilometers from Chuna; for 1000 to 1500 prisoners. Address: Zhkh-385/04.

7. Camp no. 019, for 2500 to 3000 prisoners assigned to a wood-processing plant. It is located about 2.5 kilometers from the railroad tracks. Address: Zhkh-385/019.

8. *Vikhorevka;* on the Taishet-Bratsk railway line.

9. Camp no. 042, 1500 to 2000 prisoners assigned to logging duties. It is located about 10 kilometers from Vikhorevka. Address: Zhkh-385/042.

10. Camp no. 307, for approximately 1000 prisoners also assigned to logging duties. It is located about 30 to 35 kilometers from Vikhorevka. Address: Zhkh-385/307.

11. Camp no. 308, for approximately 1000 prisoners assigned to logging duties. The facility is located about 40 to 45 kilometers from Vikhorevka.

12. Isolation prison no. 410 in *Vikhorevka* for 250 to 300 prisoners. Address: Zhkh-385/410.

13. Camp hospital in *Vikhorevka,* for 1000 to 1200 prisoners.

14. *Bratsk,* a city built by prisoners.

15. Camp of unknown designation. Prisoners here are assigned to construction work in Bratsk.

16., 17., 18. *Bodaibo,* goldmining and labor camp center.

19. *Irkutsk,* capital of Irkutsk Region.

20. Pre-trial detention prison of the K.G.B. in "Ozerlag".

21. Prison of the district K.G.B.

22. Forced-labor camp; prisoners assigned to manufacture track ties.

23. Forced-labor camp; prisoners assigned to machine-repair workshops.

24. *Angarsk*—two strict regime camps.

25. Camp located at construction site of chemical plant designed to produce synthetic gasoline.

ARKHANGEL'SK REGION
(area: 587 000 sq. km.; pop.: 1 400 000)

The greater part of Arkhangel'sk Region, a territory lying astride the Arctic Circle, is an icy, mountainous wasteland. In the south, however, there are large tracts of forest as well as significant deposits of metal ores, especially aluminum bauxite.

Life in these difficult climatic conditions is so hard that volunteers refuse to work here. For this reason, the Soviet state sends thousands of prisoners to the labor camps of Arkhangel'sk Region instead. Today, there are no less than 100 000 prisoners in the three major forced-labor camp complexes – *"Oneglag", "Kargapol'lag",* and *"Sol'lag".*

1. *"Oneglag",* whose administrative headquarters designated as no. 350) may be found in *Plesetsk,* includes 50 strict-regime and seven special strict-regime camps and a total prisoner population of approximately 60 000. The camp complex services the "Boksitstroitrest" (Bauxite Construction Trust; chief engineer is Vera Georgievna Fokht, who resides in Navolok) and the "Onegspetsles" (Onega Special Lumber Company), which provides lumber for use in the Soviet Union or for export to the West.

163

"Oneglag" extends from Onega to Konda and Nyandoma and may be reached by car from Leningrad and Petrozavodsk. The highway leading into this area will also take you to the administration of the complex in *Plesetsk,* site of most of the camps.

The bauxite dredges situated along the Puksa and Iksa rivers are primarily located in *Navolok.* An aluminum industrial plant is under construction in the vicinity of *Puksoozero.* A women's strict-regime camp may be found in Navolok. In *Plesetsk,* there is a transit camp and a prison for inmates transferred here from the "Oneglag" facilities.

Large factories in which prisoners produce bricks by hand for local construction, especially for the construction of an aluminum industrial plant, may be found in *Obozerskii* and *Kodino.* A large plant in which metal fittings are manufactured is located near the plant.

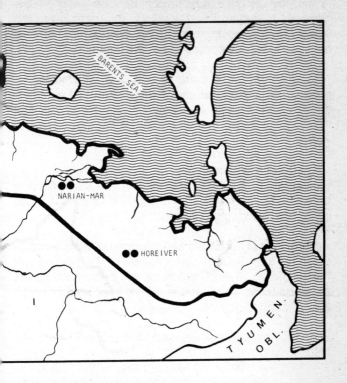

In the entire breadth of the area between *Porog* and *Konda*, prisoners are assigned to logging and to preparing the felled timber for rail transport. Here work not only prisoners but also ex-convicts from the camps who, following their release, were moved to so-called volunteer settlements, of which there are at least 150.

A special colony of Germans established by the state in *Kukoff*, which is located in the same area, may be reached from Plesetsk.

2. The logging industry also draws its labor force from the prisoners of the *"Kargapol'lag"* complex, the administration of which is located in *Kargapol'*, a city on the highway to Leningrad.

In the forests surrounding Kargapol', there are approximately 30 strict-regime camps of about 20 000 prisoners. The camps, in each of which there are 500 to

700 prisoners, are moved about from one logging area to the next as the situation requires. The prisoners are assigned to cutting down, loading, and transporting the timber as well as to building the new camps as they continue to be moved further into the depths of the forest.

In *"Kargapol'lag"*, there is also a wood-working industrial plant, the products of which are used either for construction projects in *"Oneglag"* or in the mines of *"Sol'lag"*, a camp complex near *Sol'vychegodsk* and *Kotlas.*

3. In *Kotlas,* which may be reached by train from Leningrad via Vologda, you will find a transit prison, a transit camp, and a camp that supplies labor for various construction projects in the city.

Northwest of Kotlas lies *Sol'vychegodsk,* administrative center of the "Sol'lag" camp complex. The prisoners of the estimated 15 strict-regime camps in the complex are assigned to the underground mining of potassium chloride.

Apart from these three camp complexes, there are also an additional number of strict-regime and special strict-regime camps distributed throughout Arkhangel'sk Region. In *Nar'yan-Mar* and *Khoreiver,* both in the northeastern part of the region, we have knowledge of only four camps. The number of facilities there, however, is significantly higher.

The prisoners in the camps in Arkhangel'sk itself are assigned to work in construction in the city and at the port. There, you will also find a large prison with a pre-trial detention and an isolation section.

At the ports of *Severodvinsk* and *Mirnyi,* prisoners from the camps of these cities are assigned to clean the nozzles of atomic submarines. The prisoners are neither informed of, nor are they given protective clothing against, the radioactivity to which they are exposed.

Here are a few eyewitness reports on the camps of the region as told by former prisoners.

1. M.K., an electronics engineer released from *"Oneg-lag"* in 1976, recounts:

"I was in a privileged group of specialists assigned to build tracks for the bauxite dredges and to plan the relocation of the logging camps. This gave me the opportunity to observe the conditions under which the prisoners in several 'Oneglag' camps lived. To begin with, the prisoners were kept hungry and were denied fresh vegetables, which, under sub-polar conditions, can cause scurvy. The 'struggle' against scurvy was carried out at our camp with the use of local remedies. Barrels of spruce-needle extract, which the prisoners drank as a source of 'vitamins', were available in the living areas of the camps. This measure, however, did not prevent the prisoners from losing their teeth.

"At winter temperatures of −40° or −50°C., the work in the logging areas was unbearable, and the production quotas were high. Failure to fulfill these quotas was punishable by incarceration in the isolation cell on reduced rations. A prisoner so punished, however, was at least withdrawn from his work duties.

"In the camps, I often saw desperate prisoners who had resorted to self-mutilation in order to escape the work that was sending them to their graves. Some placed a leg under a falling log, others chopped off a finger. Some even deliberately allowed a hand to become frostbitten so that it would have to be amputated. An atmosphere of hopelessness and despair reigned in the camps. Only the religious prisoners were able to stand above the human degradation. They believed that they were being tested by God and that they had to endure their sufferings. The others, however, fought each other over food or reduced themselves to acts of homosexuality or even sodomy. There were no women at the camps. The barracks at the camps were built of damp wood, which the prisoners had to dry with their own bodies. Not even the heating ovens were of any help against the dank winter cold.

"Even though we lived in the forest, we did not always have firewood for the ovens. The supervisors were more interested in fulfilling their work plans than in sending the prisoners out to gather firewood for the camps.

This was left to the disabled prisoners. The camp rations condemned us, moreover, to permanent hunger. Because of the impassability of the roads in the winter, it was not always possible for the authorities to deliver provisions to the camps, which made matters much worse. In such cases, helicopters sometimes dropped packages of zwieback from the sky. In the summer, swarms of midges, tiny gnat-like insects, plagued and literally devoured the prisoners. Even the protective nets on our headgear were of no help. The netting was coarse enough for the insects to penetrate. Yet the quotas had to be met and the prisoners had to continue working — swollen from illness, bloodstained, and hungry.

"When I was released from this horror after three years (I was unexpectedly rehabilitated), I could not for a long time believe that I had come out alive. And now, I can hardly believe that this horror continues to exist today. But it does exist. I still correspond with friends I left behind in the camp in *Puksoozero.*"

2. Z. L., an eyewitness, reports:

"Having been convicted as a recidivist, I was sent to a strict-regime camp in *Nokola* of the 'Kargapol'lag' complex. I was sentenced to toil under strict regime for having attempted to illegally cross the borders of the Soviet Union a second time. When I arrived with my group at the transit prison in *Kotlas,* we were all greeted with insults and intimidations, 'The taiga is the law here, and the bear the prosecutor!'

"I was soon convinced that they were not joking. Every day, I witnessed prisoners being beaten up for the slightest infraction of the rules or for arguing with the supervisors. Those, however, to whom the supervisors wanted to mete out an even worse punishment than the isolation cell underwent frightful humiliations. A prisoner, for example, might be locked in a barracks alone at night with homosexuals. Following such an incident, the homosexuals knew that their victim could be exploited. The prisoner was thus dispossessed of his very soul.

"I do not know exactly how many camps there were in 'Kargapol'lag'. I was aware, however, of ten or twelve such camps in the area where I was imprisoned."

168

3. "In September 1973, I was brought to a strict-regime camp in *Bestuzhevo,* which was part of the *Sol'vychegodsk* camp system, as punishment for having attempted to escape from a facility in Vologda.

"We were transported from Kotlas to the camp by train and then by prison river barge. The hold of the barge was overfilled with prisoners, who were forced to sit in a doubled-up position. There was hardly any air to breathe. We were not allowed to go to the toilet; the sick urinated without leaving their places. Upon arriving at the camp (in the taiga), we were led into cold bathrooms where our hair was cut off with blunted electric clippers. We were issued old camp clothing, and, on the very next day, we were herded off to the logging area. We were driven there in such a way that, by the time we arrived, we were half dead from exhaustion.

"Our meals consisted of boiled beets and sauerkraut There was no bread; we were given a kind of black flat cake instead. Yet everything was still relatively tolerable-until the advent of the frost and snowstorms of November. We were driven back as usual into the forest to continue our work. A slogan was hung up on the watchpost, »There is no frost in the forest!« For fear of ending up in the isolation cell or at being put on hunger rations, we devoted all our energies to doing the work assigned to us, sinking into the deep snow in the process. We dripped with sweat in the cold. There was indeed no frost in the taiga! After work we were escorted soaking wet back to the camp. We ran all the way back to the camp so as not to become numb from the cold. We ran, we fell, we cried. And when we finally got back, we still had to fall into formation so that the guards could take count of us. Whenever they lost count, we had to remain standing until they were finished.

"The escort guards were sometimes good to us. They would light up a campfire so that we could keep warm while performing our duties. There were times, however, where they were absolutely bestial. Spotting a new prisoner, they might send him to fetch something from outside the working area, which was marked off with red signal flags. On reaching the marked-off area, the prisoner would be shot for attempting to escape. The guard who fired the shot would then be given leave as a reward.

"I do not know exactly how many camps there were in the 'Sol'lag' complex. Next to our camp there were another three facilities. Further into the taiga, however, there were more." From the testimony of I.L. (archives of the Research Center).

*

Penal facilities in Arkhangel'sk Region

1. *Arkhangel'sk* city (pop.: 400 000), regional capital and major port on the Barents Sea (Arctic Ocean). A men's strict-regime camp, no. UG-42-1/5, for 1200 prisoners; a large pre-trial detention prison for 1000 to 1500 inmates; two camps near the harbor of the city (we do not know their precise address). The prisoners of the camp no. UG-42-1/5 are assigned to construction work in the city. Directions: from Leningrad or Moscow by train or car via Vologda.

2. *Onega* – men's strict-regime camp for 1500 prisoners assigned to work at the port. Directions: southwest of Arkhangel'sk, accessible by train or car.

3. *Severodvinsk* – men's camp for 2000 to 2500 prisoners assigned to construction work in the military sphere or to duties in the harbor area. Directions: west of Arkhangel'sk, 18 kilomters by train or car.

4. *Ust'-Pinega* – men's strict-regime camp for prisoners assigned to logging. Directions: 81 kilometers by train or car south from Arkhangel'sk.

5. *Nar'yan-Mar* – men's special strict-regime camp for 1000 to 1500 prisoners assigned to construction in the military sphere. Directions: may be reached by airplane from Arkhangel'sk or by steamship (approximately 600 kilometers) along the Pechora River. (See the attached photographs: incidents involving prisoners on the Pechora River).

6. *Khoreiver* – special strict-regime camp for 800 to 1000 prisoners assigned to construction in the military

sphere. Directions: accessible only by plane (approximately 1000 kilometers northeast of Arkhangel'sk) or by ship from Pechora along the Usa River.

7. *Kotlas* – strict-regime camp of 1800 to 2000 prisoners assigned to construction work in the city; transit prison for 2000 to 2500 inmates; transit camp for 1500 to 2000 prisoners. Directions: accessible from Vologda via Vel'sk or from Arkhangel'sk, which lies approximately 500 kilometers to the southeast.

8. *Sol'vychegodsk* – administrative center of the "Sol'lag" camp complex. We know of three camps that supply labor for the logging industry. Prisoners from the remaining eight to ten camps are put to work in the salt mines. Directions: 19 kilometers by train or car from Kotlas.

9. *Kargapol'* – administrative center of the "Kargapol'-lag" complex. We know of about 15 camps that supply labor for the logging industry. The total number of camps in this complex is apparently much higher. Directions: approximately 350 kilometers by train or car south of Arkhangel'sk; by train from Leningrad.

A camp of the "Kargapol'lag" complex

Above left: Barracks near Arkhangel'sk

Above middle: Watchtower at a camp near Irkutsk

Below left: Sergeant Simon V., one of the officials there.

MURMANSK REGION
(area: 144 900 sq. km.; pop.: 860 000)

In *Murmansk* city itself (pop.: 390 000), there is an ordinary-regime pre-trial detention prison for 2 000 inmates and an "inner prison" in the K.G.B. building for approximately 500 inmates. Two strict-regime camps of 1 500 prisoners; each may be found in the northern outskirts of the city on the road towards *Polyarnyi*. The camps supply labor for construction, road repair, logging, and the unloading of apatite shipments. The 2 000 prisoners of an intensified-regime camp located on the outskirts of Murmansk on the road towards *Zapolyarnyi* are assigned to construction work in the military sphere. Strict-regime camps are also located in *Polyarnyi* and *Zapolyarnyi*. Each having 1 000 prisoners, they supply labor for the construction and repair of roads leading to military installations.

In *Olenegorsk* (southeast of Murmansk, accessible by train), 1 000 prisoners from a strict-regime camp are put to work in the mines or in construction. Camp commander is Major Kostyuchenko.

In *Monchegorsk,* which lies a further 40 kilometers to the south, there is a strict-regime camp of approximately 1800 prisoners assigned to work in apatite, copper, and nickel ore mines and in a copper-and-nickel industrial plant. The prisoners here wear striped and numbered prison uniforms and are forced to work under extremely severe conditions. Camp commander is Major Prosin.

Located between *Monchegorsk* and *Olenegorsk* is a strict-regime camp for 4000 prisoners assigned to work in apatite or iron ore mines or on military construction projects. Camp commander is Lieutenant Colonel Chesnov.

Two strict-regime camps located in *Lovozero* (southeast of Murmansk) supply a labor force of approximately 6000 prisoners for work in the iron ore mines, in a mineral ore enrichment plant, or on various military construction projects.

In *Voron'e,* which lies north of Lovozero, there is a strict-regime camp of 1500 prisoners assigned to military construction projects.

In both *Kirovsk* and *Apatity,* there is a strict-regime camp of up to 2000 prisoners who are put to work in the mining and transport of apatite.

In both *Kandalaksha* and *Lesozavodskii,* there is a camp of approximately 1500 prisoners assigned to work in lumber, brick, alumina, and superphosphate plants. In *Kandalaksha,* there is also a prison for 500 to 600 inmates confined here as a punishment for having violated the rules of the camp from which they were transferred. A children's camp for about 800 prisoners assigned to manufacture wooden packaging labels may be found in the same city.

Between *Monchegorsk* and Lovozero (a distance of approximately 40 kilometers), a series of military installations and clandestine cities in which only military personnel are quartered is under construction. Approximately 3000 inmates, all of whom have been sentenced to a 15-year term in a strict-regime camp, supply the labor force for these projects. Their duties include constructing missile silos, underground airfields, and roads connecting the installations.

We have named here only 15 camps and three prisons in this region. We know that there is at least another camp north of the Arctic Circle that supplies a work force for construction in the military sphere, but we have not been able to determine its exact location.

*

KIROV REGION
(area: 120 800 sq. km.; pop.: 1 800 000)

Kirov Region has a frightful reputation among the prisoners of the Soviet Union. The cruelty and arbitrariness of the administration and the lack of any rights of the prisoners characterize the penal facilities of this region.

Let us begin with *Kirov* city, the capital of the region (pop.: 400 000), in which there is a generally well-known transit prison designed for approximately 5 000 to 6 000 inmates. I.S., an eyewitness, reports: "When our group of political prisoners and ordinary offenders arrived at the transit prison in Kirov, I felt as if I had landed on an ant hill. Escort guards led groups of prisoners through the facility, doors and locks clanged, supervisors shouted, prisoners shouted. And all this piercing through a stench that had built up over the decades."

The K.G.B. building in the center of the city also contains a prison for 500 to 600 inmates.

On *Pervomaiskaya Street* (in Zarech'e), 2000 to 2500 prisoners in an intensified-regime camp are divided into work groups and assigned to various construction projects or to loading and unloading duties, such as in a transport equipment plant. Camp commander is Lieutenant Colonel Zemlyakov. There are 15 or 20 prisoners at the camp who were arrested for practicing their religion. Directions: bus no. 4.

KIROV REGION

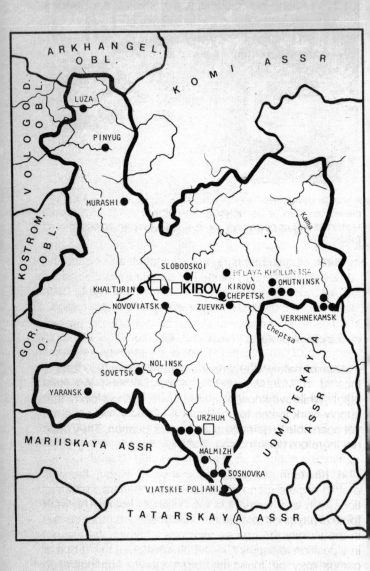

Approximately 1500 prisoners in an ordinary-regime camp (no. 216/4) in *Slobodskoi* are assigned to manufacture hardware items in the city for local industry. Camp commander is Major Pelov. Directions: bus no. 31.

In both *Luza* and *Pinyug* (in the northern part of the region), there is a strict-regime camp of approximately

A woman doing "light" work at a camp (Kirov Region; about 400 kilometers northeast of Gor'kii, European part of the R.S.F.S.R.). More women as well as guards can be seen in the forest in the background (photo 1976).

1000 to 1200 prisoners assigned to work on military construction projects in restricted areas.

Approximately 800 prisoners from camp no. 216/2, located in *Murashi,* work in a woodworking industrial plant. While we know of other camps in the vicinity that supply work forces for the logging industry, we have not yet been able to determine their exact location. They have not therefore been indicated on the map.

In *Khalturin,* 60 kilometers west of Kirov, there is a strict-regime camp of up to 2000 prisoners that functions both as a forced-labor and transit facility. The work force is assigned to a lumber mill. There are other camps in the vicinity the precise locations of which we are not in a position to supply. The administration of this group of camps may be found on Lenin Street. Administration supervisor is Colonel Okhlopkin.

The cities of *Novovyatsk, Kirovo-Chepetsk,* and *Belaya Kholunitsa* each accommodate a camp of up to 1500 prisoners assigned to logging and peat farming. In *Sovetsk,* 600 to 800 prisoners of an ordinary-regime camp are assigned to the military construction industry. In *Yaransk,* there are two strict-regime camps of 1000 prisoners each that supply labor forces for the logging and phosphate mining industries. Strict-regime camps of 800 to 900 prisoners each may also be found in *Nolinsk, Urzhum* (three facilities), *Malmyzh, Sosnovka* (two facilities), and *Vyatskie Polyany*. The prisoners of these camps are assigned to the logging and woodworking industries. A number of lumber mills are also to be found here. We know from eyewitness reports that the prisoners here are subjected to arbitrary and humiliating treatment. Many of the inmates in these camps were arrested for practicing their religious faith, conducting secret prayer meetings, or providing religious instruction for children.

In *Zuevka,* approximately 100 kilometers southeast of Kirov, is a women's intensified-regime camp for about 1800 prisoners assigned to make camp clothing and military uniforms in a sewing factory. A number of the women maintain custody over their infant children (two years of age or less).

In seven camps (nos. 216/18, 216/19, 216/20, 216/21, 216/22, 216/23, and 216/24) located northeast of *Verkhnekamsk* and *Omutninsk,* approximately 10000 prisoners are assigned to the mining and enrichment of uranium ore. These are death camps. Prisoners contaminated by radiation are removed from these camps and brought to facilities for invalids to die. This is not done for philanthropic reasons but to prevent those still healthy prisoners unaware of the hazards of their work from becoming demoralized (see map of the death camps).

*

KRASNOYARSK TERRITORY
(area: 2401600 sq.km.; pop.: 3000000)

We know of 68 camps, six prisons, and two psychiatric prisons in this remote territory.

Tourists will hardly find it possible to visit the camps in Krasnoyarsk Territory located north of the Arctic Circle.

KRASNOYARSK TERRITORY

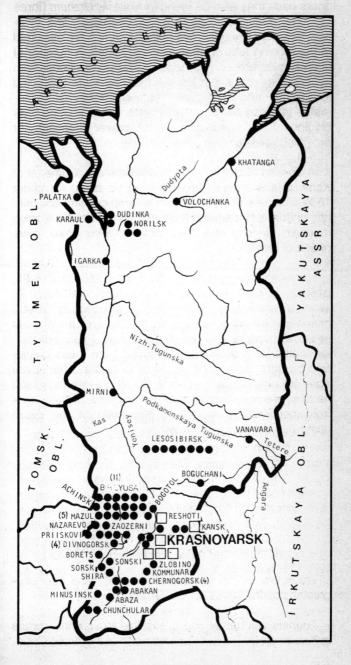

Women at work in Krasnoyarsk Territory, a logging region (Siberia, on the Enisei River). Equal rights for women, a dream that women in the free world are struggling for (photo 1976).

Built on the bones of its prisoners, these facilities may be found in *Noril'sk, Igarka, Dudinka,* and *Khatanga.* The settlement of *Karaul* (guard, "help!") received its highly picturesque name from the prisoners. These camps supply labor for the molybdenum, manganese, chrome, and nickel mines. Request permission to visit *Mirnyi,* where diamonds are mined.

Penal logging camps may be found further to the south in *Lesosibirsk, Birilyussy, Bogotol, Boguchany* (also a place of exile for those released from camp imprisonment), *Kansk, Achinsk, Mazul',* and *Reshety* (the administration of the *"Kraslag"* complex and a transit prison are located here). The number of camps and prisoners here assigned to the logging industry is known only to the K.G.B. One of the guard officers recently "boasted" that there were more than 150 camps here. But we shall only name those that have precisely been identified by eyewitnesses – 34 facilities assigned to the logging industry.

Here is the testimony of M.P., a political prisoner in the taiga camp in *Birilyussy.* "In 1975, I was one of a group of about 50 or 60 prisoners being transported from

Krasnoyarsk to a camp in Birilyussy via a transit prison in Reshety. For two or three days, we were also held in a transit camp in Birilyussy itself. There were no more than 300 prisoners in the camp. We did not have to work; we simply waited to be transferred to another facility. We were then freighted into the taiga. It was a jolting ride of 20 to 25 kilometers on a path cut through the forest rather than one on an asphalt road.

"The camp is enclosed by a mere barbed-wire fence and by watchtowers.

"The barracks are made of logs. It is damp inside; the logs are not dry. Some of the older prisoners explained that they had recently built the camp themselves. Because they had once been in a camp nearer to the city, the prisoners had to walk ten to 15 kilometers to their work areas in the taiga. The camps here are relocated after a section of the forest has been cleared.

"The 1200 to 1300 prisoners in our camp were taken every day to the logging sites. I was given responsibility for the campfire. I was happy to receive such a light duty. Soon I realized, however, that my work was quite hard. I had to drag branches cut down by the logging details to various locations in the area and light a campfire. Because they were damp, they often failed to catch fire. My eyes smarted from the smoke; my legs sank into the snow. I worked up a sweat until I was all wet. If you didn't have the branches cleared away in time, the other prisoners would scream at you. They, too, had to drag branches aside, sort them, and stack them up, all for which they needed extra room.

"We worked under all frost conditions, even at well under −40°C. At the watchpost at the camp gates, however, there was a sign that read, 'There is no frost in the taiga!' In other words, the work would warm you up. Thus, we worked up a sweat in frost temperatures. The prisoners, as a result, were coming down with pneumonia the whole time. It was almost impossible, however, to get permission from the medical assistant to be relieved from work. The camp supervision set the maximum number of prisoners permitted on sick call at ten. Those who were weakened by the cold were finished off by hunger. We were given putrid cabbage, frozen potatoes, and stinking herring to eat. Prisoners were allowed to receive parcels (five kilograms a year) from their families only after having served half their terms of imprisonment."

In *Krasnoyarsk* city, capital of the territory (pop.: 800000), there is a pre-trial detention prison for 3000 inmates, a special K.G.B. prison for 1000 inmates, and two psychiatric hospitals (in fact, psychiatric prisons). One of the hospitals is located in the center of the city at *Kurchatov Street 14,* the other in *Poimo-Tiny* (see map on psychiatric prisons of the Soviet Union).

In addition, there are three ordinary-regime camps of 1500 prisoners each in Krasnoyarsk. The prisoners are assigned to work in two saw mills, a heavy machine construction plant (camp commander: Major Zozulin), a self-propelled combine plant (both, in effect, are arms plants), and at construction sites in the city. In the morning, you can observe cargoes of prisoners being transported to a military construction site in the suburb.

In *Achinsk* and *Abakan,* there is a women's camp of 1800 prisoners assigned to work as seamstresses and a children's camp of 14 to 18-year-old inmates assigned to woodworking workshops. Commander of the children's camp is Captain Gusev. A men's strict-regime camp of 2500 prisoners assigned to underground uranium mining may also be found in *Achinsk* (see special map on the "death camps").

In *Mazul',* approximately 8000 prisoners in five camps are assigned to the logging industry or to underground manganese mining.

In *Chernogorsk,* south of Krasnoyarsk, approximately 6000 prisoners from four strict-regime camps work in coal mines. Ordinary-regime camps, each having 1200 prisoners assigned to farm work, may be found in *Sorsk* and in the sovkhozes of *Sonskii* and *Shira.* Approximately 10000 prisoners in four ordinary-regime camps in *Divnogorsk* are assigned to the construction of a hydroelectric power plant and to other construction projects. In both *Kommunar* and *Priiskovyi,* there is a strict-regime camp for prisoners assigned to extremely hazardous work in underground copper mines.

In *Abakan,* 1600 prisoners in a men's camp are assigned to a woodworking industrial plant. Prisoners in the camps in *Abaza, Chunchular,* and *Minusinsk* are put to work in various woodworking shops (track tie production, veneering, housing construction, etc.). In *Nazarovo,* 1500 prisoners from a special strict-regime camp work in an open-pit coal mine. The working conditions and the regimen of the camp are extremely severe. A. V., an eyewitness employed at the camp as an electrician reports: "The prisoners worked without special protective clothing and were always so dirty that they were horrifying to look at. They were constantly hungry. Appeals for a piece of bread were heard incessantly."

About ten kilometers outside of *Noril'sk* on the right-hand side of the road from *Igarka,* you will see a rather large camp. Its barracks, watchtowers, and barbed-wire fences are open to plain view. Prepare yourself to take a photograph as you approach the camp. This is one of the facilities that rebelled against the authorities in 1953. The desperate prisoners, who were assigned to the mining industry, went on strike and asked for an improvement in their living conditions as they were being worked and starved to death. At first, the authorities negotiated with the prisoners. Members of the Soviet government even flew in from Moscow. (They needed the nickel, molybdenum, and chrome mined by the prisoners for the arms industry.) Having witnessed the perseverance of the prisoners, however, these murderers did not hesitate to open fire on or bombard them from airplanes.

"Order" was thus reestablished, and the work of the camp was reassumed. New prisoners arrived.

Some day, a monument will be erected here to the memory of those who without the hope of victory rose up against tyranny, sacrificing their lives in the process.

*

KRASNODAR TERRITORY

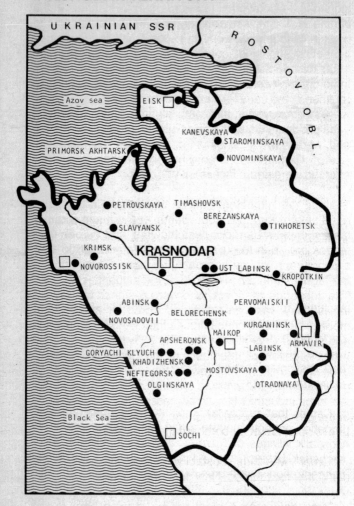

KRASNODAR TERRITORY
(area: 83 600 sq. km.; pop.: 4 600 000)

Krasnodar Territory lies in the south of the Soviet Union between the Black Sea and the Sea of Azov and is known for its health resorts *(Sochi, Tuapse,* and *Gelendzhik)* and its government dachas.

At the same time, however, there are also numerous prisons and concentration camps here. The prisoners are

A camp fence, a watchtower of the camp guards, a mined forbidden zone, a house for the soldiers of the camp guard. And all around a bumpy field of black soil. The rich soil of Krasnodar Territory is used in the camp. This is a camp in the Cossack city of Ust'-Labinsk, where the Laba River flows into the Kuban, northern Caucasus (photo 1978).

assigned to farm labor, irrigation and construction projects, oil production, and factory work. Three prisons may be found in *Krasnodar* city (pop.: 590 000): an ordinary-regime pre-trial detention prison, a secret K.G.B. prison, and a psychiatric prison. Prisons are also located in *Sochi, Eisk, Armavir, Novorossiisk,* and *Maikop.*

Camps that supply labor for the farm industry and for irrigation projects may be found in *Tikhoretsk* and in the Cossack villages of *Novominskaya, Kanevskaya, Belorechensk, Labinsk,* and *Ust'-Labinsk.* There is also a large concentration camp for tubercular prisoners in *Ust'-Labinsk.* Prisoners in camps located in *Maikop, Primorsko-Akhtarsk, Pervomaiskii, Armavir,* and in the Cossack villages of *Otradnaya, Starominskaya, Petrovskaya, Yazhenskaya, Goryachii Klyuch, Timashevsk, Berezaika, Kurganinsk,* and *Mostovskoi* are put to work in local industry, such as in the production of tools, packaging materials, furniture, compression springs, and farm machinery. Prisoners are also used for repair and construction projects.

Prisoners in the camps in the Cossack villages of *Apsheronsk, Khadyzhensk,* and *Neftegorsk* are assigned to oil production.

The number of prisoners in each camp varies. Camps assigned to the farm industry have between 300 and 600 prisoners. Camps that supply labor for construction projects are larger, having 500 or 1000 inmates. Those prisoners working in local industry are confined in camps having a population ranging from 500 to 1500. Camps designed to supply labor for the oil industry have between 500 and 800 prisoners.

Prisoners who become mentally ill are transferred either to a camp in *Primorsko-Akhtarsk* or in *Apsheronsk*. Both were designed for approximately 1000 inmates.

About 800 inmates are confined in the psychiatric prison in *Krasnodar*. Among them are Christians arrested for practicing their faith or giving religious instruction to their children. Other prisoners include those who demanded justice or the punishment of a functionary who had somehow broken the law.

In *Ust'-Labinsk, Maikop,* and *Belorechensk,* there are children's camps of between 800 and 1500 prisoners each. A women's camp of 2000 prisoners is located in *Ust'-Labinsk,* while another camp of 1200 prisoners may be found in *Berezaika.*

Some 4000 inmates are confined in an ordinary-regime prison in *Krasnodar.* There are about 1000 inmates in the secret K.G.B. prison. In the prison in *Novorossiisk,* there are approximately 1500 inmates. The prison in *Maikop* has 300 to 500 inmates, whereas another 2000 are confined in a special prison in *Armavir* for having violated the rules of the camp where they were previously held.

All in all, there are eight prisons and 34 camps, including two women's and three children's facilities, in this "health resort area".

All of the above-mentioned cities and Cossack villages are indicated on Soviet road maps and train schedules and are easily accessible from Krasnodar.

SMOLENSK REGION
(area: 49 800 sq. km.; pop.: 1 200 000)

On *Vyazemskaya Street* in *Smolensk* city (pop.: 280 000; approximately 400 kilometers from Moscow), about 1200 children in an ordinary-regime camp (no. IS-61/1) are assigned to mechanics workshops. Camp commander is Major Kostromin.

An inner prison and special pre-trial detention isolation facility for 300 to 400 political prisoners in the K.G.B. building is located in the center of the city. A pre-trial detention prison of the Ministry of Interior holds up to 2000 inmates.

There is also a men's camp in the city, the address of which, however, we do not know.

In *Velizh*, you may visit a men's camp of 800 to 900 prisoners assigned to a reinforced concrete factory.

In *Rudnya*, 1000 to 1100 prisoners in a strict-regime camp are assigned to work in quarries.

In both *Roslavl'* and *El'nya*, we know of a camp of 700 to 800 prisoners put to work in road construction and farming.

In *Dorogobych* (east of Smolensk), 1500 prisoners of a strict-regime camp are assigned to a textile industrial plant in which special clothing is manufactured. In *Safonovo*, located north of *Dorogobych*, 1000 to 1200 prisoners in camp no. 100/1 work in a lumber mill.

In *Vyaz'ma*, located halfway from Smolensk to Moscow, you may visit a men's strict-regime camp in which 1500 prisoners are assigned to a woodworking industrial plant. Camp commander is Major Slepov. In the same city, you will find a special strict-regime prison for 400 to 500 inmates.

In *Sychevka*, 70 kilometers north of *Vyaz'ma*, 800 to 900 prisoners from a strict-regime camp work in a brick factory.

In the same city, you will also find a special psychiatric

SMOLENSK REGION

prison about which the free world uninterruptedly receives shocking information. The facility is overrun by drunken, criminal hospital attendants who carry out the will of K.G.B. psychiatrists. Dissidents and religious prisoners here are subjected to systematic beatings, humiliations, and to the forced administration of neuroleptic drugs, which transmutes them into living corpses.

*

RYAZAN' REGION
(area: 39000 sq. km.; pop.: 1500000)

In *Zarech'e* near *Ryazan'* city (regional capital; pop.: 430000), there is an ordinary-regime camp of 1500 prisoners assigned to housing construction. An ordinary-

regime prison for 1800 to 2000 inmates is located on the outskirts of Ryazan' on the road to Moscow. Pretrial detention jails may also be found in both the K.G.B. and the Ministry of Interior buildings.

In *Kasimov*, you may find an ordinary-regime camp for 1200 to 1500 prisoners assigned to a woodworking plant. Camp commander is Captain Sergeichuk.

In both *Rybnoe* and *Mikhailov*, there is an ordinary-regime camp of 500 to 600 prisoners assigned to farm work.

In *Ryazhsk*, there is a transit prison, a part of which is maintained under strict regime for camp inmates sent here for some infraction in their former place of internment. A camp for 300 to 500 prisoners assigned to construction work in the city is located near the prison.

In *Sasovo,* 500 to 600 prisoners of a strict-regime camp mine building stones.

In *Shatsk,* 1200 to 1300 prisoners work in a wood-working industrial plant. Camp commander is Major Peskov.

*

KALININGRAD REGION
(area: 15100 sq.km.; pop.: 732000)

Kaliningrad Region, formerly the northern half of the German province of East Prussia, was occupied by Soviet troops in 1945 and has since been a part of the U.S.S.R.

After the flight of the German population, the territory was settled by Soviet citizens and covered with secret military bases.

We know little about the camps in this region as they are located at the site of military construction projects rather than in urban areas.

Nevertheless, you will find an old prison (modernized by the Soviets) of up to 5000 inmates in *Kaliningrad* city (formerly Königsberg, pop.: 320000). Common offenders, political prisoners, and pre-trial detainees are confined under special regime. The inmates of this facility are subjected to terrible beatings. Eyewitness A.Sh. reports: "I was confined in the prison in Kaliningrad in 1977. I remember once when we (a group of female pre-trial detainees) were led out of our cells and told to clean the floors of the corridors outside the isolation lockups in the cellar. The guards left us alone for a while in the corridor. Out of curiosity, we began to look through the peep-windows. When I got to steal a look into one of the cells, I saw a young man in a military uniform lying gagged on the floor as two other men in black smocks beat him with canes, using violent backhand strokes in the process. A man in a white smock and an officer were also present. Horrified, I closed the peep-window and told

the women in the corridor of what I had seen. They, too, looked through the peep-window. Meanwhile, the boy continued to be beaten. The men then came out of the cell and washed their hands. The two who did the beating – they turned out to be sergeants – took off their black smocks and hung them up in a closet. Then they all left. A groaning could be heard from the cell. We did not succeed, however, in talking to the boy. The corridor guards arrived. Only some time later did we learn that several soldiers at the local garrison were arrested for refusing to carry out certain orders. Perhaps the one whom we saw beaten was one of them."

There are three men's strict-regime camps in *Kaliningrad*: at the northern highway exit of the city on the right as you drive towards *Baltiisk*, you will see two camps of 600 to 800 prisoners each assigned to construction projects in the downtown area; at the western highway exit of the city as you drive in the direction of *Svetlogorsk,* you will see a strict-regime camp for 1000 to 1200 prisoners assigned to the secret production of spare parts for the military industry in large mechanics workshops.

The special psychiatric prison in Chernyakhovsk (formerly Insterburg, East Prussia; Kaliningrad Region). See the special map of psychiatric prisons and the accompanying notes.

In *Gvardeisk,* 1000 to 1100 prisoners in an ordinary-regime camp are assigned to the woodworking industry. In *Sovetsk* (formerly Tilsit; located in the northern part of the region), there is a strict-regime camp for 500 to 600 prisoners assigned to the manufacture of furniture.

In *Chernyakhovsk,* there is a notoriously frightening special psychiatric prison (see accompanying photograph). You may read about conditions in this facility in the notes to the *Guidebook*'s map of Soviet psychiatric prisons. There is also a psychiatric prison at *Aleksandr Nevskii Street 73 A* in *Kaliningrad.*

And so, we can see how the Soviet state has "assimilated" and "developed" this occupied part of Germany: five camps, one prison, and two special psychiatric prisons for dissidents.

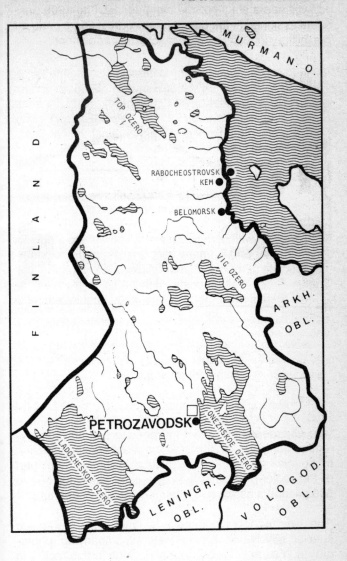

KARELIAN A.S.S.R.
(area: 172 400 sq. km.; pop.: 750 000)

Our information on this part of the Soviet Union is most incomplete. Here there are several secret military bases and camps hidden from the eyes of observers.

In *Petrozavodsk* (regional capital; pop.: 230000), we know of a prison for 1500 to 1600 inmates and a camp for 1200 inmates assigned to construction work in the city.

In the north, there are three men's strict-regime camps: in *Rabocheostrovsk* (approximately 1500 prisoners), *Kem'* (approximately 1800 prisoners), and *Belomorsk* (approximately 1200 prisoners). Special escort guards accompany the prisoners to military construction sites.

*

GOR'KII REGION
(area: 74800 sq. km.; pop.: 3700000)

You are now in a region in which you will find a developing industry and... many religious people. The state is conducting a massive anti-religious propaganda campaign here. Yet Baptists, Jehovah's Witnesses, and Pentecostals nevertheless continue to acquire secret adherents.

Note, for example, the receipt of the authorities: "a fine of 50 rubles for belief in God". Fifty rubles represent a half-month's salary for an engineer.

Many people in the Soviet Union are arrested for their belief in God or lose custody of their children, who are then "reeducated".

Receipt for a fine of 50 rubles (half-month's wages) "for belief in God".

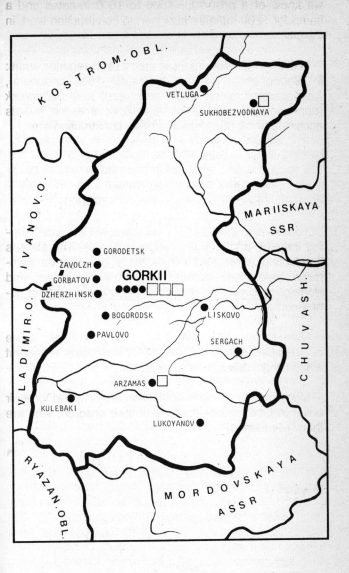

Let us now examine the camps in *Gor'kii* city and region in which religious citizens as well as dissidents seeking to bring democracy to this unhappy country are imprisoned with ordinary offenders.

In *Gor'kii* city, we know of five camps, three prisons,

and one psychiatric prison. In a men's camp near the suburb of *Bor* (camp no. UZ-62/1; bus nos. 64 and 65), more than 3000 prisoners are assigned to construction projects in the city or to auxiliary duties (loading and unloading) in a woodworking industrial plant. Some of them are used as loggers.

In the city's *Avtozavodskii* District, you will find a women's camp of 1500 to 1600 prisoners, some of whom maintain custody of their children while serving their sentences. They work as seamstresses. (See the testimony of A. Sh., who was imprisoned here until 1979, in the notes to the chapter on women's and children's camps.)

In a children's camp of 1200 to 1300 prisoners located in the same area, the children are forced – as in other, similar facilities – to work on starvation rations and endure the usual mockery and humiliations. For directions to the camp, see the map of Gor'kii city.

In *Gor'kii,* there is a huge prison of more than 10000 prisoners confined under extremely severe conditions. In addition to the many pre-trial detainees, there are also prisoners here who were sentenced to the isolation area for having committed a misdemeanor in a labor camp. Directions: bus nos. 7, 26, or 37 to *Gagarin Street.*

In the building of the regional K.G.B. located in the center of the city on *Vorob'ev Street,* there is another prison for political pre-trial detainees of approximately 800 inmates. "Investigations" of those detained here for their belief in God are made to last for months in order to persuade them to renounce their faith. Dissidents here are subjected to provocations or are threatened with reprisals against their families. Those "sentenced to insanity" are sent from this facility to a special psychiatric prison (see notes to the map of psychiatric prisons in the Soviet Union). In *Komsomol'skii* settlement, a part of Gor'kii, you will find a psychiatric hospital containing a special prison ward. Directions: bus no. 17 along the highway that leads to *Bogorodsk.* (Request to see section 16 in which the mentally healthy are tortured and driven to insanity.)

While we have knowledge of camps located in the vicinity of Gor'kii that supply labor for the lumber industry, we cannot provide the reader with their exact addresses.

Harsh and arbitrary conditions reign in camp no. UZ-62/10, located in *Sukhobezvodnoe* (120 kilometers by train north of Gor'kii). More than 2000 prisoners in this strict-regime camp are assigned to construction or farm work. Nearby is a prison of up to 500 inmates who had violated some rule while interned in the camp. Prisoners have good reason to fear this facility and the hunger, despair, and brutality that pervade it.

In *Vetluga*, about 250 kilometers northeast of Gor'kii, 1500 prisoners in a strict-regime camp (no. UZ-62/12) are assigned to the logging and woodworking industries.

In both *Zavolzh'e* and *Gorodets,* you will find an ordinary-regime camp of 500 to 600 prisoners assigned to the woodworking industry. This labor force is augmented by prisoners drawn from other camps.

In *Dzerzhinsk,* 1000 to 1100 prisoners from an intensified-regime camp work in a farm machinery plant. L.T., who spent three years there (until 1978), reports: "I did not work in the main production area but was assigned instead to paint finished products with nitrolac. We worked eight hours a day during which we applied the nitrolac with spray containers. Because, however, our protective masks were always defective, we could not avoid inhaling the acetone fumes. By the end of our work shift, we were intoxicated from the poison. I remember how my friend, Sergei *Kargach,* was overwhelmed by the poisonous fumes and lost consciousness. We carried him to the medical section. One of the supervisors said, 'He's drunk!' Within an hour and a half, Sergei was dead."

An ordinary-regime camp of 500 to 600 prisoners assigned to work in brick or cement plants may be found in *Bogorodsk, Pavlovo,* and *Lyskovo.*

In *Arzamas,* 1200 prisoners from an ordinary-regime camp are assigned to the manufacture of spare parts in a mechanics workshop for the Gor'kii Automobile Plant.

There is also a large prison of 3000 inmates here.

Approximately 1500 prisoners in an ordinary-regime camp in *Kulebaki, Sergach,* and *Lukoyanov* are assigned to work in woodworking plants.

*

GOR'KII CITY
(pop.: 1300000)

No. 1 on the city map represents Gor'kii Square, the center of the regional capital. From Gor'kii Square, you may walk along Sverdlov Street until you reach the K.G.B. prison on the corner of *Vorob'ev* Lane (which connects Krasnoflotskaya and Sverdlov Streets). Directions: bus nos. 1, 26, 40, 43, and 45; trolley bus nos. 3, 6, 9, and 12; tram nos. 3, 5, 18, and 24. Some 500 to 600 prisoners are incarcerated here.

A special prison for political prisoners is housed in the K.G.B. building (no. 3). Across the street is the K.G.B. club (no. 13), in which employees of the organization amuse themselves after "work".

No less than 10000 inmates languish in a huge prison (no. 8) at *Gagarin* Prospekt 26. (See testimony of A. Sh., an eyewitness, in the notes to the map on women's and children's camps). As you approach the prison, you

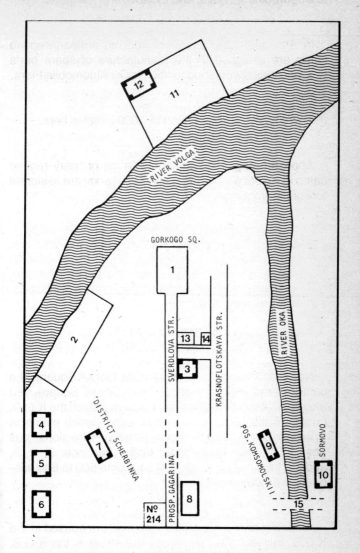

will see its high, red walls. Directions: bus nos. 4, 26, and 37; trolley bus nos. 17 and 62 (to Universitet stop).

Three camps are located near the automobile plant (no. 2): a women's camp (no. 6) of 1500 to 1800 prisoners – including mothers who continue to maintain custody of their infant children – assigned to work in a sewing factory; a men's camp (no. 4) of 3500 prisoners assigned to toil under conditions hazardous to their health in foundry or lacquer enamel workshops in the automobile plant; a children's camp (no. 5) of approximately 800 prisoners assigned to mechanics workshops.

The camps are easy to recognize. They are surrounded by barbed-wire fences and watchtowers manned by guards. Directions: bus nos. 1, 26, and 40; trolley bus nos. 3, 6, 9, and 12; tram nos. 3, 5, and 18.

In *Shcherbinka* District, a large, new prison (no. 7) designed for 8000 inmates – the prison for 10000 inmates was apparently not enough – was built by work gangs from the labor camps. Directions: bus nos. 9 and 45 or trolley bus no. 13.

Across the Oka River in *Sormovo,* (part of Gor'kii), approximately 2000 prisoners from a camp (no. 10) are assigned to industrial construction. They have recently begun to build a new bridge across the Oka connecting *Sormovo* to the rest of Gor'kii. Directions: bus nos. 43 and 45 or tram nos. 5 and 24.

Dissidents and religious people ("Only the insane believe in God!" say the K.G.B. "doctors") are confined in a large psychiatric hospital (no. 9) in the *Komsomol'skii* settlement, which is part of *Sormovskii* District. Directions: bus nos. 9 and 45 or trolley bus no. 13 to Komsomol'-skii posëlok (Komsomol'skii settlement) stop.

In the new suburb of *Bor,* which is located on the other side of the Volga River from Gor'kii, about 3000 prisoners in a strict-regime camp (no. 12) are building a plant for plastics and glass. Prisoners are also assigned to work under conditions hazardous to health in those shops of the plant that are already in operation.

In Gor'kii, there are altogether three large prisons, five camps, and a psychiatric hospital in which prisoners of the K.G.B. are confined – a most worthy "monument" to the writer *Maksim Gor'kii,* who praised the Soviet state while ignoring the camps and the atrocities of Bolshevism.

TOMSK REGION
(area: 316900 sq. km.; pop.: 850000)

We know of two prisons and 15 camps in this remote region of the Soviet Union, a relatively small number of penal facilities for a population of 850000...

Tomsk is most easily accessible by airplane. The journey by train is fatiguing. (It is also instructive. The observant passenger would be able to see much on a 3000-kilometer journey from Moscow.)

In *Tomsk* city (regional capital; pop.: 440000), there is a prison for 2000 prisoners. In a special section of the facility, many practicing Christians are confined with other prisoners under strict regime.

The K.G.B. building in Tomsk houses a pre-trial detention isolation prison in which as many as 200 political prisoners are incarcerated.

The prisoners in the camps in Tomsk work primarily in the military construction sphere. Five of the seven camps here supply labor for underground military plants in *Tomsk*-2 and *Tomsk*-3. Up to 5000 prisoners from these camps are confined underground under strict regime and are rarely transferred to other facilities, except to special isolation prisons as an additional punishment.

Two intensified-regime camps in *Zarech'e* of 1500 prisoners each supply labor for construction projects within the city.

In *Prokhorkino,* in the northern part of the region, 1500 to 1800 prisoners of a strict-regime camp produce concrete pipes and reinforced concrete slabs.

Oil is produced in *Negotka, Parabel',* and *Kolpashevo.* We know of four camps of approximately 4000 prisoners that supply labor for the production and pumping of oil and for the construction of facilities connected with oil production.

In *Parbig,* 800 to 900 prisoners from an ordinary-regime

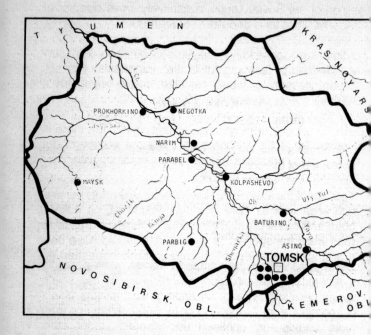

camp work as loggers or load and unload lumber materials.

In *Maisk,* 1200 prisoners are assigned to work in the military construction sphere.

In *Baturino,* 1500 prisoners are put to work in woodworking and track tie plants.

In *Narym,* 500 to 600 prisoners from a strict-regime camp work in a quarry. In the same city, you will also find a prison that was designed for up to 1500 inmates. Known for the brutality of its administration, the prison serves as a facility for camp internees found guilty of some infraction. Practicing Christians are among the inmates confined here.

KOMI A.S.S.R.
(area: 415 900 sq. km.; pop.: 1 100 000)

In Stalin's time, the population of Komi A.S.S.R. solely consisted of the prisoners and guards of the camps here. No one was willing to settle in these subpolar regions. The aim of the state, however, was to exploit this mineral-rich area with its coal *(Vorkuta, Pechora)*, oil *(Ukhta)*, gold, and metal ores. Thus, hungry prisoners dressed in rags were transported to an area that would have been a horrifying experience for even properly nourished human beings. The prisoners of the *"Rechlag", "Pechlag"*, and *"Vorkutlag"* complexes, which represented hundreds of camps, first built additional camps, then settlements, and finally cities. Ditches were dug and industrial complexes for the refining of oil and the processing of wood were erected.

The population centers now have a civilized appearance, and the number of camps has been reduced. There are now "only" 36 camps and four prisons for an area having a total population of 1 100 000. There used to be hundreds of camps here. Thus, a "democratization" of the regime has taken place. The reduction in the number of camps was not the result of kindness on the part of the state. The cities and mines had already been built, life had more or less become normalized, and the released prisoners "voluntarily" remained here to take up an occupation. In addition, people from other areas come to the cities and mines of Komi to live and work.

Yet these places are nevertheless so horrifying that the state is hardly likely to allow you, as a foreigner, to visit them. No one, however, is going to deny your at least trying to taking a trip there.

203

KOMI A.S.S.R.

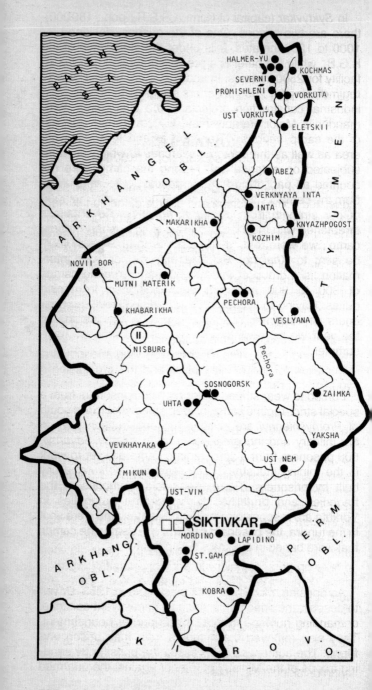

BARENT SEA

ARKHANGEL. OBL.

T Y U M E N

HALMER-YU
KOCHMAS
SEVERNI
PROMISHLENI
VORKUTA
UST VORKUTA
ELETSKII

ABEZ

VERKNYAYA INTA
INTA

MAKARIKHA
KOZHIM
KNYAZHPOGOST

NOVII BOR
①
MUTNI MATERIK

PECHORA

KHABARIKHA
VESLYANA

②
NISBURG

Pechora

SOSNOGORSK

UHTA
ZAIMKA

YAKSHA

VEVKHAYAKA

MIKUN
UST NEM

UST-VIM

☐☐ ●SIKTIVKAR
MORDINO
LAPIDINO
ST.GAM

PERM. OBL.

ARKHANG. OBL.

KOBRA

K I R O V O.

Here is a list of what you may see:

In *Syktyvkar* (capital of Komi A.S.S.R.; pop.: 180000), there are two prisons. One of the prisons, designed for 1000 to 1200 inmates, falls under the jurisdiction of the K.G.B., while the other is a pre-trial detention and transit facility for 2500 inmates. In addition, there is an ordinary-regime camp for 1500 prisoners assigned to housing and industrial construction projects in the city. Camp commander is Major Peremyshlev. L.F., a former prisoner of the camp, reports: "Transport to and from the work area as well as the personal searches to which we were subjected on entering and leaving the camp were not counted as part of our official workday. We were away from the camp for altogether twelve hours a day. Sapped of our strength from the work, we were nevertheless threatened with much worse. 'This is an ordinary-regime camp', we were told. 'If you get into trouble here, you'll be sent to *Khal'mer-Yu.*' *Khal'mer-Yu,* for your information, is a group of three special strict-regime camps of 800 to 900 prisoners each assigned to mining duties. Having to live north of the Arctic Circle, the prisoners of Khal'mer-Yu often joke, 'Twelve months of the year we have winter. The rest of the time we have summer.'"

Forced to wear striped uniforms, 1200 prisoners from a special strict-regime camp located somewhat to the south of *Promyshlennyi* are assigned to construction work in the military and industrial spheres. In nearby *Severnyi,* 600 prisoners from a strict-regime camp are put to work in the mining industry. To the east lies *Vorkuta,* a city built by prisoners. There are untold memories of the tragedies and brutalities for which the authorities in Vorkuta are responsible: the innocent men who were shot in the tundra, the prisoners who froze to death, the camps that were buried in the snow by a blizzard.

An uprising, moreover, took place here in 1953. Driven to despair, the prisoners in the coal mines went on strike, demanding humane treatment and proper nourishment. They also removed the numbers from their prison uniforms. The authorities suppressed the uprising by sending troops of the Ministry of Interior against the unarmed prisoners. Frightened by the incident, however, the authorities removed the numbers from the uniforms and reduced the severity of camp conditions. They needed the coal, after all.

Today, in 1980, numbers can once again be seen on the clothing of the prisoners. Secretly taken photographs of the camps will testify to this.

Today, we know of only two strict-regime camps in *Vorkuta.* One is located near the *Tsentral'nya* mine, the other in the vicinity of the cement plant. The prisoners, of which there are 1000 to 1200 in each camp, are assigned to construct and repair the mine. *Vorkuta* also has a special prison for 1500 to 2000 inmates. The facility houses a pre-trial detention section and a section for prisoners transferred from the camps as a punishment.

Many of the inmates of the camps and prisons of *Vorkuta* were not arrested for having committed a crime but for believing in God.

In *Kochmas,* located north of Vorkuta, 600 to 700 children (aged 14 to 18) in an intensified-regime camp make minepit props and wooden packing labels. Major Karnaukhov, the camp commander, is known for his cruelty. The supervisors, or so-called "guardians", beat the children up and train them to denounce each other. The older boys rape the younger ones and turn them into homosexuals.

The prisoners of the strict-regime camps in *Abez', Inta, Verkhnyaya Inta, Knyazhpogost, Kozhim, Pechora,* and *Pechora Severnaya* are assigned to coal mining, construction projects, and wood processing. A camp hospital in *Pechora,* moreover, was designed for the prisoners of these facilities. The combined population of the camps ranges from 1000 to 1500.

The prisoners in the ordinary-regime camps south of

Pechora – that is, those in *Veslyana, Sosnogorsk, Khabarikha, Novyi Bor, Zaimka, Yaksha, Ust'-Nem, Ust'-Vym'*, and *Vevkhayanka* – are assigned to the logging industry. These relatively small camps have a population of 500 to 700 prisoners each. The prisoners in the ordinary-regime camps in *Mikun', Mordino,* and *Lopydino* repair machines and mechanical devices in mechanics workshops. The prisoner population in each camp ranges from 1000 to 1500.

The prisoners in the camps in *Gam* and *Kobra,* located south of *Syktyvkar,* are assigned to work in lumber mills and woodworking industrial plants. The plywood made in these facilities is exported. There is also a plant here for reinforced concrete products. About 2000 to 2500 prisoners are held in each camp.

The prisoners in the group of camps in *Ukhta* are assigned to the oil and oil products industries.

Speaking of the camps in and around *Vorkuta,* we should mention the incident involving Evgenii *Rusinovich* that took place in 1954. Mrs. Rusinovich had traveled

As you can see, there are large houses and broad streets in Vorkuta (northern Urals, 110 kilometers north of the Arctic Circle, Komi A.S.S.R.). These, however, are cemeteries of slaves. Under the asphalt lie the countless remains of the prisoners who built the city. The photograph shows the K.G.B. building and a building of the Ministry of Interior. Prisons are concealed in both (photo 1975).

Above: Barges on the Pechora River in which prisoners from Arkhangel'sk Region are transported. (The photograph was taken from near the city of Nar'yan-Mar on Pechora Bay, 110 kilometers north of the Arctic Circle.) According to B., a former prisoner, these barges become jammed in the ice as a result of the winter frosts. The prisoners would then be led away from the barge without warm clothing or nourishment. During the winter, 2000 of the 6000 prisoners died in tents (Photo 1969).

Below: The tents or "chumy" (nomad tents covered with animal fur or hide) to which the prisoners from the barges were brought and where they had to spend the winter (photo 1968).

4000 kilometers to visit her husband in the camp, but the guards refused to let her see him. Friends of Rusinovich thereupon arranged for a secret meeting at the building site where he worked. The guards, however, found them out and beat them. They cut Mrs. Rusinovich's hair off, hanged her from the barbed-wire fence in the forbidden zone, and made fun of her. Driven raving mad, Rusinovich attacked a guard at the building site with an ax and killed him. Seizing the latter's machine gun, he shot down the remaining guard (!), thus freeing the other prisoners. Having taken additional loaded magazines, this hero went to a neighboring camp, killed the guards, and freed the prisoners there. Word of his armed campaign spread to the other camps in Vorkuta. The security guards in the area, however, did not rush to attack Rusinovich. They jumped into their cars instead and fled Vorkuta like cowards!

Only after three or four hours had passed was a division of security forces of the Ministry of Interior fielded against Rusinovich, who, in the meantime, had occupied the top floor of the "Vorkutalag" building. He returned fire for 24 hours.

With his last bullet, Rusinovich shot himself in the heart.

Should you ever visit Vorkuta, think of Evgenii Rusinovich of Minsk.

*

TULA REGION
(area: 25 700 sq. km.; pop.: 2 000 000)

Driving in the direction of *Yasnaya Polyana* (once the home of Lev *Tolstoi*) as you exit from *Tula* city (regional capital; pop.: 520 000), you will see a large prison of the Ministry of Interior standing on the left side of the road near a stadium. Approximately 1500 to 1800 prisoners are incarcerated in it. From the street, you will have a good view of the upper floors of the prison as well as the windows, which are kept boarded so that the prisoners may not be seen from the outside. The prison is known

TULA REGION

for its underground isolation cells and the terrible stench that pervades it. The K.G.B. building in the center of the city houses a special isolation prison designed for 200 to 300 political prisoners.

In the suburb of *Kosaya Gora,* located on the southern outskirts of Tula (again in the direction of *Yasnaya Polyana),* approximately 2000 prisoners work in a metallurgical plant or at construction sites. Turn your attention to the smokestack of the plant and to the tension wires supporting it. A prisoner once tried to escape by descending one of the wires, but he was spotted by a guard and shot down. He fell dead to the ground.

In *Aleksin,* in the northern part of the region, approximately 2500 prisoners in a strict-regime camp are assigned to work under hazardous conditions in a military chemical industrial plant or to construction duties connected with the plant. The camp lies in the city's *Zarech'e* District.

In *Revyankino,* 500 to 600 prisoners in an ordinary-regime camp are assigned to the manufacture of special clothing.

In *Yasnogorsk,* 1500 to 1800 prisoners from an intensified-regime camp are assigned to the military construction sphere.

In *Venev,* 1000 to 1200 prisoners from an ordinary-regime camp sew protective covers for artillery weapons produced in military plant no. 535 in *Tula.*

In *Novotul'skii,* approximately 800 prisoners from a labor camp are assigned to mechanics workshops for the benefit of local industry.

In *Novomoskovsk,* located east of Tula, approximately 1500 prisoners from a strict-regime camp work in military industrial and farm machinery plants under conditions hazardous to health.

In *Kimovochi* and *Severo-Zadonsk,* which are located further to the south, prisoners of two ordinary-regime camps are assigned to farm work to replace those who had fled the miserable conditions of the kolkhoz'. In *Donskoi,* approximately 1500 prisoners from an ordinary-regime camp work in the "Ventilyator" machine plant.

In *Shchekino* and *Lipki* (about 70 kilometers south of Tula), more than 3000 prisoners in two strict-regime and one intensified-regime camp assigned to the construction and operation of gas wells and to related construction projects.

In *Skuratovo,* approximately 600 prisoners from an ordinary-regime camp are assigned to construction in the military sphere.

In *Suvorov,* 800 to 900 prisoners of an ordinary-regime camp work in a brick factory.

In *Odoev,* 1000 prisoners of a strict-regime camp produce reinforced-concrete slags.

In *Belev,* approximately 1000 prisoners are assigned to a woodworking plant.

In *Gorbachevo* and *Chern'*, there are two ordinary-regime camps of approximately 500 prisoners each assigned to farm work. In *Plavsk*, approximately 2000 prisoners in a strict-regime camp (no. 400/5) work in a ventilator plant. Camp commander is Lieutenant Colonel Sidorov.

In *Uzlovaya*, an ordinary-regime camp for 600 to 700 prisoners supplies labor for road construction and repair.

In *Bogoroditsk*, there is a camp for 800 to 900 invalid prisoners.

In *Tovarkovo*, 1500 prisoners in a camp are assigned to housing and industrial construction.

In *Turdei*, there is a camp hospital for 1500 to 1600 prisoners.

In *Efremov*, there is a strict-regime camp for 1500 prisoners assigned to a woodworking plant.

Altogether, there are 26 camps and two prisons in this region of 2000000 inhabitants.

*

VOLGOGRAD REGION
(area: 114100 sq.km.; pop.: 2400000)

Volgograd city (regional capital; pop.: 950000) was formerly called *Tsaritsyn* and later renamed *Stalingrad*. The city is known for its resistance against Hitler's forces in World War II. Few tourists, however, know of the hundreds of thousands of prisoners who were brought here immediately after the war to rebuild the city, to construct a hydroelectric power plant, and to connect the Volga

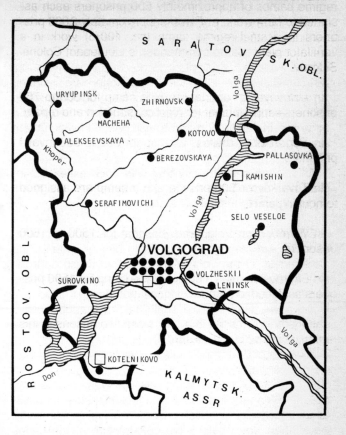

and Don Rivers (Volga-Don Canal) or were sent to toil away at construction sites in *Leninsk, Volzhskii,* and *Kamyshin.* These prisoners worked many years in Volgograd; it is only thanks to them that the city was able to rise from the rubble again.

You will not, however, hear a single word from the state to the memory of these victims.

May our modest list of the existing camps and prisons in Volgograd serve as a reminder of those whose bones lie beneath the foundations of the city's buildings or at the bottom of the Volga-Don Canal.

In and around Volgograd city itself, we know of twelve ordinary-regime camps of about 15000 prisoners. They are located in *Zarech'e* and *Slobodka*. Directions: tram nos. 16, 29, or 41; bus nos. 7, 11, and 14. These facilities include a camp for 1500 women prisoners, some of whom continue to maintain the custody of their infant children while serving out their sentences. The women work in a knitted-wear industrial plant located next to the camp. Directions: bus nos. 12 or 35. Male prisoners are assigned to construction, farm work, or to hazardous duties in military plants (foundries, plastics plants). In the city is a large pre-trial detention and transit prison in which there are about 5000 inmates.

As we can see, the city that was once called Stalingrad has earned the name and memory of the tyrant and murderer.

Our report on Volgograd-Stalingrad would be incomplete without mentioning that Stalin himself ordered the construction of the Volga-Don Canal, in which approximately 150000 prisoners using wheelbarrows and spades participated. The number of those who died in the process is unknown. Perhaps we shall learn the tragic figures once this infernal regime has fallen. *Solzhenitsyn* estimates that as many as 60000000 prisoners have died in 60 years of Communist rule in Russia.

This frightful construction project was directed by Colonel Barabanov, a sadist who took pleasure in humiliating intellectual political prisoners. This is the same Barabanov, who, before the construction of the canal, had already gained a reputation for his brutality in *Salekhard*. Acting on orders from Stalin, he directed the construction of a railroad with the use of the labor of prisoners in the sub-polar permafrost area between *Vorkuta* and *Salekhard*. (See the notes to the map of Tyumen' Region, especially on the prisoner uprising that took place there.) Colonel Barabanov's cruelty had driven the prisoners to such desperate lengths that they organized a rebellion against his rule – without any hope of succeeding. When the secret police learned of the plot, they executed the leaders by firing squad and sent hundreds of others to special strict-regime prisons and camps in Siberia. This took place between 1950 and 1952. Today, the waters of the canal flow peacefully. Intourist will gladly entertain you among the unmarked graves.

Do not forget to tell Intourist that you know what lies under the waters of the canal. Take a picture of the canal in memory of the victims.

Near Volgograd, you will find the cities of *Volzhskii* and *Leninsk,* in which there is considerable industry. Teams of prisoners are brought here from several camps to work. We know the location, however, of only two of these facilities.

1. *Volzhskii* – camp no. 154/12; 1200 prisoners in this intensified-regime facility are put to work in a tractor plant (directions: bus no. 45). Camp commander is Major Malov; supervisor of K.G.B. operations is Lieutenant Colonel Moskalenko. Many of the prisoners in the camp, primarily Jehovah's Witnesses, Pentecostals, Jews, and Moslem Darghins (from Daghestan) were arrested for practicing their religious beliefs. There are more than 20 such prisoners here.

2. *Leninsk* – camp no. 154/14, in which 1500 prisoners are assigned to industrial and housing construction projects.

In *Vesëloe,* located somewhat north of Volgograd, about 5000 prisoners of a women's ordinary-regime camp make military uniforms, bedsheets, protective covers for tanks, parachute pouches, and cartridge pouches in a large sewing factory. Camp commander is Lieutenant Colonel Rostin. More than 200 of the women maintain custody of their infant children. When the children reach two years of age, they are mercilessly taken away from their mothers. (See the notes to the special map on women's and children's camps and accompanying photographs.)

There are two prisons in Volgograd Region: a transit prison in *Kotel'nikovo* for 1500 prisoners and a special isolation prison in *Kamyshin.* (See a detailed discussion of prisons of this type in the section on Vladimir.)

In the northern part of Volgograd Region, you will find camps in *Uryupinsk, Serafimovich, Kamyshin, Berezovskaya, Zirnovsk, Pallasovka, Machekha, Kotovo,* and *Alekseevskaya.* Prisoners in these camps are assigned to various duties: oil production in *Serafimovich,* loading and unloading in *Kamyshin,* and woodworking in *Berezovskaya.* In the camps of the other cities and settlements, the prisoners are assigned to road repair and construction or to farm work. In the kolkhozes, there is a constant shortage of labor as a result of the migration of peasant population to the cities. It is not easy, however, to migrate. The kolkhoz peasants do not possess passports, without which it is impossible to register with the local police as required by law. Without proper registration, it is impossible to find a job.

It is not uncommon that the half-starving population in the countryside is tempted to assist the K.G.B. in maintaining order in the camps. For the discovery and aid in the recapture of a camp runaway, the K.G.B. offers a reward of 16 kilograms of flour and a sheep.

Such acts of betrayal take place throughout the entire Soviet Union.

*

KEMEROVO REGION
(area: 95500 sq. km.; pop.: 3000000)

Relatively small geographically, Kemerovo Region is saturated with penal facilities: 39 camps and six prisons.

This can be explained by the region's severe climate conditions, the absence of a network of services for the population, the constant shortage of provisions and clothing. All these factors impede work. For these reasons,

KEMEROVO REGION

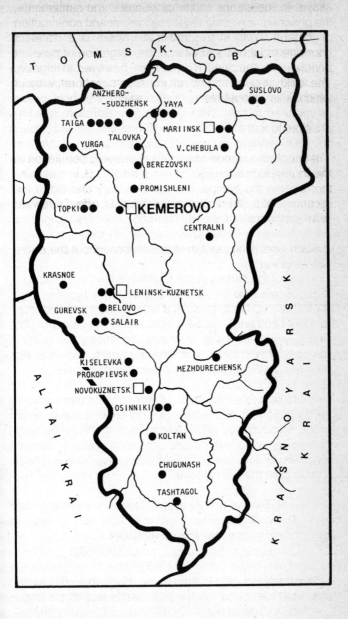

the necessary labor supply for mining and industry must be provided by camp prisoners, exiles, and former camp inmates who, having served their sentences in the region's facilities, are unable to acquire permission to leave

217

the area. They are therefore said to have "voluntarily" assumed residence and employment in the region.

Kemerovo city, the capital of the region (pop.: 480000), is a major railroad juncture on the Tom' River connecting *Tomsk, Barnaul,* and *Novosibirsk.* It is the center of the Kuznets coal basin and of the mechanical engineering and military industries.

We know of three prisons in Kemerovo: a K.G.B. prison of 1000 inmates, a pre-trial detention prison of 2000 inmates, and a special psychiatric prison of no less than 500 inmates.

In addition, there is a strict-regime camp in the railroad settlement of the city for 2500 prisoners assigned to construction or forced to work under hazardous conditions in either a coking plant or in an electromotor factory.

Most of the camps in the region are for male prisoners, but you will also be able to find women's facilities here. In Kemerovo itself, there is a women's camp of approximately 1200 prisoners who work in a sewing factory. (The many prisoners here who also continued to maintain custody of their infant children were amnestied on 21 November 1979. Perhaps they have since returned...)

In *Novokuznetsk,* south of Kemerovo, approximately 1000 prisoners of a women's strict-regime camp (which once was and may still be a women-and-children's camp) are assigned to loading and unloading duties at the railroad or to the production of spun and woven goods. Camp commander is Major Tomilin.

In both *Suslovo* and *Anzhero-Sudzhensk,* located north of Kemerovo, there is a camp of 800 to 900 women prisoners assigned to farm work.

Mariinsk is the administrative center of all the camps in the northern part of the region. Here you will find two men's strict-regime camps that supply labor for a woodworking industrial plant and the mines (auxiliary duties). A special prison for 600 to 800 inmates is also located here.

Prisoners in the men's camps in *Suslovo, Yaya,* and

Verkhnyaya Chebula are assigned to underground coal mining.

Four camps in *Taiga* and another two in *Yurga* supply labor for the logging industry. About 500 to 600 prisoners are confined in each camp.

In *Talovka*, 1200 prisoners in an ordinary-regime camp work in a woodworking industrial plant.

In *Berezovskii*, 1500 prisoners are assigned to woodworking, such as the production of track ties and minepit props.

In both *Promyshlennaya* and *Tsentral'nyi*, 800 to 900 prisoners in a strict-regime camp are assigned to mechanics workshops or to underground coal mining.

Two camps in *Topki* and *Leninsk-Kuznetskii* each and one in *Krasnoe* supply labor for the underground coal-mining and construction industries. There are about 1000 to 1200 prisoners in each camp.

Camps of 1000 to 1100 prisoners each in *Gur'evsk, Salair, Belovo,* and *Kiselevsk* supply labor for the construction and repair of mine shafts.

In *Prokop'evsk, Mezhdurechensk,* and *Osinniki*, there are camps of 1200 to 1500 prisoners each assigned to construction, woodworking (at a housing construction industrial plant), and mine-shaft repairing (auxiliary duties).

Strict-regime camps of 800 to 1000 prisoners each in *Kaltan* and *Tashtagol* supply labor for the logging industry.

In *Temirtau*, about 800 to 900 prisoners in a strict-regime camp are assigned to underground coal mining. Many of the prisoners here are Christians, primarily Pentecostals, Baptists, and Jehovah's Witnesses, who were arrested for their belief in God.

In *Chugunash*, 1000 to 1200 prisoners of a strict-regime camp work in a metallurgical plant.

219

In *Novokuznetsk,* there is an extremely severe special strict-regime prison for 1000 to 1100 inmates. It is interesting to note that the inmates here are assigned to construct special traps made of metal wire for use in the border areas of the Soviet Union.

The horror of everyday life in the camps and prisons in this remote part of the Soviet Union is indescribable. V.P., one of the political prisoners here arrested for their religious beliefs, reports: "I was in the camp in *Chugunash,* Kemerovo Region, from 1974 to 1977. The camp grounds were ancient, and the barracks were filthy and rotted through. The religious prisoners number 30 or 35 among the thousands of recidivist criminals. We were also considered recidivists as each of us had already once been convicted of 'belief in God' and of not belonging to the official church. The administration persecuted us in every way possible. We were given the hardest work; and only we were assigned, moreover, to clean the toilet bowls.

"There were those in our group who chose not to eat in the dining area; they limited their diet to bread. In the summer, they tried to plant a small kitchen garden on the camp grounds: onions, peas, garlic, even potatoes. The guards first allowed everything to grow and then destroyed the plants.

"There were also Old Believers in our group. Knowing that Old Believers do not eat pork, the guards would dip a small piece of pork fat into their soup. The Old Believers would then stop eating and leave.

"The guards also incited the criminals against us. Among them were horrible people who carried out the will of the supervisors. They even beat us up, abused us in every way possible, and mocked our religion. The hard and dangerous work that we were given made things even worse."

Here, then, is an example of how horrifying everyday camp life can be for innocent prisoners.

SARATOV REGION
(area: 100200 sq. km.; pop.: 2500000)

In *Saratov* city (regional capital; pop.: 880000), you will find a prison for 600 to 800 inmates in the K.G.B. building on Dzerzhinskogo Street. The inmates here are political prisoners. In addition, there is an ordinary-regime prison in the city with a section for prisoners in transit. The flow of prisoners destined for camps in the East is channeled through Saratov from transit prisons in *Balashov, Rtishchevo,* and other cities. Very few of them are not aware of what "Saratov transit" means: filth, hunger, beatings. Up to 5000 inmates are confined in the prison, and sometimes more.

I.P., an eyewitness, reports: "In 1976, I was transitted through Saratov on my way to the camps in the East. Before having to enter the disinfection chamber, I was subjected to a personal search, during which the guards tried to tear off the cross that I wore around my neck. Yet I refused to let them have it. The guards remained quiet as there were many other prisoners there. On being led away from the area, however, to be taken to our cells (this was after our clothes had been disinfected), I was separated from the others in order to be escorted alone. The guards once again began to reach for my cross. I still refused to give in even though there were three of them. I tried to swallow the cross, but then they grabbed it from me. During the struggle, I bit into someone's hand, whereupon they beat me up brutally, tore off my clothes, and threw me into a cold underground isolation cell."

A camp for 800 to 900 prisoners assigned to construction work in the city may be found near the transit prison.

SARATOV REGION

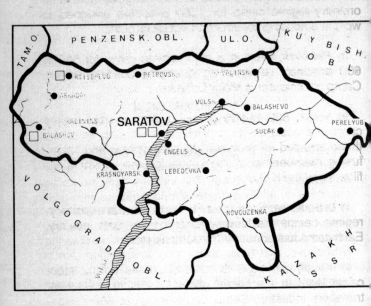

Approximately 1500 prisoners in an ordinary-regime camp in *Engels* work in a woodworking plant. Camp commander is Major Okulin.

In *Balashov* and *Rtishchevo,* as we have already indicated, there is a transit prison of 1200 to 1500 inmates each. In *Balashov,* 500 to 600 prisoners in a forced-labor camp work in a brick plant, whereas another 600 to 700 inmates in a camp in *Rtishchevo* are assigned to industrial construction.

In *Arkadak,* there is a strict-regime camp for 1000 to 1100 prisoners who work in the military construction sphere.

In *Kalininsk,* approximately 1200 prisoners in an ordinary-regime camp are assigned to construction or farm work. Many of the prisoners here were arrested for their belief in God, including Jehovah's Witnesses, Evangelists, and Baptists. Camp commander is Major Fomin.

In *Krasnoarmeisk,* located south of Engels, there is an ordinary-regime camp for 1500 prisoners assigned to work in a housing construction industrial plant.

In *Petrovsk,* there is a strict-regime camp for 500 to 600 prisoners assigned to quarrying building stones. Camp commander is Major Lebedev.

In *Vol'sk,* 800 to 900 prisoners from a strict-regime camp are assigned to a brick plant. Among them are those arrested for their religious convictions and for refusing membership in the official church, which is infiltrated by the K.G.B.

In *Lebedevka, Sulak,* and *Perelyub,* there are ordinary-regime camps that supply labor for the farm industry. Each camp has about 600 to 800 prisoners.

In *Khvalynsk,* 1000 to 1200 prisoners from a labor camp work in mechanics repair shops for the water transport industry. Camp commander is Major Konstantinov.

In *Balakovo,* 1000 to 1100 prisoners in an ordinary-regime camp work in a woodworking plant.

In *Novouzensk,* 800 to 900 prisoners in a strict-regime camp are assigned to secret military construction projects.

ASTRAKHAN' REGION

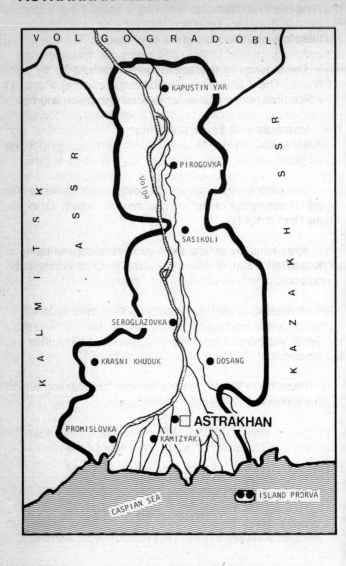

ASTRAKHAN' REGION
(area: 44 100 sq. km.; pop.: 870 000)

The major industries of Astrakhan' Region, which is located on the Caspian Sea, are fishing, caviar production, oil shipping, and the loading and unloading of tankers arriving from Baku. Prisoners of the camps in Astrakhan'

Region – in *Astrakhan'* city, *Kamyzyak* (no. NUD-249/7-A), *Promyslovka* (no. N-249/8), and on the island of *Prorva* (two facilities; nos. NN-249/14 and 16) – are therefore assigned to work in these areas.

The industry in this region was also built up by prisoners. The Lenin Fish-Processing Industrial Plant, in which prisoners continue to work, serves as an example.

Prisoners of the camps in *Dosang, Seroglazovka,* and *Krasnyi Khuduk* (north of Astrakhan') are assigned to the oil fields.

The camps in *Sasykoli, Pirogovka,* and *Kapustin Yar* (all in the northern part of the region) supply labor for the farm industry.

Approximately 800 prisoners in a strict-regime camp in *Kharabali,* located north of Astrakhan', work in stone quarries.

In *Astrakhan'* city (regional capital; pop.: 460000) itself, there is also a pre-trial detention and transit prison. Designed for approximately 1000 prisoners, it always has more than 2000 inmates confined in its cells.

Thus, there are altogether ten camps and one prison in the region.

*

VOLOGDA REGION
(area: 145700 sq. km.; pop.: 1300000)

Every prisoner knows the saying, "The guards in Vologda don't like to joke. (We shoot without warning!)"

That is the "law" in Vologda Region – a frightening "law". The guards nevertheless like to have their "fun". An inexperienced prisoner might be told to fetch something from outside the guarded area. He goes, not anticipating what is about to befall him. A shot is soon fired, and the prisoner falls dead. For "preventing an escape", the guard who fired the shot is given two weeks' leave. That, too, is the law.

225

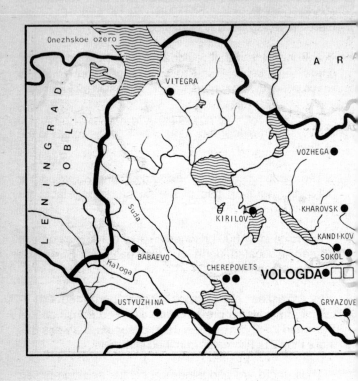

The region is covered with camps.

Let us begin with *Vologda* city (regional capital; pop.: 250 000), located north of Moscow and east of Leningrad. Here, there are two prisons: a K.G.B. facility for political prisoners designed to hold 500 to 600 inmates and a pre-trial detention and transit facility for 4 000 inmates. In addition, there are two men's strict-regime camps of 2500 prisoners each. Situated on both sides of the highway at the northern entrance to the city, the camps supply labor forces for a large woodworking industrial plant, a plywood factory, mechanics workshops, and construction projects within the city.

On *Vokzal'naya Street,* there is an intensified-regime camp for 1000 to 1200 children assigned to manufacturing containers for canned goods or to making stools.

226

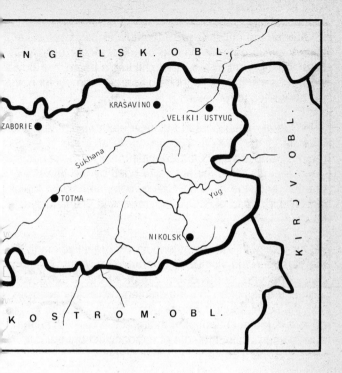

V.L., a physician who had been to the children's camp to conduct medical examinations, reports: "The children were emaciated. Their behavior was passive. Intimidated, some of them were afraid to answer the simplest questions. They were 14 to 18 years of age. After a few visits to the camp, I ascertained that many 14 and 15-year-old boys had been turned into passive homosexuals by the older youths and had become infected with syphilis or gonorrhea through the anal passage. The older boys had warned the younger ones against complaining or against reporting their illness. In addition to being forced to commit acts of homosexuality, the younger boys were also made to perform involuntary favors for the older prisoners, the supervisors, and the guardians. The children toiled in factory shops, and, after work, they were run through military drills that completely sapped them of their strength. Both guardians and supervisors beat the children prisoners without the slightest embarassment. Their explanation: 'Give them half the chance and they'll walk all over you!'

"Among the children were those who had been taken from their parents for having been raised to believe in God. Initially sent to a special children's home, the boys were subsequently brought here as a punishment for having attempted to run away."

In *Cherepovets,* located 140 kilometers west of Vologda by train or car, 600 to 700 prisoners of a men's strict-regime camp are assigned to build houses or make bricks. The buildings that they erect are used by the Ministry of Interior and the K.G.B. Camp commander is Major Grechikhin; head of K.G.B. operations is Captain Vyaz'-mov.

Our attention, however, should be drawn primarily to the camps in the vicinity of *Cherepovets.* Approximately 5000 prisoners of the death camps of the *Cherepovets* vicinity are assigned to mine uranium, which is necessary for the construction of Soviet atomic bombs. The prisoners are not supplied with protective clothing so that, after a short while, they die of radioactive contamination. More prisoners arrive to take their place.

The remaining camps of *Vologda* Region supply labor for logging, lumber transport, woodworking (in the many woodworking industrial plants), timber-rafting, and the shipment of commercial lumber for domestic use or export.

Ask well-known businessmen whether they purchase lumber from the Soviet Union. If they answer yes, ask them whether they have never seen the words, "Help! SOS!", inscribed in blood on the wood.

Driven to such desperate lengths by hunger, humiliation, and injustice the prisoners of the camps will sometimes chop off a finger and insert it under the bark of a piece of wood or in a split log that would then be sent to the free world. This would serve as a sign that enslaved prisoners had cut down the tree.

S.V., a former soldier of the Soviet Army who stood

guard in a watchtower at a camp in *Tot'ma,* reports: "I had not given much thought to whom I was guarding or to who was imprisoned in the camp. I stood in the tower until I was relieved and then rested up. Once, however, an emaciated and fairly elderly man approached the tower in which I was posted and began to ask, 'Soldier, do you have a mother and father?' I remained silent as it was forbidden to speak while on duty in the tower. And then, he began to talk about his past, about his being tried and convicted for no reason at all, and about his term of camp imprisonment being inexplicably extended and re-extended. He had been imprisoned for 14 years, yet no end was in sight. Plagued by hunger and forgotten by his family, he had become indifferent to the world. Then he reached for an ax hidden under his pea jacket and said, 'I'm not sorry for myself', whereupon he lopped off his left hand."

It is worth thinking about those who desperately cry for help.

*

TADZHIK S.S.R.
(area: 143 100 sq. km.; pop.: 3 300 000)

This mountainous part of the Soviet Union is bordered on the west by *Uzbekistan,* on the north by *Kirghizia,* on the south by *Afghanistan,* and on the east by *China.* We know very little about this remote Soviet republic. In *Dushanbe* (republican capital; pop.: 480 000), for example, we know of only one special prison, which is located in the city's K.G.B. building and is designed to hold 500 to 600 inmates. We can also confirm that there is a prison of the Ministry of Interior in *Dushanbe,* though we do not know its exact location.

Four intensified-regime camps are located in the southern part of the republic – in *Kulyab, Kuibyshevskii, Kalininabad,* and *Kurghan-Tyube.* Approximately 6 000 prisoners from each camp are assigned to construct military installations in the area and the roads leading to them.

In *Pochati,* a settlement in the eastern part of the province near *Khorog,* approximately 2 000 prisoners from a

TADZHIK S.S.R.

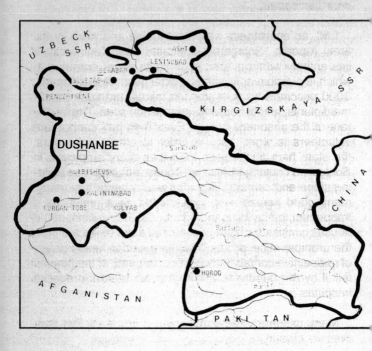

strict-regime camp (no. YuAS-3/5) are assigned to construction in the military sphere. Many of the prisoners confined here were arrested for practicing their religious beliefs. Camp commander is Major Sapogov.

In *Pendzhikent,* there is an ordinary-regime camp for 500 to 600 prisoners assigned to farm or irrigation work.

In *Sovetabad, Zervashan, Bekabad, Leninabad,* and *Asht,* a total number of approximately 10000 prisoners in strict-regime camps are serving sentences of ten years or more. The long term of imprisonment, has apparently to do with the fact that the inmates here are put to work in the uranium mines – that is, they are assigned to duties that will prove fatal for them. Some of the prisoners are also given work at construction sites in the above-mentioned cities as well as in *Sotsgorod,* which is located near *Leninabad.*

I. M., an eyewitness who used to live and work in this area, reports: "Sotsgorod is located near Leninabad. It lies entirely within a special off-limits zone, entrance to which is possible only with a special pass. Approximately 3 000 prisoners work in uranium mines, uranium enrichment plants, and at housing construction sites. The fatality rate of the prisoners is high. Even high pay cannot lure volunteers to work here. In order to attract volunteers, the state had declared in 1975 that every employee in *Sotsgorod* could build his own house with cost-free building stone and cement. The offer was accepted by many; many good homes were constructed as a result. As it happened, the building material for the foundations of the houses consisted of trailings that had been extracted from the uranium mine shafts. Thus exposed to heavy doses of radioactive contamination, the occupants of the houses fell ill by the hundreds and had to be treated in special hospitals."

Many prisoners and employees of the state lost their lives as a result.

Fence enclosure of a death camp in Leninabad (southeast of Tashkent, on the Syr-Dar'ya River, Uzbek S.S.R.). The photograph shows a watchtower with guards, barbed-wire fencing around the isolation cells (the fencing is electrically charged), and the forbidden zone (which is mined) near the fence enclosure (photo 1976).

231

CHUVASH A.S.S.R.

CHUVASH A.S.S.R.
(area: 18 300 sq. km.; pop.: 1 300 000)

The capital of Chuvash A.S.S.R., *Cheboksary* (pop.: 320 000), lies approximately 800 kilometers east of Moscow.

Our information on this autonomous republic is most incomplete. We know of only three camps and two prisons here. In the neighboring *Gor'kii* Region, there are at least 18 penal facilities.

In *Cheboksary*, there is a prison of the Ministry of Interior for 2500 inmates and a pre-trial detention, isolation prison of the K.G.B. There is also a camp located on the outskirts of the city on the road to *Tsivil'sk*. Approximately 1800 prisoners there are assigned to mechanics workshops.

In *Kozlovka,* about 90 kilometers southeast of *Cheboksary* by car, there is a strict-regime camp (no. YuL-34/5) for 1500 prisoners assigned to the logging industry. Here are many Christians arrested for practicing their religion, giving their children religious instruction, refusing military service, etc.

In *Alatyr',* located in the southern part of the autonomous republic, there is a prison for 500 to 600 inmates tried by special courts and sent here as an additional, severer punishment for having committed certain transgressions.

Next to the prison is a camp for 2000 prisoners assigned to work in a sawmill. The lumber is then rafted along the Sura River. Camp commander is Major Dovzhenko.

In a special fenced-off area of the camp, there is a special children's zone. Approximately 600 minors here are assigned to manufacturing packaging labels from the scrap wood.

*

KALMYK A.S.S.R.
(area: 75900 sq.km.; pop.: 290000)

Kalmyk A.S.S.R. is located on the Caspian Sea. A railroad line extending all the way to *Astrakhan'* crosses through the autonomous republic in an east-westerly direction. Another line connects *Elista,* the capital (pop.: 80000), with *Volgograd* in the north.

Upon your arrival in *Malye Derbety* from *Volgograd* by train, you may visit two forced-labor camps:

1. a strict-regime camp of 1200 prisoners who work in an asbestos pipe plant or in road construction. Camp commander is Major Kapitonov. Many Christians are imprisoned here: six Baptists, four Pentecostals, ten Old Believers, and 15 Jehovah's Witnesses. Jews accused of advocating Zionism, including Iosif *Dvornikov,* a former officer in the Soviet Army, are also confined here.

KALMYK A.S.S.R.

2. an intensified-regime camp of 1000 prisoners assigned to soil-enrichment and farm work. (The farm products are delivered to the camps in the area.) Among the prisoners here are seven Baptists, three Pentecostals, as well as a number of Jews who, wishing to emigrate to Israel, had refused induction into the Soviet Army. Anatolii *Malkin* is one such Jewish prisoner.

Further to the south in *Bol'shoi Tsaritsyn,* there is an ordinary-regime camp of 800 prisoners assigned to construction and farm work. Those imprisoned for their belief in God include four Baptists, two Seventh-day Adventists, three Old Believers, and a number of Jews, such as Leo *Epstein,* arrested for seeking emigration to Israel. Camp commander is Major Ivanov; local K.G.B. chief is Captain Shiverskii.

Near the railroad tracks in *Sarpa,* approximately 2000 prisoners in a strict-regime camp are assigned to secret military construction projects.

In *Yusta,* located 70 kilometers east of *Sarpa,* prisoners from another strict-regime camp are assigned to the construction of a secret military installation.

In *Tsentral'nyi,* located south of *Sarpa,* there is an ordinary-regime camp for 1500 prisoners assigned to road repair and construction and to soil-enrichment projects.

In *Tselinnyi,* approximately 50 kilometers from *Elista,* 500 to 600 prisoners from a labor camp are assigned to farm work.

In *Elista,* 1100 to 1200 prisoners in a men's strict-regime camp are assigned to duties in mechanics workshops. A separate section of the camp is maintained for prisoners waiting for transfer to other facilities. There is also a prison in the city in which approximately 2500 inmates are held. Among them are political prisoners, including those arrested for practicing their religion.

Three camps of 500 to 600 prisoners each are located in *Chernozemnyi, Prikumskii,* and *Artezian* (all south of *Elista*). The prisoners are assigned to soil-enrichment and irrigation projects as well as to farm work.

Three strict-regime camps are located in *Egorlyk, Solenoe,* and *Bashanta.* Unconfirmed information suggests that another two camps may be found in *Solenoe.* Prisoners from the three known camps are assigned to constructing potassium chloride mines and to road building.

Altogether, we know of 16 camps and one prison in this small area of the Soviet Union.

ROSTOV REGION

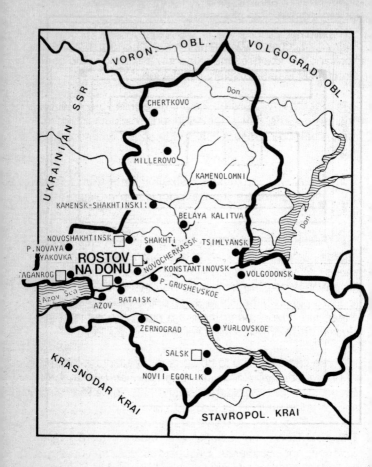

ROSTOV REGION
(area: 100 800 sq. km.; pop.: 3 900 000)

In *Rostov-on-Don* (regional capital; pop.: 900 000), you will find a prison on the corner of Gor'kii Street and Universitetskii Prospekt (see accompanying map). More than 2 000 inmates, including pre-trial detainees and prisoners in transit, are incarcerated in it. In addition, 200 to 300 inmates are confined in the special Pre-Trial Isolation Prison (SIzo: Sledstvennyi Izolyator) located in the K.G.B. building. An ordinary-regime camp (no. YaYa-398/19) for 600 to 700 prisoners located on Tonnel'naya Street

236

PRISON IN ROSTOV CITY

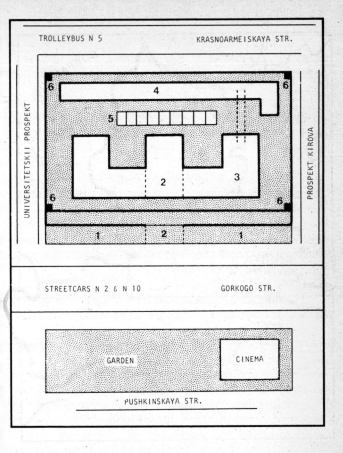

supplies labor for a packaging plant and for construction.

In *Novocherkassk,* about 40 kilometers northeast of Rostov, there is a prison that became well known in the Soviet Union in connection with an uprising in the city in 1962. (See special map of and notes on the prison in *Novocherkassk*.)

There is also an ordinary-regime camp of approximately 1000 prisoners located on the road to *Bagaevskii* on the outskirts of *Novocherkassk.* The prisoners produce reinforced-concrete slags.

In *Grushevskoe, Arsai* District (south of *Novocherkassk*), 1000 to 1100 prisoners in camp no. YaYa 398/6 are assigned to construct an irrigation system.

In *Novaya Yakovka, Matveev Kurgan* District (west of *Rostov*), approximately 800 prisoners of an ordinary-regime camp (no. YaYa-398/5) work in the farm industry.

In *Taganrog,* located further to the south, there is a prison for 400 to 500 inmates sent here from the camps as a punishment and an ordinary-regime camp of 500 to 600 prisoners who perform loading and unloading duties.

In *Bataisk,* located south of *Rostov,* 800 to 900 prisoners of an intensified-regime camp work on the construction of military installations.

In the port city of *Azov,* 500 prisoners from an ordinary-regime camp (no. YaYa-398/14) are assigned to road repair and construction.

In *Zernograd,* 1200 prisoners from camp no. YaYa-398/17 are assigned to construct granaries and storehouses.

In both *Novyi Egorlyk* and *Sal'sk,* there is a camp of 800 to 900 prisoners who are put to work on the construction of irrigation canals. There is also a prison in *Sal'sk* in which transit prisoners as well as former camp inmates sent here as a special punishment are confined. The latter group includes many religious prisoners who were penalized for conducting group prayers and for possessing anti-Soviet literature – the Bible – in the camps. (See the law on the confiscation and burning of Bibles.)

In *Yurlovskoe, Sal'sk* District, approximately 600 prisoners in camp no. YaYa-398/3 do farm work.

In *Shakhty,* 800 to 900 prisoners of an intensified-regime camp (no. YaYa-398/9-1) are assigned to construct surface mines.

In *Novoshakhtinsk,* 1500 prisoners from a strict-regime camp (no. YaYa-398/11) work in mines. Those prisoners found guilty of violating camp rules are sent to a prison in the city designed to hold 400 to 500 inmates.

238

In *Konstantinovsk*, located east of *Shakhty*, 1200 prisoners in camp no. YaYa-398/7 work in a woodworking industrial plant.

In both *Tsimlyansk* and *Volgodonsk*, there is an ordinary-regime camp of 600 to 700 prisoners; they are assigned to various projects dealing with the construction and repair of canals.

In *Belaya Kalitva*, 400 to 500 prisoners of a strict-regime camp (no. YaYa-398/12) work in a brick factory. Camp commander is Captain El'tsov.

In *Kamensk-Shakhtinskii*, approximately 500 prisoners of an ordinary-regime camp are assigned to the construction and repair of mine shafts.

In *Kamenolomni*, 600 prisoners of a special strict-regime camp are assigned to the quarrying of building stone.

In *Millerovo*, 800 prisoners in an intensified-regime camp work in a woodworking plant.

In *Chertkovo*, located in the north of the region, 600 prisoners of a strict-regime camp are assigned to chalk mines and lime pits.

Altogether, we know of 20 camps and five prisons in a region having 3 900 000 inhabitants.

*

NOVOCHERKASSK CITY (ROSTOV REGION)
(pop.: 180 000)

We now wish to present a map of the prison in *Novocherkassk* that became known to the outside world in con-

PRISON IN NOVOCHERKASSK CITY

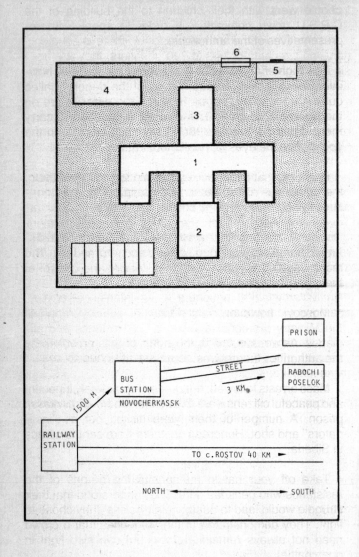

nection with an uprising. Hundreds of insurgent prisoners were brought to this facility, as a result, to be shot.

In 1962, hunger riots broke out in *Novocherkassk* as a result of Soviet government actions. Hunger was prevalent throughout the entire region, but only the inhabitants of *Novocherkassk* dared to stage a demonstration, demanding from the government, "Give us and our children bread!" The demonstration was peaceful. The people went with their children to the building of the C.P.S.U. town committee in order to speak with representatives of the authorities.

Too frightened to meet with the demonstrators, however, the "elected representatives of the people" called out the troops. The troops received the order to fire on the peaceful, unarmed crowd, but they refused to carry it out. Their commander then committed suicide on the spot before the eyes of the demonstrators.

Realizing that they had no back-up force behind them, the authorities asked Moscow to despatch special non-Russian K.G.B. troops from Asia immediately. Upon arriving, the Asian troops fired on the peaceful demonstrators, who then charged the troops. The people disarmed some of the child murderers and returned fire. The much-vaunted K.G.B. troops fled, leaving the control of the city in the hands of the insurgents.

Moscow, however, sent additional special troops of the Ministry of Interior and the K.G.B. in tanks and airplanes. As a result, the uprising, which was provoked by the authorities themselves, was drowned in blood.

Mass arrests followed; hundreds of completely innocent and peaceful citizens were thrown into the *Novocherkassk* prison. A number of them were picked out as "instigators" and shot. Hundreds of others were sent to camps in Siberia.

Take off your hat in memory to the heroes of the resistance who perished here. They understood that their struggle would lead to death; nevertheless, they chose to fight. They demonstrated to the authorities that a crowd need not always remain a crowd but can also fight in open battle!

Refer to the accompanying map for directions to the prison in *Novocherkassk*. Take the city's central bus terminal, located 1.5 kilometers from the train station and serviced by coach lines from *Rostov* 40 kilometers away, as a starting point. Board a bus marked "Rabochii Posëlok" and ride for three kilometers until you get to the end of the line. Arriving in Rabochii Posëlok, you will see the prison building on the left.

Do not forget to photograph the prison. It will remind you of what once took place here. Dissidents, including those arrested for their belief in God or for attempting to flee this "Soviet paradise", continue to languish today in *Novocherkassk* prison.

*

BELGOROD REGION (and Valuiki city)
(area: 27000 sq. km.; pop.: 1300000)

After arriving in *Valuiki* from *Belgorod, Khar'kov,* or *Voronezh* by train, you will be able to walk to two men's camps in the city (no. YuS-321/1 and LTP) without any difficulty. The prisoners of these facilities, of whom there are about 2000, work in a brick plant, a lime-production facility, and in clay and lime quarries. Commander of the camps is Major Vladimir Voronov.

There is also a children's intensified-regime camp (no. YuS-321/2; see map) here of approximately 500 prisoners assigned to work in a foundry shop under conditions hazardous to health.

In *Belgorod* itself, there is a prison with approximately 600 inmates and a camp (no. YuS-321/3) of about 2000 prisoners assigned to construct a tractor plant or produce hardware items for local industry.

In *Shebekino,* approximately 500 prisoners in camp no. YuS-321/5 are assigned to farm work.

In *Gubkin,* about 500 to 600 prisoners in a camp are assigned to construction work. A similar camp is also located in *Staryi Oskol.*

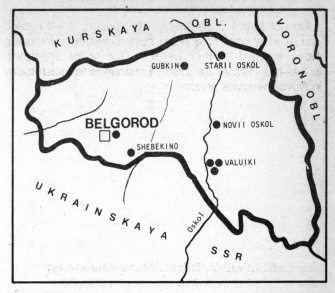

In *Novyi Oskol,* approximately 1000 prisoners in a women's camp (no. YuS-321/4) are assigned to exhausting work in the textile industry. Some of the women here maintain custody of their infant children.

*

VALUIKI
(Belgorod Region; camp no. YuS-321/1, camp LTP, and children's camp)

In passing through *Belgorod* Region on your way from *Khar'kov* to *Voronezh,* you may wish to make a stop in the small provincial town of *Valuiki.* We turn your attention to this inconspicuous town because in it you will be able to see three concentration camps at once – two men's camps and a children's facility for 14 to 16-year-olds.

We have provided the reader here with a map of the one-and-a-half-kilometer route from the train station to the camps, which are located on the periphery of the city. We have also added a map of the main men's camp in which 1500 prisoners are assigned to work in a brick factory, lime pit, or clay quarry.

VALUIKI CITY

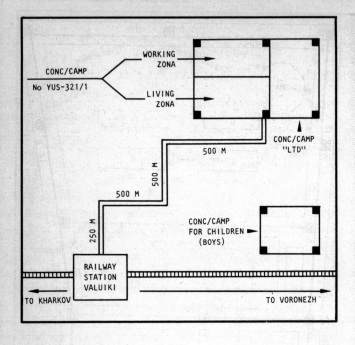

The production methods here are, characteristically enough, not mechanized. Bricks are made in the plant by hand as in the days of the Pharaohs of Egypt.

Even a view of the camps from the outside will show you how cramped the living conditions here are for 300 prisoners forced to huddle around the plank-beds in the small barracks.

Key to the map of the camps

I. Living area of camp no. YuS-321/1 (barracks 1, 2, 3; kitchen 13)

II. Living area of camp LTP

III. Work area of the camps (6 – lime pit; 7 – clay quarry; 8 – brick plant; 9 and 10 – lime plants; 4 – camp administration, where camp commander Major Vladimir

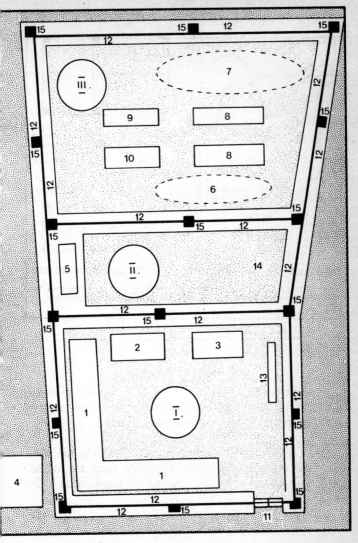

Voronov may be found; 15 – watchtowers; 12 – forbidden zone and mine fields; 11 – gates of the camps)

As you approach the children's camp, in which there are approximately 500 prisoners, you will be able to see from the outside that the work done there is hazardous to health. The children are assigned to duties in a foundry shop.

VLADIMIR REGION

VLADIMIR REGION
(area: 29 000 sq. km.; pop.: 1 500 000)
THE ISOLATION PRISON IN VLADIMIR CITY

In the ancient Russian city of *Vladimir* (regional capital; pop.: 300,000), there is a prison that was built during the reign of Empress Catharine II. The Soviet authorities found the facility useful and renamed it the Special Political Isolation Prison OD-1/ST.2. Its capacity, however, proved to be too small.

No. 1 on the diagram of the prison is the entrance to the administrative building (No. 3). No. 2 indicates the gates allowing cars transporting prisoners into the prison. No. 5 is the ancient prison building (now known as Section 3). No. 9 contains bathhouses, kitchens, storage rooms, and the living quarters of those prisoners who perform staff services within the facility. Nos. 4, 6, and 7 are prison buildings constructed during the Soviet regime

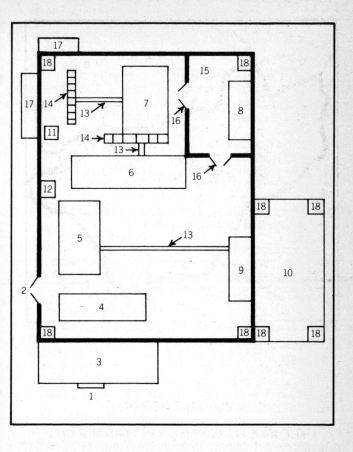

(Sections 4, 2, and 1 respectively). Prison building No. 6 also contains the hospital wards.

It is most telling that the old building contains large window openings. No attempts were made before the revolution to deny prisoners daylight. Today, the windows are sealed off halfway up and are barred. Translucent screens on every window prevent the prisoners from looking out onto the prison courtyard. A kind of twilight reigns in the cells.

The windows of the newer buildings are smaller than those of the older prison. The ancient prison is made of brick; its floors are of wood. The new Soviet structures, on the other hand, are built of reinforced concrete, which represents a serious hazard to the health and lives of the inmates.

The added section (No. 10) is a prison camp maintained independently of the prison. Its four corners, as well as those of the prison, contain watchtowers (No. 18) for armed guards. Returning to the prison proper, we see the prison warehouse (No. 12) and the morgue (No. 11).

From this morgue, the corpses of prisoners are given to students in the medical institutes. Prior to delivery, however, the corpses are decapitated to prevent their being recognized.

No. 14 represents the small courtyards of the prison. The inmates are permitted to take a 30-minute walk every day in the small walled-off, roofless pathways around the facility. No. 13 indicates overhead connecting corridors used for transferring prisoners.

The final section of the prison, in the upper right corner of the diagram, is the work brigade area (No. 15) and the gates entering it (No. 16). In the same area, is the workers' prison building (No. 8). The two sections in the upper left of the diagram are far from the least important in the Vladimir prison: they house the Officer's School of the M.V.D. and its dormitory (No. 17).

The prison in *Vladimir* is reputed to be the strictest political isolation facility under the administration of the K.G.B. Inmates here are often not able to find out who is locked up in the neighboring cell.

The walls of this facility have come to know the tragic fate of many people. One of the most tragic cases here has been that of Raoul Wallenberg, the former Swedish diplomat. Kidnapped by the Communists in Budapest 35 years ago, this completely innocent human being, who rescued many Hungarian Jews at the end of World War II, has since been held prisoner in the camps and prisons of the Soviet Union.

Our Research Center has been able to trace Wallenberg's secret journey through the Soviet penal system. Soviet authorities have made two official statements on the case thus far; "Soviet authorities know nothing of the fate of Raoul Wallenberg" and "Raoul Wallenberg died in a K.G.B. prison in 1947".

We have found a number of witnesses, former political prisoners from the Soviet Union, who could name a series of camps and prisons in which Raoul Wallenberg was confined: on *Vrangel'* (Wrangel) Island; in a secret camp for foreigners in *Zabaikal'e,* a prison in *Verkhneural'sk,* and the prison in *Vladimir.* We can confirm that Wallenberg was in building no. 4, cell no. 23. And he may still be there today.

The list of former inmates in *Vladimir* prison also includes Francis Gary *Powers,* the American pilot, and Vasilii *Stalin,* a son of the late Soviet dictator. More recent inmates of the facility have included *Bukovskii, Shcharanskii,* and other well-known political prisoners.

A.V., an eyewitness, describes life in this horrible prison: "Upon arriving in 1970, we were told by the prison authorities that we would first be put into quarantine. This meant living on starvation rations in a cell without mattresses, blankets, pillows, and without personal possessions or books. We were subsequently placed under strict regime for six months. The first of these six months was spent under isolation-cell conditions (approximately 800 calories).

Nadezhda Shumuk was arrested in 1976 for supporting Ukrainian independence. Her husband, D. Shumuk, and her brother, I. Svetlichnyi, were also arrested. Her small son, N. Shumuk, was taken away from her upon her arrest. His fate is unknown.

"All this was done to break the spirit of the inmates at the outset of their imprisonment. After six months of stupefying hunger, you could hardly think about anything except a piece of bread. The people were reduced to humiliation, torpidity, and brutality. I witnessed a few prisoners who cut open a vein in order to dip bread in their blood as a means of satisfying their hunger. I once even saw a prisoner who cooked a piece of flesh that he had cut from his own leg. He started a fire with the use of pages torn from a book by Karl Marx that he had obtained from the library.

"Except for the herbs that the inmates were allowed to eat in the camp in the summer and from which at least a few vitamins could be gotten, I was never given any vegetables or greens during my whole three years in Vladimir prison."

Such are the conditions in Soviet prisons. One cannot help but recall the "sufferings" of Angela Davis or of those other American prisoners who went on strike to protest against the monotonous prison food. They were fed chicken every day; when they demanded steak, they got it!

Pray for the martyrs of the *Vladimir* prison!

Generally speaking, there is "almost" nothing else to see in *Vladimir* Region. Only in *Vladimir* city itself (on the outskirts of town on the road to Gus'-Khrustal'nyi), there is a small ordinary-regime camp of 600 to 700 prisoners assigned to mechanics workshops in which hardware products are made for local industry (locks, door knobs, etc.).

In *Vladimir,* there is also a pre-trial detention prison. At least 40 of approximately 1500 prisoners here were jailed for political reasons. Other prisons in the region may be found in *Aleksandrov, Kovrov,* and *Murom.* Apart from ordinary offenders in these facilities, there are also those tormented here for having practiced their religion or simply for thinking differently. Being forced to live among criminals is often the worst aspect of imprisonment.

*

ESTONIAN S.S.R.
(area: 45100 sq. km.; pop.: 1500000)

Our knowledge of this part of the Soviet Union is incomplete and imprecise. We know of only five camps, two prisons, and one psychiatric hospital.

In *Tallinn* (republican capital; formerly called Reval; pop.: 420000), there is an ordinary-regime camp (no. ITK-5) for 1000 to 1200 prisoners at Tisleri Street 31–32. Camp commander is Major Kitaev. This is a camp for ordinary criminals, but there are also Estonian and other dissidents here (ask, for example, about Viktor *Matveyuk*, a political prisoner) as well as those arrested for their belief in God. The prisoners of the camp are assigned to work in industrial construction.

There are two prisons in *Tallinn*. One is a pre-trial detention facility for approximately 1000 inmates; it is known for its brutal regimen, its isolation cells (which are penetrated by moisture from the sea), and its special cells, in which thugs, incited by the K.G.B., beat up political prisoners and extract confessions from them. Located in the vicinity of *Kaubasadam* on Suur-Patarei Street the prison may be reached by tram nos. 1 and 2.

The other prison is housed in the K.G.B. building, formerly the stock exchange, at Pagari Street 2 and can hold 500 to 600 inmates. Only political prisoners are incarcerated here.

In *Tartu* (formerly called Dorpat; located in the southeast of the republic), there is a strict-regime camp for 800 to 900 prisoners assigned to the construction of military installations. Camp commander is Major Kapustin.

251

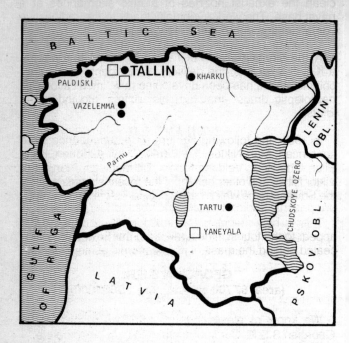

South of *Tartu*, there is a psychiatric hospital (in fact, a psychiatric prison) in which Estonian nationalists involved in the struggle for the independence of their country and against the Soviet occupation of it are confined. Konstantin Päts, the former president of independent Estonia, recently died here.

In *Vasalemma*, 50 kilometers southwest of *Tallinn*, there are two camps: an ordinary-regime facility in which approximately 1500 prisoners produce spare parts in an excavator plant; a strict-regime camp for 600 to 800 prisoners who work in a quarry or in a lime pit. Work conditions here are extremely severe.

In *Harku*, about 30 kilometers southeast of *Tallinn*, 300 to 400 prisoners in a women's camp manufacture and grind buttons. The work is very damaging to the lungs.

On *Paldiski* Bay, prisoners from a forced-labor facility (mentioned on our list of death camps) are assigned to clean the exhaust nozzles of atomic submarines at a naval base. The work eventually leads to the radioactive contamination and death of the prisoners.

At the State University of *Tartu,* Professor Juri Saarma, a K.G.B. expert on the delivery of dissidents to the psychiatric prison, has been developing new "medications"—neuroleptic drugs—that turn his victims into indifferent idiots.

In 1981, the following fighters for independence were sentenced: Mart Niklus, Yurii Kukk, Vinvi Akhonen, Kalle Eller, Otto Bool, Veldzho Kalen, Tiit Madison, Alan Sinp, Viktor Nitso, and other heroes of the recent struggle against the Soviet regime which has occupied Estonia since 1940.

This is how the peaceful and friendly Estonia would appear to the tourist, if he knew what the Soviet state concealed behind the mask of its "economic achievements".

GEORGIAN S.S.R.
(area: 67700 sq. km.; pop.: 5000000)

We know of eleven camps and two prisons in the Georgian S.S.R. Our information may not be complete.

In *Tbilisi* (republican capital; formerly called Tiflis; pop.: 1100000), there are two prisons: a pre-trial detention facility of 2500 inmates; a facility of up to 800 inmates located in the Georgian K.G.B. building.

Nationalism in Georgia is a highly developed force. The state, however, is moving to eradicate it. For this reason, arrests and persecutions are systematically pursued. The authorities are employing brutal and dirty methods in the process to humiliate prisoners under investigation. In these facilities, there are special cells in which criminal thugs beat up political prisoners and use physical violence to force them to commit homosexual acts. Their advice to their victim: "Confess to what you've been accused of; there is no other way out of this cell!"

Camps in *Rustavi* and *Telavi* (having 1500 and 1200 prisoners) supply labor for metallurgical factories. The prisoners are assigned to loading and unloading duties under conditions hazardous to health.

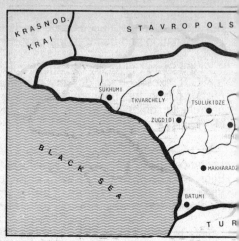

Prisoners in the ordinary-regime camps ın *Batumi,* *Makharadze,* and *Tsulukidze* are assigned to farm work in sovkhozes. The authorities in these leniently run facilities accept bribes from the prisoners in return for allowing them to accept additional food packages from their relatives. There are 500 to 600 prisoners in each camp.

Prisoners in the intensified-regime camps in *Zugdidi,* *Kutaisi,* and *Khashuri* are assigned to farm work (1200 to 1500 in each facility). The cities in which these facilities are located are easily accessible by car and by train. Whether you wish to visit them or not depends entirely on you. Soviet law does not forbid such visits.

ARMENIAN S.S.R.
(area: 29 800 sq. km.; pop.: 3 000 000)

In this Transcaucasian republic, we know of the following penal facilities: In *Erevan* (republican capital; pop.: 920 000), there is a pre-trial detention prison of approximately 1500 inmates, a special K.G.B. prison of 500 to 600 inmates, and a camp (no. 2) for 1500 to 1600 prisoners assigned to industrial construction in the surrounding areas of the city. Located at Sovetashenskoe High-

way 20, the camp is designated as a penal facility for ordinary offenders. Nevertheless, there are also political prisoners here. Ask, for example, about Shagen *Artyunyan,* an Armenian freedom-fighter. (His wife, Asya Nachapetyan, lives in Erevan at Chernyshevskaya Street 23/5. Pay her a visit and ask her about the struggle of the Armenians for their separation from the Soviet Union.)

In *Sovetashen,* located south of *Erevan,* 600 to 800 prisoners in a camp are assigned to construction work.

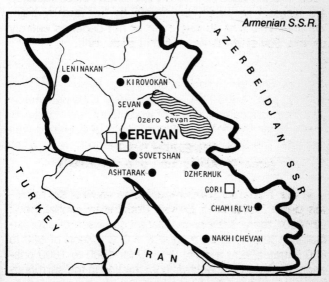

Armenian S.S.R.

In both *Dzhermuk* and *Nakhichevan'*, there is a camp of 500 or 600 prisoners assigned to farm work. (*Nakhichevan'* is the capital of the *Nakhichevan* A.S.S.R., which is in fact an exclave of Azerbaidzhan wedged in between *Armenia* and *Iran. – trans.*)

In both *Leninakan* and *Kirovakan,* found in the northern part of Armenia, there is a camp for 1000 prisoners assigned to industrial construction.

The political activity of those fighting for the independence of Armenia and its separation from the Soviet Union is growing. Several political dissidents, as a result, have been arrested and even executed in the last few years. It would be useful to keep this in mind when your amiable Intourist guide (trained by the K.G.B.) tries to deceive you with the ostensible prosperity that reigns in Armenia.

*

AZERBAIDZHAN S.S.R.
(area: 86000 sq. km.; pop.: 6000000)

On the territory of this southern republic, which stretches across the mountains and plains lying along the Caspian Sea, there are at least 16 concentration camps and two prisons. Our information, however, is far from complete.

Nevertheless, there is something for the tourist to see here:

1. In *Chёrnyi Gorod,* a suburb of *Baku* (republican capital; pop.: 1600000), approximately 1000 prisoners in two women's camps, some of whom continue to maintain custody of their infant children, work in a knitted-wear factory. There is also a children's camp here of about 600 prisoners assigned to mechanics workshops.

2. In *Mardakyan,* located 50 kilometers from *Baku,* more than 1000 prisoners in a children's camp (no. 38/11) work in joiner's shops.

3. In *Zakataly,* located northwest of *Baku,* 500 to 600 prisoners in a children's intensified-regime camp are assigned to mechanics workshops.

4. In *Bekshir,* located near *Baku,* approximately 3000 prisoners in a men's ordinary-regime camp work in the woodworking industry. Among them are those arrested for their belief in God, including Baptists, Seventh-day Adventists, Jehovah's Witnesses, and Pentecostals.

5. In *Beyuk Shor,* located near *Baku,* approximately 300 prisoners in camp no. 38/6 are assigned to manufacture inlaidwood products, such as small jewel boxes or "shesh-besh" parlor game sets. Some of the products are exported.

6. In *Akhmedli,* located north of *Baku,* more than 1500 prisoners from a strict-regime camp (no. 38/7) work in a machine factory in which spare parts for weapons are manufactured. Production is secret.

257

7. In *Agdam,* located west of *Baku*, approximately 1200 prisoners in an ordinary-regime camp (no. 38/13) are assigned to industrial construction.

8. In a suburb of *Baku,* located near *Bina,* more than 3000 prisoners from an ordinary-regime camp (no. 38/2) are assigned to industrial construction.

9. In *Shusha,* located southwest of *Baku*, approximately 1000 prisoners in camp no. 38/10 are assigned to industrial construction.

10. In *Neftechala, Lenkoran', Masally,* and *Sal'yany,* all of which are located in the south of Azerbaidzhan, there are camps that provide labor for the oil production and refining industries. The exact number of prisoners in the camps is not known.

11. In both *Sumagally* and *Dashkesan,* there is a camp of 500 prisoners assigned to road construction and repair.

12. In *Baku*, there are two prisons: a pre-trial detention prison of the Ministry of Interior in which up to 2000 inmates are confined; an inner prison of the K.G.B. of up to 300 inmates.

The above represents a sober, statistical survey of the camps and prisons in this republic. But how much suffering and how many tears, how many ruined lives are concealed by these figures?

It is interesting to note that many Christians from central Russia arrested for practicing their religious beliefs are sent to camps in Azerbaidzhan. This tactic apparently stems from the fact that Christians are not likely to find sympathy and support from the local population, which is predominantly Moslem.

*

DAGHESTAN A.S.S.R.
(area: 50 300 sq. km.; pop.: 1 600 000)

This part of the Soviet Union lies north of *Azerbaidzhan* along the Caspian Sea.

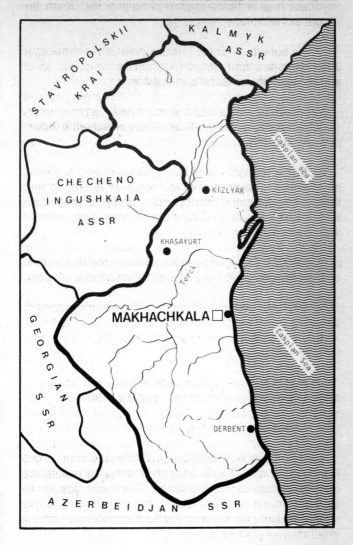

We know very little about the penal facilities here and believe that our information on them is incomplete. You may at least become acquainted with those facilities of which we already have knowledge.

In *Makhachkala* (capital; pop.: 210 000), there is a large prison for 2 000 to 2 500 inmates as well as three intensified-regime camps of approximately 1 000 prisoners each. The prisoners in the camps are assigned to work in oil production, housing and industrial construction, and the plastics industry.

In *Khasavyurt,* located 100 kilometers northwest of *Makhachkala,* approximately 1000 prisoners from an ordinary-regime camp are assigned to the construction industry. Camp commander is Lieutenant Colonel Sergeev.

In *Kizlyar,* located 100 kilometers north of *Khasavyurt,* 500 to 600 prisoners in a strict-regime camp work in a brick plant.

In *Derbent,* south of *Makhachkala,* 500 to 600 prisoners make slag blocks for construction purposes or quarry building stone in the mountains west of the city.

Thus, we know of "only" six camps and one prison in Daghestan. Our knowledge of the area is obviously incomplete. We will have to wait for additional data from tourists.

*

TATAR A.S.S.R.
(area: 68000 sq. km.; pop.: 3500000)

In *Kazan'* (capital; approximately 700 kilometers east of Moscow; pop.: 970000), there are two prisons, a special psychiatric prison for dissidents, and three camps, one of which is for children. In addition, there is also a special prison for political prisoners in the K.G.B. building.

Here are the addresses of these horrifying places:

1. Special prison in K.G.B. building on Lenin Street; approximately 500 prisoners.

2. Special psychiatric prison UZ-148-ST.6, Ershov Street 49. Directions: tram no. 5 or 11 to stop marked "Oktyabr'skii gorodok"; approximately 1500 prisoners.

3. Prison of Ministry of Interior, corner of Krasin and Bol'shaya Krasnaya Streets (Baumanskii District). Direc-

tions: public transportation to stop marked "Aviatsionnyi institut"; approximately 2000 prisoners.

4. Prison of the Ministry of Interior, Privolzhskii District. Directions: tram no. 8 to stop marked "Medsanchast' SK-4".

5. Ordinary-regime camp in the vicinity of Vakhitov Street; 2000 prisoners manufacture metal fittings and bolts in a machine plant. Camp commander is Lieutenant Colonel Sikaev.

6. Strict-regime camp of approximately 2000 prisoners assigned to construction work within the city. Located in the vicinity of Promyshlennaya Baza. Directions: public transportation to stop marked "Prombaza".

7. Children's intensified-regime camp of approximately 1800 prisoners aged 14 and older. Located in Leninskii District directly behind the "Orgsintez" Plant in which the children make boxes used for the shipment of goods.

In *Tetyushi* and *Buinsk,* there is a group of camps; we have precise information, however, on only two of them. In *Buinsk,* 1500 prisoners work in a cotton factory or lumber mill. In *Tetyushi,* 1500 prisoners are assigned to lumber-rafting on the Volga River or to duties in a lumber mill.

Three strict-regime camps of 1200 to 1500 prisoners each located in *Al'met'ievsk, Leninogorsk,* and *Bugul'ma* supply labor for the oil industry and for construction projects connected with it. In addition, there is a prison for 500 to 600 inmates sent here as a punishment for having committed an infraction of the rules at a camp. These "infractions" include, for example, common prayer and the demand for the establishment of a normal, humane regimen.

Approximately 2 000 prisoners in each of four camps in *Mendeleevsk, Menzelinsk, Naberezhnye Chelny,* and *Nizhnekamsk* (in the northern part of the autonomous republic) are assigned to lumber mills, housing construction industrial plants, and plywood plants.

In *Mamadysh,* 1500 prisoners in an ordinary-regime camp work in a paper cellulose industrial plant. Camp commander is Major Esipov.

In *Elabuga,* located in the northeastern part of the autonomous republic, approximately 1800 prisoners from a strict-regime camp work in a lumber mill. There is also a prison here for 400 to 500 inmates serving sentences of various lengths. They were transferred here from the surrounding camps.

Elabuga is known throughout the world as the city in which the exiled poetess, Marina Tsvetaeva, took her life.

In *Baltasi,* located in the north of Tatar A.S.S.R., 800 to 900 prisoners of a special strict-regime camp work in a lumber mill. Camp commander is Captain Il'ichev. The punishment meted out to the prisoners in this facility differ in no way to those suffered by the victims of the Nazi concentration camps. The inmates here are forced to wear striped and numbered uniforms and are made to endure hunger, beatings, and a hopeless existence. Here is an extract from the testimony of an eyewitness who was imprisoned here in 1977: "I was afraid of the difficult time facing me as a result of being imprisoned with habitual criminals. Instead, however, I found myself among many devout Christians imprisoned for practicing their religion (or for refusing induction into the army or being a member of an unregistered sect). These people proved to be of great help to me when they discovered that I was arrested on trumped-up charges in connection with my desire to emigrate to Israel. They became enraptured with Israel and dreamt themselves of going there.

"I saw more than enough arbitrariness and injustice at the camp. Hungry people were herded ten or twelve kilometers to and from work on foot in both rain and snow through the forest. The prisoners were practically forced to run the whole way. Those who fell behind were beaten. It was almost impossible for the sick to be released from their duties. The slightest retort would earn a prisoner a night on the naked cement floor of the isolation cell. Forced to run to work on an empty stomach the next morning, the prisoner would, together with other isolation-cell victims, be kept separate from the remaining inmates so that no one could throw him a piece of bread."

In *Chistopol'*, 140 kilometers east of *Kazan'*, there is an ordinary-regime camp for 1000 to 1100 prisoners who work in a ship repair factory. Here you will also find a special prison of the K.G.B. (union level). The authorities have been transferring political prisoners to this facility from the K.G.B. prison in *Vladimir* since 1978. (See the notes to the special map of Vladimir.) The prison in *Chistopol'* carries the numeral designation UZ-148-ST.4. Prison commander is Lieutenant Colonel Malofeev; chief of K.G.B. operations is Major Ismagilov; K.G.B. liaison is Ferdinand Valeev. The prison, in which there are approximately 300 inmates, is located on the eastern edge of town and consists of three buildings. The prisoners here work in the cells in which they live. They assemble watches or clocks, weave or sew sacks, cobble shoes, or work with metal. The cells are poorly illuminated. The light is not switched off during the daytime. The authorities censor the prisoners' family and especially their foreign correspondence. Meetings between the prisoners and their families are severely hampered. The transfer of many political prisoners to this facility, which is located a long way from Moscow, was clearly connected with the approaching Olympic games.

Shcharanskii, Mendelevich, and *Ogurtsov,* all of whom were once in the prison in *Vladimir,* are now confined in this facility.

Try to arrange a meeting with them. Let the Soviet authorities know that you are aware of the whereabouts of these martyrs.

*

UZBEK S.S.R.
(area: 449600 sq. km.; pop.: 15400000)

In this wealthy part of the Soviet Union, you will be shown examples of the happy and prosperous existence of the population. The official guides will "neglect", however, to mention the hatred of the Uzbeks of foreign domination, their desire to achieve independence, and their opposition to Russification. We know of 20 camps, five prisons, and two psychiatric prisons in Uzbekistan.

Let us begin with *Tashkent* (republican capital; pop.: 1700000), in which there is an ordinary-regime prison of the Ministry of Interior (3000 inmates), a special K.G.B. prison (800 inmates), and a special psychiatric prison (no. UYa-64/PB; 1500 inmates). On the road to *Chimkent* (still within Tashkent), there is an ordinary-regime camp divided into two zones – one for men (3000 prisoners) and one for women who continue to maintain custody of their infant children while serving their sentences (2000 prisoners). The men are assigned to work in a cotton-cleaning factory, whereas the women work in a textile industrial plant.

264

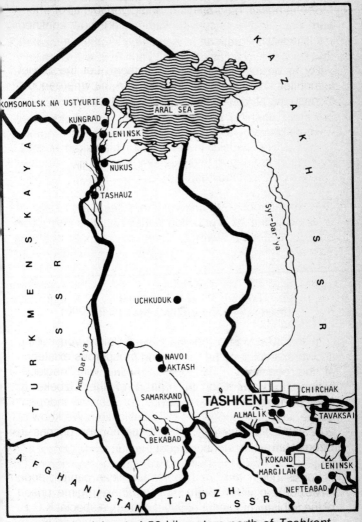

In *Tavaksai*, located 50 kilometers north of *Tashkent*, 1500 prisoners in a strict-regime camp are assigned to making reinforced-concrete pipes.

In *Chirchik*, located north of *Tashkent*, there is a prison in which approximately 800 inmates are held for having broken a regulation in the camp where they were previously confined. Many of the inmates are here for having practiced their religious beliefs.

In *Kokand,* located south of *Tashkent,* dissidents, Uzbek nationalists, and religious people are confined by the K.G.B. in an ordinary-regime psychiatric hospital (in fact, a psychiatric prison).

In *Almalyk, Zeravshan, Margilan, Fergana, Andizhan,* and *Leninsk,* all located east of *Tashkent,* approximately 10000 prisoners in at least six camps (nos. UYa-64/2, UYa-64/4, UYa-64/6, UYa-64/8, UYa-64/9, and UYa-64/37) are assigned to work in uranium mines without protective clothing. It is only a matter of time before they become contaminated and die of leukemia. The diseased prisoners are usually transferred to the camp hospital in *Nukus,* located in the western part of the republic, where they await their death.

In *Nefteabad,* 1500 prisoners in a camp are assigned to work in the oil-production sphere or in construction projects connected with it. Camp commander is Major Baruzov.

In *Bekabad,* 1600 prisoners in an ordinary-regime camp (no. UYa-64/21) are assigned to saw logs into planks. There are many Baptists here.

In *Karaul-Bazar,* 1200 prisoners from a special strict-regime camp quarry building stone and granite.

In *Samarkand,* 1000 to 1100 prisoners in camp no. UYa-64/10 work in construction.

In *Bukhara,* there is an ordinary-regime camp for 2000 prisoners assigned to construction work. One of the projects on which they worked was the construction of an Intourist hotel, which, as you can see, was photographed before its completion. Note the forbidden zone and watch-towers. Compare. Is this where you are staying?

In *Aktash,* there is a camp hospital for 1500 to 1800 prisoners.

In *Urga,* 1500 juveniles in a children's camp make boxes for fruit and vegetables.

In *Navoi,* there are two camps. Camp UYa-64/29, which was designed to hold 2000 prisoners, supplies labor for construction projects in the city. The prisoners are assigned, among other things, to build a secret chemical industrial plant (the police prohibit cars driving past the construction site to slow down) or work in work-shops of the plant that have already been completed. There is also a children's camp here for 1500 prisoners assigned to the textile branch.

In *Zing-Ata,* 2500 prisoners in a men's ordinary-regime camp work in a cotton-cleaning industrial plant; another 2500 prisoners from a women's ordinary-regime camp work in the textile branch. Many of the women here maintain custody of their infant children.

In *Kungrad, Tashauz, Leninsk,* and *Komsomol'sk-na-Ustyurte,* 500 to 600 prisoners in each of four strict-regime camps are assigned to the construction and repair of irrigation canals and irrigation systems.

In *Uchkuduk,* there is a strict-regime camp for 2000 prisoners assigned to a machine plant. Working condi-tions here are so severe that, in 1977, the prisoners went on strike demanding an improvement of the situa-tion. The authorities called out troops who then fired into the camp zone with machine guns. More than 20 pris-oners were killed. Many were sentenced to additional terms of imprisonment. Now there is "peace and quiet" here, as Major Gazurov, the camp commander, once said in 1978 on greeting a new group of prisoners.

An Intourist hotel under construction in Bukhara (Uzbek S.S.R.), south-west of Tashkent; here there is an irrigation canal that flows to the Amu-Dar'ya River 220 kilometers away. Perhaps you will be put up in this hotel after the camp fences and watchtowers are removed and the prisoners transferred (photo 1975).

TURKMEN S.S.R.

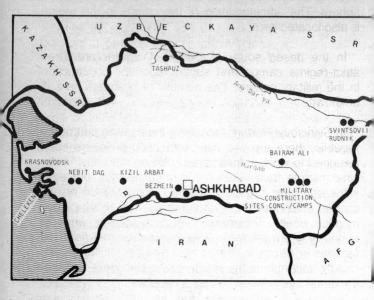

TURKMEN S.S.R.
(area: 488100 sq. km.; pop.: 2800000)

In *Ashkhabad* (republican capital; pop.: 300000), there are two prisons: a K.G.B. prison for 400 to 500 (political) prisoners and an ordinary-regime pre-trial detention facility for 1200 to 1500 inmates. There is also an ordinary-regime camp in the city in which 1500 prisoners are assigned to woodworking and cotton-cleaning plants.

In *Bezmein,* a suburb of *Ashkhabad*, there is a strict-regime camp of 2000 prisoners assigned to industrial construction or to plants in which reinforced concrete slags are made.

In *Krasnovodsk, Cheleken,* and *Nebit-Dag,* approximately 2000 prisoners are assigned to the oil-production industry.

In *Kizyl-Arbat,* 1500 prisoners in an ordinary-regime camp are assigned to construction, road building, and the digging of irrigation canal systems. Camp commander is Lieutenant Colonel Sukhov.

In *Bairam-Ali,* there is a strict-regime camp for 1000 to 1200 prisoners assigned to the military construction sphere. The administration of the camps in the region is also located here.

In the desert south of *Bairam-Ali,* there are three strict-regime camps that supply labor for construction in the military sphere. The number of prisoners here is unknown.

In *Svintsovyi Rudnik,* located in the eastern part of the republic, there are two camps of 2500 prisoners each assigned to work in lead mines. We do not know under what regime these camps are administered, but eyewitnesses have reported that they are unaware of any case in which a prisoner had returned from these camps in good health. Prisoners from these camps who fall seriously ill are delivered to a hospital located near the facilities in *Bezmein.* They report that the mining of lead rapidly undermines the health of the prisoners and that the death rate in these camps is very high.

I.B., an eyewitness and former prisoner, reports: "In the hospital, I spoke with one of the prisoners from *Svintsovyi Rudnik.* He explained that the administration rarely found fault with the prisoners and only demanded that the mining quota be fulfilled. The prisoners were rarely locked up in the isolation cell and were not deprived of their right to receive parcels. The dangers involved in working underground, however, were great. After a year of work, the human organism would become languid and generally weak. Additional nutrition would not strengthen it. The prisoner would eventually become indifferent to everything. My conversation partner had heard from the others that a prisoner, who demonstrated impotence during a visit from his wife, was probably suffering from the effects of the lead poisoning."

Having heard such eyewitness testimony, one begins to understand why the Soviet state requires slave labor.

*

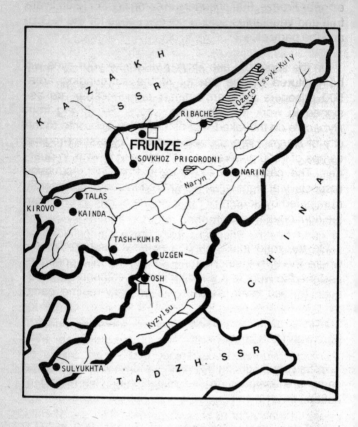

KIRGHIZ S.S.R.
(area: 198 500 sq. km.; pop.: 3 500 000)

As a tourist, you will encounter no difficulties in traveling to *Frunze* (pop.: 500 000), the capital of Kirghizia. Once you begin sightseeing, however, you will not want to limit yourself to visiting museums. Take a drive, for example, along the road towards Lake *Issyk-Kul'* to the death camp located in the mountains outside the city. Here you will find 2500 prisoners in a strict-regime camp forced to mine uranium without any protection against the deadly rays. After about a year and a half in the mines, the prisoners die. In the center of *Frunze,* you will find two prisons: a penal facility of 1200 (political) prisoners in the K.G.B. building; an ordinary-regime pretrial detention facility of 1500 inmates, a number of whom are political prisoners. In the *"Prigorodnyi"* sovkhoz located near *Frunze*, 800 prisoners in camp no. 36/12 cultivate fruit and vegetables sold in special shops for the K.G.B. and the party elite.

On the shore of Lake *Issyk-Kul'*, where your eyes will be captured by the beauty of the surrounding area, 500 prisoners from an ordinary-regime camp are assigned to work in auto repair shops. By driving from *Rybach'e* on the lake towards *Osh*, you will come to the city of *Naryn.* Here you will find two large strict-regime camps of 1000 prisoners each assigned to work in quarries. The camps are easily seen from the mountains (especially at night when the forbidden zones are brightly illuminated by searchlights), from the highway, and from the right on entering the city.

On the road to *Osh*, you will pass through *Uzgen*, where there is a strict-regime camp for 1200 prisoners assigned to work in a plant for reinforced concrete products. In *Osh* itself, there is an ordinary-regime camp for 800 to 900 prisoners assigned to make boxes for fruit in a packaging plant. You will also find a prison here with 1200 to 1500 inmates.

In *Sulyukta*, 500 to 600 prisoners in an ordinary-regime camp are assigned to the planting and harvesting of cotton.

In *Talas*, located southwest of *Frunze*, 900 to 1000 prisoners in a strict-regime camp work in a brick plant.

In *Kainda*, located south of *Talas*, 1000 prisoners in camp no. 36/1-P are assigned to work in local sovkhozes.

In *Kirovo*, approximately 700 prisoners in camp no. 36/8 are assigned to farm work.

In the camps in *Talas*, *Kainda*, and *Kirovo*, there are many who were imprisoned for their belief in God.

In *Tam-Kumyr*, 1000 to 1200 prisoners from a strict-regime camp (no. 36/6) are assigned to road repair and construction.

Altogether, we can count twelve camps and three pris-

ons in Kirghizia. We are not certain that our information is complete.

*

CRIMEAN REGION
(area: 27 000 sq. km.; pop.: 1 900 000)

The population of the Crimea is "served" by four prisons and seven camps, not a very high number of penal facilities when compared to those in other regions of the Soviet Union. The state apparently felt that it had to consider the presence of the many health resorts and tourists.

In *Simferopol'* (regional capital; pop.: 300 000), there are two prisons: a K.G.B. prison; an ordinary-regime pre-trial detention prison on Lenin Street near the railroad station. Both facilities were designed for 1000 prisoners. Camp no. ITK-8 in *Simferopol'*, located on the road leading to *Nikolaevka,* is an ordinary-regime facility of approximately 1500 prisoners assigned to construction work in the city. Camp commander is Captain Semënov.

In *Feodosiya,* there is a strict-regime camp for 500 to

600 prisoners assigned to work in quarries. A pre-trial detention prison for 400 to 500 inmates is also located here.

In *Kerch'*, 800 to 1000 prisoners in an ordinary-regime camp are assigned to construction at the port or to road-building and repair. Approximately 500 prisoners are confined in an ancient prison here under strict regime for having violated the rules at the camp where they were previously held.

In *Sevastopol'*, there is a large prison for 2000 to 2500 inmates. Part of the facility is reserved for arrested sailors. One thousand five hundred prisoners in a strict-regime camp here are assigned to construction work at the port, to loading and unloading duties, or to work at the quarries.

In *Dzhankoi*, up to 800 prisoners in an ordinary-regime camp are assigned to farm work or to soil-enrichment projects. Camp commander is Major Kostin.

In *Evpatoriya*, approximately 500 prisoners in an ordinary-regime camp work in mechanics shops for local industry. Camp commander is Captain Virtok.

In *Gvardeiskoe*, approximately 1500 to 1800 prisoners in an ordinary-regime camp are assigned to construction in the military sphere.

As you can see, everyone is "satisfied". Every prisoner has work.

If, instead of visiting a model children's camp in the Crimea, you should like to see a special children's home, in which young people are confined under camp or prison-like conditions, then ask to be taken to the *Arabatskaya Strelka*, the land tongue jutting out into the Sea of Azov. Here you will find more than 500 children abandoned to the arbitrariness of the sadist supervisors. (See the special map of women's and children's camps and the accompanying notes.)

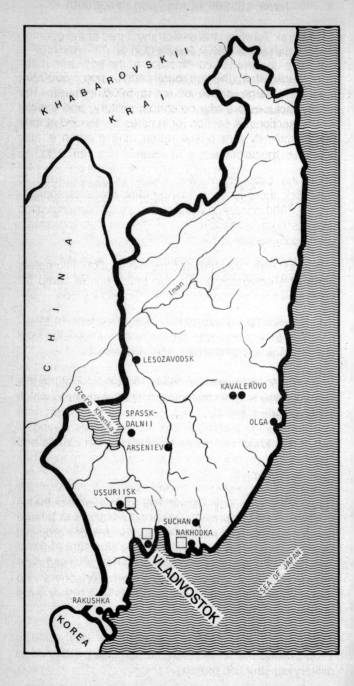

PRIMORSK TERRITORY
(area: 165 900 sq. km.; pop.: 1 800 000)

Primorsk Territory, the easternmost part of the country, forms a part of the Soviet Pacific Coast.

In *Vladivostok* (the territorial capital; pop.: 550 000), there is a large prison of up to 5 000 inmates. The facility includes pre-trial detention, military, and special K.G.B. sections. A section for inmates sentenced at their trial specifically to a prison rather than a camp is also housed in the facility.

On the outskirts of *Vladivostok* along the road to *Ussuriisk,* there is an ordinary-regime camp of approximately 1 800 prisoners assigned to various construction projects both in the city and in the surrounding areas. Camp commander is Major Semënov.

In *Ussuriisk,* located approximately 700 kilometers north of *Vladivostok,* there is a strict-regime camp for 1 500 prisoners assigned to mechanics workshops.

In *Spassk-Dal'nii,* located 80 kilometers north of *Ussuriisk,* 500 to 600 prisoners in a camp are assigned to road repair duties on the Vladivostok-Khabarovsk highway.

About 150 kilometers north of *Lesozavodsk* along this very highway is a woodworking industrial plant to which 1 500 prisoners are assigned. The wood is brought here from the camps located in the vicinity of *Lesozavodsk.* We do not know the precise location of the camps and have therefore not drawn them onto the map. They exist nevertheless.

On *Nakhodka* Bay (about 100 kilometers southeast of *Vladivostok*), approximately 2 000 prisoners in a large transit camp are assigned to various construction projects. There is also a prison here for 1 200 to 1 500 inmates. The facility houses pre-trial detention, military, and punishment wards. The latter is intended for prisoners who have broken the rules of the camps in which they were previously confined.

In *Suchan,* located north of *Nakhodka* Bay, 1 000 to 1 200 prisoners of a strict-regime camp are assigned to military construction projects.

In *Vershino*, approximately 1500 prisoners in a women's camp are assigned to a sewing factory. The camp is located due east of *Spassk-Dal'nii*.

On *Ol'ga* Bay (on the Pacific Ocean) as well as in the settlements of *Kavalerovo* (north of Ol'ga) and *Shamor* (in the northernmost part of the territory), approximately 10000 prisoners in four special strict-regime camps mine uranium for use in the military industry. For details about these death camps, see the notes to the special map on these facilities.

On *Rakushka* Bay, located southwest of *Vladivostok*, there is another death camp in which prisoners are assigned to clean the nozzles of atomic-powered submarines.

Here is the testimony of A.K., a military physician stationed at the military hospital in *Vladivostok*. His duties included inspecting the living conditions of servicemen at the bases located near the camps and uranium mines.

"As a member of a team of three military physicians, I inspected the military camps in the vicinity of Ol'ga Bay, Kavalerovo, and *Shamor* Bay in order to determine whether the servicemen stationed here were exposed to radioactive contamination. Their camps were not in the contamination zones; we could not therefore establish any danger to the soldiers or officers. We were, however, able to establish deadly radiation in the uranium mine areas. I inspected the labor camps and saw that the barracks were located within the radiation zone. I asked the officer who accompanied us, 'How do the prisoners and guards here live?' His answer was merely to shrug his shoulders. I realized immediately that I had touched upon a dangerous subject. I became silent."

*

NOVGOROD REGION
(area: 55300 sq. km.; pop.: 730000)

Novgorod Region lies between Moscow and Leningrad and is easily accessible by car or train.

In *Novgorod* (regional capital; pop.: 180000), a city of

ancient monuments, you may visit a pre-trial detention prison located on the outskirts of town on the road to *Staraya Russa* as well as the prison in the regional K.G.B. headquarters building. In addition, there is an ordinary-regime camp located on the outskirts of town near *Podberez'e*. Here, 1500 prisoners are assigned to work in a woodworking industrial plant. The facility lies in the direction of Leningrad.

Two camps in the vicinity of Lake *Il'men* supply labor for the military construction industry: a strict-regime camp of 800 to 900 prisoners in *Staraya Russa* and an ordinary-regime camp of 500 to 600 prisoners in *Pola.*

In *Malaya Vishera,* 600 to 800 prisoners in an ordinary-regime camp are assigned to farm work for the benefit of local industry.

In *Okulovka,* approximately 1000 prisoners in an ordinary-regime camp are assigned to construction work in the military sphere.

As you can see, our information on *Novgorod* Region is most incomplete. We know of "only" five camps and two prisons for a population of 730 000.

KALININ REGION

KALININ REGION
(area: 84 200 sq. km.; pop.: 1 800 000)

Kalinin Region lies between Moscow and Leningrad and is easily accessible by car or train.

In *Kalinin* city (regional capital; pop.: 400 000), you may visit the area near *Danilovskoe* where there is a women's ordinary-regime camp for 1500 prisoners assigned to a sewing factory.

In the center of the city, there is a prison of approximately 1500 inmates, some of whom are pre-trial detainees. Some of the inmates, moreover, are also assigned to work in mechanics shops for the benefit of local industry.

North of *Kalinin* lies *Torzhok*. Look at the photograph of the Boris and Gleb Monastery in this city. Now surrounded by barbed-wire fencing and watchtowers, the monastery has become a camp. Such is the respect of the state towards religion. Visit the more than 800 prisoners here. Should you suddenly find yourself being diverted by your guide from the camp, show him the photograph and ask him where the prisoners are taken.

278

In *Krasnomaiskii*, a suburb of *Vyshnii Volochek* located north of *Torzhok*, prisoners from an ordinary-regime camp are assigned to industrial construction.

Further to the west in *Ostashkov*, there is a strict-regime camp; 1200 prisoners work in construction, road building and repair, and brick production.

In *Bezhetsk*, located in the northern part of the region, 1500 prisoners in a strict-regime camp are assigned to make reinforced-concrete blocks for use in constructing foundations for houses.

In *Krasnyi Kholm*, located north of *Bezhetsk*, 1000 prisoners in an ordinary-regime camp work in a brick factory.

In *Rzhev*, located in the southern part of the region, there is an ordinary-regime camp for 600 to 800 prisoners assigned to the construction industry. Another 500 to 600 inmates in a strict-regime prison assemble electrical switches in their cells.

I.V., an eyewitness, reports: "I was brought to *Rzhev* from the camp in *Ostashkov* after having participated in a kind of a strike for better nourishment. Up to then,

The Boris and Gleb Monastery in Torzhok (approximately 230 kilometers northwest from Moscow, Kalinin Region, on the eastern edge of the Valdai hills) was converted into a camp in which there are more than 800 prisoners. The church is used as a barracks. The fencing, the watchtower, and the forbidden zone are easily discernable. Freedom of religion – Soviet style (photo 1978).

the prisoners had been fed spoiled cabbage and frozen potatoes. I spent the first two weeks in solitary confinement in a cell that had no bed. This was called 'quarantine'. Afterwards, I was transferred to a cell in which there were already nine criminals confined. They described the prison regimen as bestial. The slightest impertinence on the part of the prisoner would get him thrown into the isolation cell, a cold vault with nothing more than a cold, damp concrete floor to sleep on. On his way there, the prisoner would be beaten. We worked in the cell, assembling electrical contacts, plugs, and outlets for electrical wiring networks. Our production quota was so high that we had to work from morning to night. We did not even have the time to stretch our limbs. Failure to fulfill our quotas meant forfeiting the right to make purchases in the prisoners' commissary (of up to three rubles a month) as well as to receive visitors. And so there we sat over our work, bent over like prisoners sent to forced-labor camps. We were hungry, after all. The opportunity to buy a packet of margarine, a half-kilo of sugar, a dry biscuit, or a little jam was a great crutch of support."

This is the reality of everyday life in a Soviet prison — a dream about a packet of margarine or a piece of bread.

Last but not least, you may visit a psychiatric hospital-prison for dissidents in *Burashevo,* where the arbitrariness of the K.G.B. and its underling physicians reigns.

YAROSLAVL' REGION

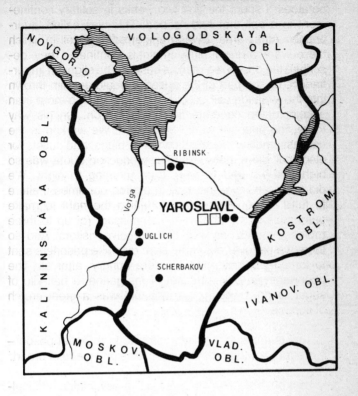

YAROSLAVL' REGION
(area: 36 400 sq. km.; pop.: 1 500 000)

Yaroslavl' Region is located approximately 150 to 200 kilometers north of Moscow.

There are two prisons in *Yaroslavl'*: an ordinary-regime facility of the Ministry of Interior for 2000 inmates in the *Zarech'e* area; a facility for 500 inmates in the building of the regional K.G.B.

There are also two camps of 1500 to 1800 prisoners each in *Zarech'e*. The prisoners work under hazardous health conditions in an India rubber plant, a rubber industrial plant, and a chemical plant.

In *Shcherbakov,* located south of Yaroslavl', 1200 prisoners from an ordinary-regime camp work in a rope factory and a sawmill. Camp commander is Major Shestov.

In *Rybinsk,* located north of Yaroslavl', there is a transit prison for 1500 inmates and next to it a camp for 2000 prisoners assigned to various duties, such as repair work in shipyards or other tasks in a lumber mill or at industrial construction sites. Near the lumber mill is a camp for 500 children assigned to manufacture containers for canned goods.

In *Uglich,* located south of Yaroslavl', 1500 prisoners in an ordinary-regime camp work at various industrial construction sites. Nearby is a cheese factory built by the prisoners of the camp. Camp commander is Major Lyadov.

In the same city, you will also find a special strict-regime camp of 800 to 900 prisoners assigned to work in a quarry. The prisoners wear striped, numbered concentration camp uniforms, and their food rations are lower than those in strict-regime camps.

*

KOSTROMA REGION
(area: 60200 sq. km.; pop.: 890000)

In *Kostroma* city (regional capital; approximately 250 kilometers northeast of Moscow; pop.: 250000), there is a prison of the Ministry of Interior *(Zarech'e area)* for 2500 inmates and a prison of the regional K.G.B. for approximately 300 inmates. In the vicinity of the freight train station, there is also an ordinary-regime camp of about 2000 prisoners serving short sentences (three to five years) and assigned to loading and unloading duties for the railroad or at the lumber industrial plant. Camp commander is Major Zyablikov.

North of *Kostroma* is a strict-regime camp for 1200 prisoners assigned to a brick plant and a lumber mill.

In *Galich,* also located north of Kostroma, there is a strict-regime camp for 1000 prisoners assigned to

industrial construction. Camp commander is Major Korot-kov.

In *Soligalich,* located in the north of the region, is an ordinary-regime camp for 1200 to 1500 prisoners assigned to logging, timber-rafting, or salt mining.

In *Kologriv,* located northeast of Kostroma, there is a strict-regime camp for 1800 prisoners assigned to a farm-machinery plant. Camp commander is Major Volodin.

In *Manturovo,* located east of Kostroma, there is an ordinary-regime camp for 800 to 900 prisoners who do farm work. A camp hospital for 1000 to 1200 prisoners may be found in a separate zone within the facility.

KAMCHATKA REGION

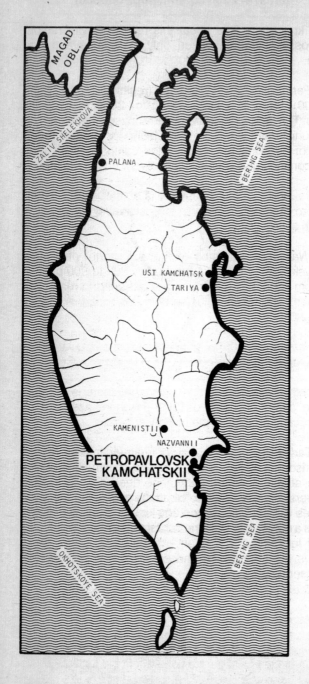

KAMCHATKA REGION
(area: 472 300 sq. km.; pop.: 380 000)

We know very little about this remote Soviet region. We possess information on only six camps and one prison.

In *Petropavlovsk-Kamchatskii* (regional capital; pop.: 210 000), there is a large prison for 2000 to 2500 inmates. The facility houses a pre-trial investigation, transit, and punishment ward, the latter being for inmates found guilty of breaking the rules of the camp in which they were confined and sentenced to severe prison regimen.

At the northern exit of the city is a strict-regime camp of approximately 1500 prisoners assigned to construction work in town.

In *Nazvannyi,* located somewhat north of Petropavlovsk-Kamchatskii, approximately 800 to 900 prisoners from a strict-regime camp are assigned to road construction and logging. Camp commander is Major Sergeev.

In *Kamenistyi,* 600 to 700 prisoners in a special strict-regime camp work in a quarry.

In both *Palana* and *Ust'-Kamchatsk,* there is a strict-regime camp of 1000 to 1200 prisoners assigned to construction projects in the military sphere.

At *Tar'ya* Bay, there is a strict-regime camp for 400 to 500 prisoners assigned to repair and construction duties at the atomic-powered submarine base next to it. The prisoners are also made to clean the nozzles of the submarines without being given any kind of protective clothing. As a result, they become contaminated and eventually die of leukemia. This is an extermination camp. Here there is no firing squad and no court that pronounces death sentences.

*

MAGADAN REGION

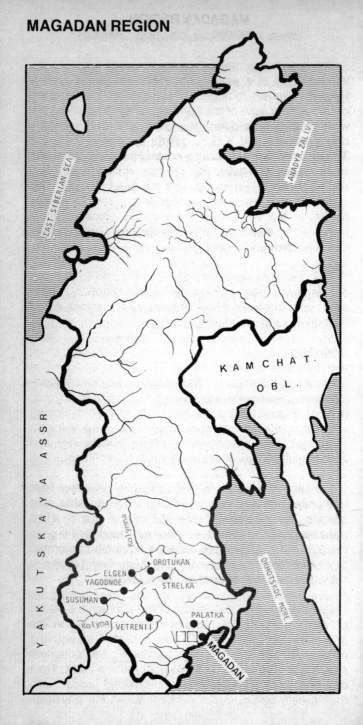

EAST SIBERIAN SEA

ANADYR. ZALIV

KAMCHAT. OBL.

YAKUTSKAYA ASSR

OKHOTSKOE MORE

Kolyma

OROTUKAN
ELGEN
YAGODNOE
STRELKA
SUSUMAN
Kolyma
VETRENII
PALATKA
MAGADAN

MAGADAN REGION
(area: 1 200 000 sq. km.; pop.: 360 000)

Our information on this remote region is very scanty. We know of one prison and eight camps. Magadan Region is known throughout the world as the "country of camps" because of the hundreds of such facilities that were located here during the Stalin era. Until recently, only prisoners and K.G.B. guards populated the area. These slaves were used to mine gold (which is deposited in the banks of what is still the free world), build cities and settlements, lay roads, and construct airfields. The state can now, however, manage with a voluntary labor market in Magadan. It is economically more advantageous when everything has already been built and ordered according to a rational plan.

The prisoners were (and still are) brought to the port of *Magadan* (regional capital; pop.: 120 000), where there is a prison of 1500 inmates and a transit camp of 1000 to 1200 prisoners.

We know of strict-regime camps in the following cities and settlements: *Palatka* (1500 prisoners assigned to gold mining), *Strelka* (1200 prisoners assigned to construction), *Orotukan* (1800 prisoners assigned to gold mining), *El'gen* (1000 prisoners assigned to gold mining), *Vetrenyi* (1500 prisoners assigned to gold mining), *Yagodnoe* (1500 prisoners assigned to gold mining), and *Susuman* (1800 prisoners assigned to gold mining).

Eyewitnesses have informed us that the prisoners here live under primitive conditions and work at exhausting tempos. The prisoners are pressed to labor at such a fast pace because the state sees an urgent need for the gold. In 1978, for example, the Moscow leadership informed the supervision in *Magadan* that gold may be mined without regard to environmental regulations.

One can imagine the effects of the work on the health of the prisoners. Z.L., a physician employed in the *Magadan* Region in 1977, was assigned to visit the mine areas. Once he saw a chain of women prisoners standing at a conveyor belt in a gold-refining plant. Their duty was to blow the dust from the refined product with their breath before it was packed. When the physician

asked why the women were given such hazardous work and whether there were any machines that could be used instead, he was told, "We don't have any machines yet; we have a gold production plan!"

It was in this horrible region that Garanin, the notorious commander of *Kolymstroi,* not too long ago ordered the prisoners lined up and every tenth one shot for failing to meet the gold production plan. The prisoners rebelled without any hope of victory and met their death in an unequal battle with the killer guards.

The crimes continue today, less frequently perhaps, but certainly no less horrifying. There are also exiled dissidents in this region. Iosif *Begun,* for example, is being held prisoner in *Susuman* under horrible conditions for having sought to emigrate to Israel.

*

SAKHALIN REGION
(Sakhalin Island and the Kurile Islands)
(area: 87 100 sq. km.; pop.: 680 000)

According to eyewitness testimony, the number of camps in this remote part of the Soviet Union has been reduced in the last ten or 15 years. The demand for labor, which has nevertheless remained constant, has been met through the enforced settlement of the camp prisoners following their release from penal servitude.

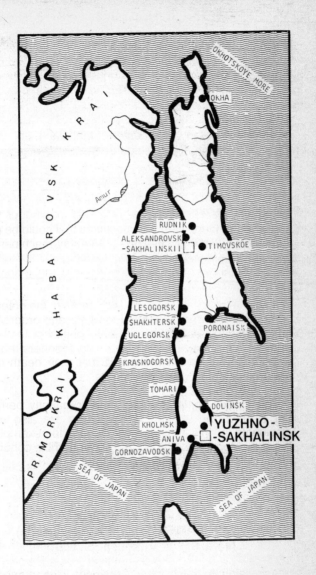

Until 1945, the Soviet Union controlled only the northern half of *Sakhalin* Island, whose capital was located at *Aleksandrovsk-Sakhalinskii*. The capital of the entire region today, *Yuzhno-Sakhalinsk* (pop.: 140 000), is located in the southern half of the island, which was a part of Japan until its occupation by Soviet forces at the end of World War II.

In *Okha,* a settlement on the northern half of the island where temperatures fall to as low as −50°C. and where strong gales are notorious, approximately 3 000 prisoners in a strict-regime camp are assigned to the oil-production industry.

In *Rudnik,* located in the center of the island, approximately 2 000 prisoners in a strict-regime camp mine coal.

In *Tymovskoe,* located east of Aleksandrovsk-Sakhalinskii, 500 to 600 prisoners in an ordinary-regime camp are assigned to farm work.

In *Aleksandrovsk-Sakhalinskii,* there is a prison in which up to 2 000 inmates are incarcerated, including pre-trial detainees, transit prisoners, and those transferred to this facility from a camp as a punishment. There is also a camp here for 1 500 prisoners assigned to construction work and to hazardous duties in a military plant for explosive materials.

In *Lesogorsk,* approximately 3 000 prisoners from a strict-regime camp are assigned to duties in a woodworking plant and a cellulose factory. Camp commander is Major Zubov; head of K.G.B. operations is a certain Zelenin.

In both *Shakhtersk* and *Uglegorsk,* there is a strict-regime camp of approximately 1 200 to 1 500 prisoners assigned to mine coal. Many of the prisoners were arrested for practicing their religious faith.

In the area surrounding *Poronaisk,* located on the eastern coast of the island, there are several camps that supply labor for the logging industry. We know of one camp in the city itself. Others are, according to those who have heard about them, to be found in the taiga. The 800 to 900 prisoners in the camp in *Poronaisk* work in a lumber yard where the wood is sorted out and sent to the lumber mill and cellulose plant in *Lesogorsk.*

Lumber arriving in this camp is sent from the forced-labor facilities located in the taiga.

In *Krasnogorsk,* there is an ordinary-regime camp for 600 to 700 prisoners assigned to a brick plant.

In *Kholmsk,* 800 to 900 prisoners from a strict-regime camp are assigned to construction in the military sphere.

In *Dolinsk,* there is a camp for 600 to 700 prisoners assigned to farm work.

In *Aniva,* 1500 to 1600 prisoners from an ordinary-regime camp are assigned to construction in the military sphere.

In *Gornozavodsk,* 2500 prisoners from a strict-regime camp are assigned to the underground mining of poly-metallic ores.

In *Yuzhno-Sakhalinsk,* 1500 to 1600 prisoners from a camp work in a furniture factory or at construction sites. There is also a prison in the city for 600 to 700 inmates.

On the island of *Shikotan,* which is one of the Kurile Islands (occupied by the Soviet Union following the defeat of Japan in World War II), approximately 6000 prisoners in a women's camp prepare preserves of cartilaginous fish, crabs, and caviar for export.

In an accompanying photograph, you will see these unhappy women. Among them are many women who were arrested for their belief in God or for their efforts to provide their children with religious instruction.

*

AMUR REGION
(area: 363 700 sq. km.; pop.: 820 000)

Our information on this region is rather incomplete, as there is no opportunity for the people here to emigrate to the free world. Thus far, we have received only fragmentary information from those who have been here. This remote part of the Soviet Union borders on *Primorsk*

AMUR REGION

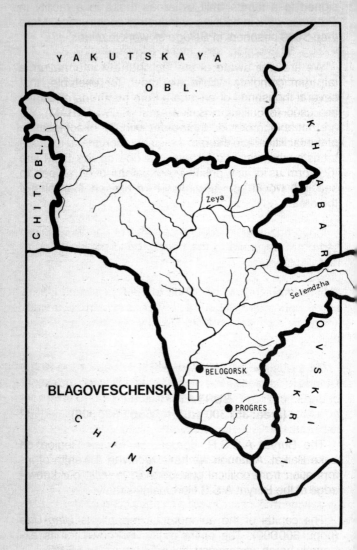

Territory and is separated by nearly 10000 kilometers from Moscow.

We know of two prisons in *Blagoveshchensk* (regional capital; pop.: 180000): a pre-trial detention facility for 1000 to 1200 inmates and a special isolation prison for 500 to 600 inmates transferred here from various camps as a punishment.

Prisoners in the camps in *Blagoveshchensk* are assigned to a lumber mill, whereas those in a facility in *Progress* work in housing or industrial construction. More than 3000 prisoners in *Bełogorsk* work in mines.

We are well aware of the fact that our information is far from complete. While we know, for example, that several thousands of prisoners from hundreds of camps are used to build the Baikal-Amur Railway (BAM), we are not able to provide the reader with the exact location of the facilities. We therefore wish to recommend to those tourists who succeed in getting a ride on the BAM line to inform us of any prisoners or camps they happen to see. We would also be grateful for any photographs of the area.

*

BURYAT A.S.S.R.
(area: 351 300 sq. km.; pop.: 830 000)

The Buryat A.S.S.R. borders on *Irkutsk* Region on Lake Baikal. Although we have received a wealth of information from political prisoners on *Irkutsk,* our knowledge of the Buryat A.S.S.R. remains scanty.

The capital of the autonomous republic is *Ulan-Ude* (pop.: 300 000). The entire region is known for its extremely harsh winters and its temperatures of −50°C.

The Buryat A.S.S.R. has long served as a transit territory for prisoners bound for Soviet camps in Mongolia. It is therefore well-known. The railroad line from *Ulan-Ude* to *Ulan Bator* (Mongolia) via *Kyakhta* was built by prisoners. Camps in the border town of *Kyakhta* continue to exist to this day and are now used as transit bases for sending slaves into Mongolia.

BURYAT A.S.S.R.

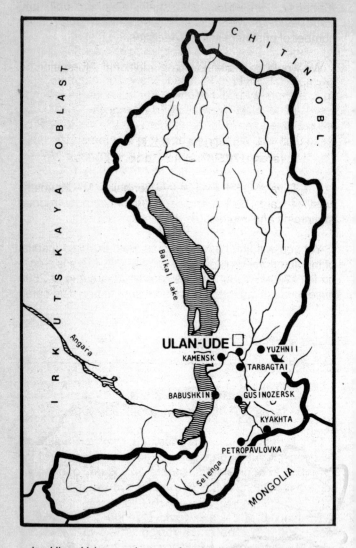

In *Ulan-Ude,* we know of only one prison (in which there are 1500 inmates). There is also a men's ordinary-regime camp for 600 to 800 prisoners who work in a railroad car plant or perform auxiliary duties in a glass-ware plant as well as a children's camp of 500 prisoners assigned to manufacture packaging containers in a meat-products industrial plant. We also know of several camps to the south and west of *Ulan-Ude* where military installations (airfields, missile silos, bases) are being construct-

ed by prisoners. The camps are located in *Yuzhnyi,
Kamensk, Tarbagatai, Babushkin, Gusinoozersk,* and
Petropavlovka. We possess no precise information on the
number of prisoners in these facilities.

We would be grateful for any additional information on
this area.

*

TUVA A.S.S.R.
(area: 170 500 sq. km.; pop.: 270 000)

The Tuva A.S.S.R. lies on the Mongolian border southwest of Lake Baikal and is characterized by rugged
mountains and impassable stretches of territory.

Yet you will find camps here as well. In *Kyzyl* (capital
of the autonomous republic; pop.: 65 000), there is a prison for 1200 to 1300 inmates as well as a camp of 2500
prisoners assigned to the construction sector. The camp

TUVA A.S.S.R.

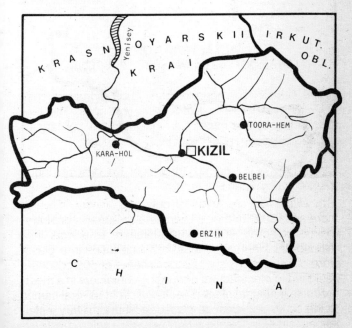

is located across from the city hotel on the opposite bank of the Enisei River.

Because the camps in this part of the Soviet Union supply forced-labor forces for the construction of military installations, their locations have largely remained secret.

We know of such camps, each having 1500 to 1800 prisoners, in *Kara-Khol', Tora-Khem, Bel'bei,* and *Erzin.* We received this information from a former Soviet service-man who had been to these areas. He reports that the prisoners in the above-mentioned camps live under the most primitive conditions in tents both summer and winter (with temperatures falling to -50°C.) and are assigned to build roads to the military installations in the area as well as dig pits for missile silos or construct underground airfields. The prisoners live a long way from population centers, which explains the irregular delivery of food and water and the resulting chronic hunger that prevails in the camps.

The above-mentioned cities are accessible only by car.

*

ALTAI TERRITORY
(area: 261 700 sq. km.; pop.: 2 700 000)

Altai Territory lies approximately 4000 kilometers east of Moscow. A large part of it is mountainous. The territory's industry and mines were built and are now largely manned by prisoners.

We know of 17 camps (of which, we believe, there are many more) and five prisons.

In *Barnaul* (territorial capital; pop.: 525 000), there is a prison of approximately 1500 inmates. A number of them are pre-trial detainees; the rest are serving normal prison terms.

There is also a children's camp in the city of approximately 1000 prisoners assigned to work in a packaging plant.

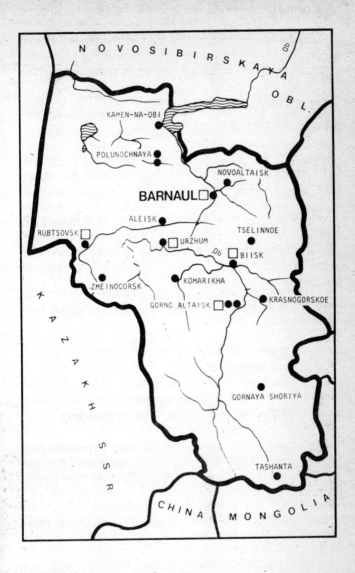

There is a prison in *Biisk* and in *Gorno-Altaisk*, both located in the southeastern part of the territory for those brought here from the camps as a punishment.

In both *Tselinnoe* and *Biisk*, there is a camp of 500 to 600 prisoners assigned to farm work. Prisoners in the camps in *Krasnogorsk, Gorno-Altaisk, Gornaya Shoriya,* and *Tashanta* mine non-ferrous metals. In *Gornaya Shoriya*, there is a camp for 1500 to 1800 prisoners convicted of "parasitism". In the Soviet Union, everyone is obligated to work. If you are unemployed for a few months, you get sent to a camp. Unemployment is not tolerated.

In *Rubtsovsk,* there is a transit prison. A pre-trial detention prison may be found in *Urzhum.*

In *Novoaltaisk,* 1500 women prisoners in camp no. UB-14/18 work as seamstresses. Many of the women maintain custody of their infant children.

Prisoners in the camps in *Rubtsovsk* and *Urzhum* are assigned to the housing construction sector, whereas those in *Komarikha* and *Zmeinogorsk* work in industrial construction.

Prisoners in *Aleisk, Kamen'-na-Obi,* and *Polunochnaya* are constructing both highways and a railroad in the north-western part of the territory.

In all the camps listed above, the arbitrariness of the K.G.B. and Ministry of Interior officials prevails. The officials see themselves as judges of all life-and-death questions over prisoners languishing in a God-forsaken place where the expressive saying, "the bear is the prosecutor; the taiga is the law", applies.

The spirit of resistance, however, continues to live everywhere. In 1954, a revolt broke out in *Barnaul* among the Chechens sent here from the Caucasus. They disarmed the troops of the Ministry of Interior and the K.G.B. and assumed complete control of the city for 48 hours. During this time, they executed dozens of K.G.B. hangmen. Special troops of the K.G.B., however, were soon despatched from Moscow. In crushing the revolt, they drowned the city of *Barnaul* in blood.

*

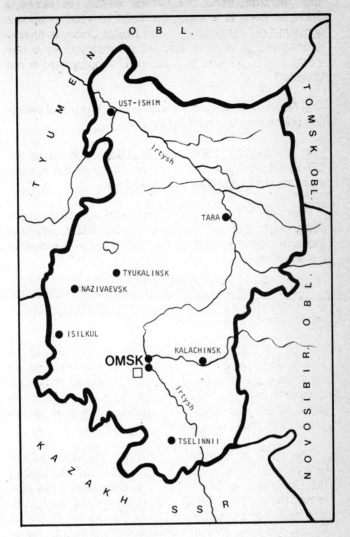

OMSK REGION
(area: 139 700 sq. km.; pop.: 1 900 000)

Omsk Region lies en route from Moscow to the Soviet
Far East and thus serves as an area through which prisoners from the western regions and the transit facilities
in *Gor'kii, Kuibyshev, Volgograd, Kirov, Kazan', Sverd-*

lovsk, and *Chelyabinsk* pass on their way to the camps in *Novosibirsk* and further on.

For this reason, there is a large prison in *Omsk* city (regional capital; pop.: 1 030 000) for approximately 5 000 inmates, some of whom are pre-trial detainees. In addition, there is an "inner" prison in the K.G.B. building for 500 to 600 inmates.

Up until 1958, there were about ten camps in *Omsk.* Now there are only two. The reduction in the number of facilities here was in no way dictated by a liberalization of the regime. Having laid the industrial foundation of the city, the prisoners were moved to other areas. Among the things that they had built in *Omsk* were a heat and power plant, an oil-refining plant, a television center, a streetcar depot, and a new residential housing area.

Camps nos. UCh-16/3 and UCh-16/8, each with 1000 to 1200 prisoners, are located in the city's *Sloboda* district (near the heat and power plant) and supply labor for housing construction projects.

Turn your attention to the tower of the television center. In 1956, one of the prisoners of camp no. UCh-16/4 (whose inmates constructed the tower) climbed up the structure and hanged himself from a conspicuous spot. From his foot hung a sign, "Unjustly convicted, sentenced to 25 years". The corpse hung from a metal crossbar that protruded sideways from the tower. No one, therefore, was willing to try to make his way up. The gathering crowd of city residents below began to express its indignation. The camp administration wanted to cut the rope by shooting through it but ordered the firing to cease when the crowd began to raise its protest. The corpse hung for two days until the arrival of spidermen. The prisoners had refused to bring the corpse down.

Camp no. UCh-16/4 today is a strict-regime facility located in *Isil'kul'.* Its 1200 prisoners are assigned to the military construction sphere.

In *Tselinnyi,* located in the south of the region, approximately 800 prisoners in an ordinary-regime camp do farm work. Directions: only by car via *Russkaya Polyana.*

In *Tyukalinsk, Nazyvaevsk,* and *Kalachinsk,* there is a strict-regime camp of 1000 to 1200 prisoners assigned to road building and military construction.

In *Ishim,* there is a special strict-regime camp for 600 to 700 prisoners assigned to a lumber mill.

In *Tara,* approximately 1000 prisoners in a strict-regime camp work in a lumber mill and in a brick plant.

The direction of the camps of the region is housed in the building of the Ministry of Interior. Director is Colonel Nikitin.

*

TYUMEN' REGION
(area: 1 435 200 sq. km.; pop.: 1 400 000)

Beyond the Urals in Soviet Asia lies the vast territory of Tyumen' Region, which extends to as far as the Arctic Ocean in the far north.

We only know of 14 camps and three prisons in this region. We can say with certitude that our information is incomplete. In *Surgut,* for example, we know of only three camps. An eyewitness, however, has informed us that there is a large group of camps near the oil fields located to the north, east, and west of the city. The 800 to 900 prisoners in each of the camps in *Surgut* are also assigned to the oil industry (extraction, piping, and refining).

301

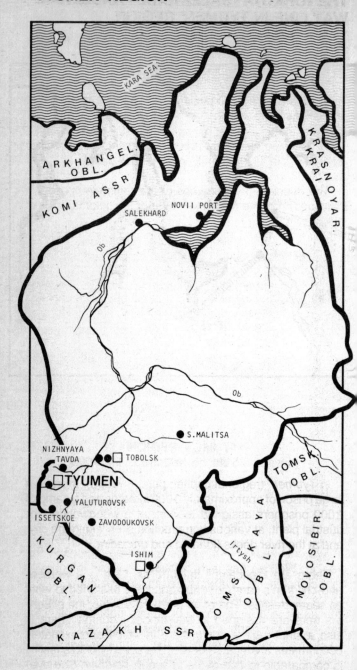

THE VORKUTA - SALEKHARD - NADIM RAILWAY LINE IN TYUMEN' REGION

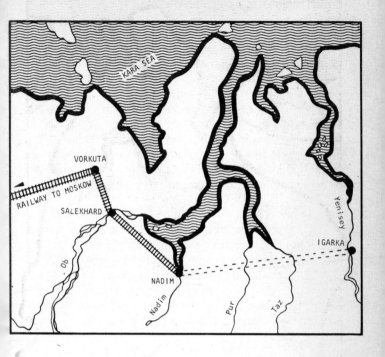

In *Tyumen'* (regional capital; pop.: 360 000), there is a large prison of approximately 3 000 inmates and a camp of 2 000 prisoners assigned to work at a woodworking industrial plant, at various construction sites within the city, and at the river docks (loading and unloading).

There are two camps in *Tobol'sk*. One is a women-and-children's camp for 1500 prisoners assigned to work as seamstresses. The other is a men's camp; the prisoners here are assigned to the lumber industry. There is also a strict-regime prison here in which approximately 600 inmates are incarcerated. (The severity of this facility is comparable to that of the prison in *Vladimir*. See eye-witness testimony in the section on *Vladimir*.)

Prisoners in camps in *Zavodoukovsk, Yaluturovsk, Nizhnyaya Tavda,* and *Isetskoe* are assigned to industry and construction duties. There are up to 1500 prisoners in each camp.

In *Ishim,* there is a camp for 800 prisoners assigned to work in timber areas or in a track tie plant.

At the port of *Nakhodka,* located north of the Arctic Circle, 1600 to 1800 prisoners in a camp are assigned to construction or loading and unloading duties at the docks as well as to the underground mining of non-ferrous metals. There are several more facilities in the area. We do not, however, know their precise location.

At the port of *Salekhard,* approximately 1500 prisoners load and unload goods at the dock or mine polymetallic ores. Many of the prisoners were arrested for their belief in God. About 5000 prisoners in two camps located near *Salekhard* are assigned to polish diamonds. The diamonds are mined in *Mirnyi.* A percentage of the final products are exported and sold in shops as "Russian Gems".

In *Malitsa,* located near Salekhard, approximately 1000 prisoners in a camp mine polymetallic ores. Many of them were arrested for their belief in God.

The sun does not appear during the six-month winter in these regions. The area is covered with frightening snowdrifts.

During the Stalin era, a railroad line was built in the *Vorkuta-Inta* vicinity in the direction of *Salekhard* by prisoners, uncounted thousands of whom perished in the process. The accompanying photograph shows this "railroad" and a locomotive buried up to its smokestack in snow.

In July 1950, a camp revolt was organized in Salekhard

by former Soviet General Belyaev, a political prisoner. The guards of the camp were overwhelmed, and their weapons fell into the hands of the rebelling prisoners, who then freed the inmates of other camps. They sought their escape by making their way to the Ural Mountains. Four hundred rebels succeeded in reaching the Urals, where they fought a month-long battle with the troops of the K.G.B. All were eventually killed through aerial bombardment in this unequal battle. Honor and glory to these heroes!

Yurii Shukhevych was not given the opportunity to raise his two sons. In September 1972, he was sentenced to ten years camp imprisonment and another five years exile after already having spent 20 years in Russian concentration camps. His crime: he is the son of General Roman Shukhevych, commander-in-chief of the Ukrainian rebel army, which fought against both Hitler and Stalin during World War II. Would you have thought this possible? It is the truth. It continues to happen in our own time — today!

The north of Russia is covered with snow almost the entire year. Prisoners construct railroad lines, build cities, and dig up mines in this polar wasteland.

The photograph shows a locomotive somewhere between Vorkuta, northern Urals, 110 kilometers north of the Arctic Circle, and Salekhard (southeast of Vorkuta, on the Arctic Circle, Tyumen' Region, R.S.F.S.R.). It is buried in the snow so that only the smokestack remains visible (photo 1975).

*

BASHKIR A.S.S.R.
(area: 143 000 sq. km.; pop.: 3 800 000)

A part of the R.S.F.S.R., the Bashkir A.S.S.R. lies southwest of the Ural Mountains and is predominated by a harsh, continental climate with temperatures falling to as low as -50°C.

The area is rich in oil. The prisoners in the many camps here are assigned to oil production and refining and to various construction projects connected with the oil industry, such as building roads leading to the various industrial sites or laying pipelines. In *Ishimbai*, center of the oil region, we know of a strict-regime camp of 1500 prisoners. Camp commander is Captain Matveenok. There are certainly several camps here about which we have not yet been informed. Prisoners have long been used here as a source of labor for this hard, dirty, and hazardous work. They have no right to refuse. By doing so,

306

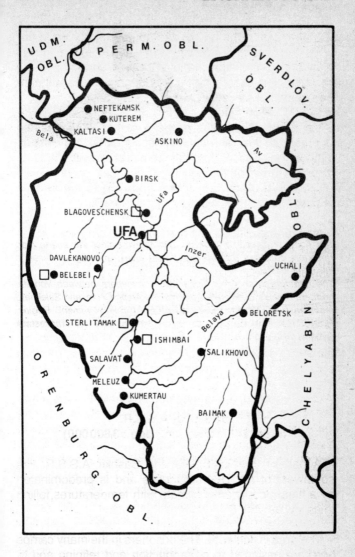

they would run the risk of being transferred to the special prison on Kirov Street in *Ishimbai*.

Strict-regime camps of 1200 to 1500 prisoners each may be found in *Sterlitamak, Salavat, Meleuz, Kimertau, Salikhovo,* and *Baimak* – all of which in the area surrounding *Ishimbai*. The prisoners of these camps are assigned to duties in the oil fields or at construction sites. We have several reports of the extremely arbitrary and harsh regimen of these camps.

The barracks in the camps are separated from one another by barbed-wire fencing. The prisoners are locked in the barracks at night and are not even permitted to use the toilet. The slightest infraction of camp rules will earn them a spell in the isolation cell.

Many of the prisoners of these camps were arrested for practicing their faith in a way not permitted by the state—without registration, through common prayers held in private homes, or through providing their children with religious instruction. Directions from *Ufa* to the various camps: 100 to 250 kilometers by car or train.

An average of 1000 prisoners from the ordinary-regime camps in *Belebei, Davlekanovo, Beloretsk,* and *Uchaly* are assigned to construction projects or to road building and repair. The above-named cities are accessible by train from *Ufa*. In addition, there is a special-regime prison in *Belebei* to which up to 500 inmates have been transferred from the camps for such "violations" as failing to fulfill their work quotas or refusing to work at all (uranium mines). Old Believers are imprisoned here for refusing to work for "Satan's regime".

In the center of the autonomous republic lies the major city of *Ufa* (capital; pop.: 950000). We know of only one camp in it, a strict-regime facility of 1800 prisoners on Zheleznodorozhnaya Street. Camp commander is Major Sergeenko. There is also a pre-trial detention prison for 2000 inmates here. The prisoners in *Ufa* are assigned to housing and industrial construction or are put to work under conditions hazardous to health in a mining equipment plant, a machine plant, an electrical appliance plant, or in the oil fields in the suburban areas. To provide such a large labor force, a large number of camps would be necessary. We have no eyewitness testimony on this question, however, and therefore ask you to take note of any camps you happen to see in *Ufa* when you visit the city and to inform us of them.

In *Blagoveshchensk*, located 74 kilometers north of Ufa, 3000 prisoners in a large strict-regime camp are assigned to a woodworking industrial plant as well as to construction projects within the city. Camp commander is Major Lapin. There is also a prison here for 1000 inmates. We have, unfortunately, no additional information on it.

The administrative center of the camps in the northern part of the autonomous republic is in *Neftekamsk*, which lies approximately 270 kilometers by train from Ufa. We know of an ordinary-regime camp in *Neftekamsk* (1800 prisoners), a strict-regime camp in *Kuterem* (600 prisoners), a special strict-regime camp in *Kaltasy* (800 prisoners), a special strict-regime camp in *Askino* (800 prisoners), and a strict-regime camp in *Birsk* (1500 prisoners).

The prisoners in all these camps are assigned to duties connected with oil production and transport (pipelines) as well as with the construction of oil–refining plants and the roads leading to them.

Altogether, we know of 18 camps and five prisons in the Bashkir A.S.S.R. In our view, these figures represent only an insignificant percentage of the camps that are likely to be scattered throughout this vast territory.

*

UDMURT A.S.S.R.
(area: 42100 sq. km.; pop.: 1500000)

On your way from *Moscow* to *Perm'* Region, where camps for political prisoners are located, you will pass through the Udmurt A.S.S.R. In *Izhevsk*, the capital of the autonomous republic (pop.: 550000), you may visit an old prison (1500 inmates) that has been "modernized" by the state. The windows of the facility have been reduced by half in size and covered with opaque screens ("muzzles"). In the same city, 1200 prisoners in a camp work in a metallurgical plant.

In *Votkinsk*, there is a camp for 2000 prisoners assigned to the logging and woodworking industries as well as to duties in a chemical industrial plant. There is also another camp here for 900 to 1000 minors assigned to make wooden packaging labels. A prison for 500 to 600 inmates transferred from the camps as an additional punishment may be found in the city.

UDMURT A.S.S.R.

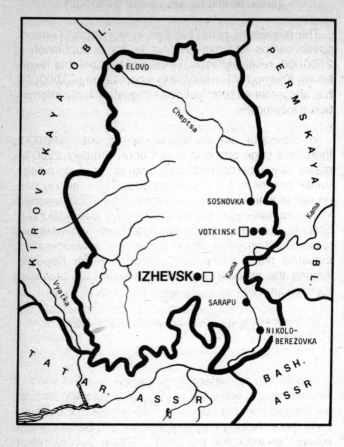

The facility serves as a transit prison as well.

In *Sosnovka*, located north of Votkinsk, 1500 prisoners in a strict-regime camp are assigned to logging. Camp commander is Major Zagolin.

In *Sarapul*, 1200 to 1300 prisoners from a camp are assigned to the military construction sector.

In *Nikolo-Berezovka*, 800 to 900 prisoners from an ordinary-regime camp are assigned to logging. Camp commander is Captain Serdyukov. Although we have evidence of other camps in the area, we have not been able to determine their exact location.

STAVROPOL' TERRITORY
(area: 80 600 sq. km.; pop.: 2 500 000)

The number of penal facilities in *Stavropol'* Territory, seven camps and five prisons, is, for a population of 2 500 000, relatively small. In view of the fact that neighboring *Krasnodar* Territory, with a population of 3 000 000, has altogether 40 such facilities suggests that our information is incomplete.

In *Stavropol'* city (territorial capital; pop.: 260 000); there is a large prison in which approximately 2500 inmates are incarcerated, including pre-trial detainees, transit prisoners, and those sentenced to a term in prison rather than in a camp. Approximately 1500 prisoners in an ordinary-regime camp located on the outskirts of *Stavropol'* on the road to *Nevinnomyssk* are assigned to construction in the city or to work in a woodworking industrial plant. Camp commander is Major Kapustin. Among the prisoners are those arrested for practicing their religion.

In *Nevinnomyssk,* located south of Stavropol', 600 to 700 prisoners in an intensified-regime camp are assigned to construction in the military sector.

In both *Cherkessk* and *Karachaevsk,* located south of Nevinnomyssk, there is a prison with 300 to 400 inmates transferred from the camps for having broken the regulations there. Among the prisoners are Old Believers who refuse "to work for the devil". These people refuse to work in the camps because they consider the entire Soviet system as an offspring of the devil. Not without reason...

Approximately 5000 prisoners in the four camps in *Prikumsk, Zelenokumsk, Proskoveya,* and *Zaterechnyi* are assigned to work in oil fields and on construction projects connected with them.

In both *Nal'chik* and *Ordzhonikidze,* there is a prison in which approximately 500 to 600 inmates are incarcerated. Among the prisoners here are pre-trial detainees.

In *Nal'chik,* 600 to 700 prisoners in a strict-regime camp work in quarries. The majority of them are Christians

arrested for practicing their religion.

It is worth noting that the entire local population of *Karachaevsk, Nal'chik,* and the surrounding area was deported to Siberia during World War II for having helped the Nazis. (In their search for deliverance from the Communists, these people fell into the hands of those who were equally monstrous.) For this reason, the people from this area have since nurtured a deep hatred of all Russians.

VORONEZH REGION
(area: 52400 sq. km.; pop.: 2600000)

There are two prisons and one camp in *Voronezh* city (regional capital; pop.: 790000). The K.G.B. prison, which was designed for 1000 inmates, is a place of confinement for political prisoners under investigation. Those suspected of having committed an ordinary offence are detained in the prison of the Ministry of Interior. Prisoners having broken a regulation at a camp are confined in a special prison of the Ministry as a punishment. A number of the inmates of this facility, however, are in fact political prisoners arrested for practicing their religion. Many of them refused induction into the army or were caught participating in common prayer meetings. The camp in *Voronezh* is an ordinary-regime facility having 1200 prisoners assigned to work in a packaging plant, a lumber storage area, and at various construction sites in the city. Directions: bus to stop marked "Tovarnaya stantsiya".

In *Semiluki,* 15 kilometers north of Voronezh, there is a men's camp for 600 prisoners who manufacture winnowing and seeding machines in mechanics workshops.

In *Ostrogozhsk, Gheorghiu-Dej (Georgiyu-Dezh), Bobrov, Novokopersk,* and *Verkhnyaya Tishanka,* all of which are located south of Voronezh, there are camps of 1000 to 1200 prisoners assigned to construction projects in the city and to a lesser extent in the military sector.

In both *Povorino* and *Borisoglebsk,* 1500 prisoners in an ordinary-regime camp work in a brick and a woodworking industrial plant.

In *Buturlinovka, Pavlovsk, Rossosh',* and *Bochugar,* all of which are located in the southern part of the region, there are camps of 500 to 600 prisoners each, who are assigned to industrial and housing construction and,

VORONEZH REGION

during the sowing and harvest seasons, to farm work as well.

A.S., a Jew imprisoned for having refused induction into the Soviet Army and having demanded the right to emigrate to Israel, reports on the practices that reign in the penal facilities in *Voronezh* city and region:

"During my journey on the train to the camp, I fell ill and came down with a high fever. Having been brought to the prison in *Voronezh* on a stopover, I was given no medical assistance. Twenty-four hours later, I was to continue on my journey. I refused, however, to leave my cell, whereupon the guards immediately seized me and put special handcuffs on me. The handcuffs were attached to a chain that, fastened around the knees, had applied such a painful squeezing pressure on the handbones that I lost consciousness. I felt as if my hands had been sawn into two. I was brought to again when the supervisor struck me in the back with his bunch of keys and kicked me in the stomach. The handcuffs were then loosened, after which I was led to the paddy wagon that was to take me to the camp. The traces of the handcuffs remained for five or six months; the pains in my hands, however, lasted several years.

"When we arrived at the camp, my escorts reported that I had offered 'resistance'. As a result, I was thrown into the isolation cell in the basement of a special barracks. There was no bed, just a freezing cold floor. (It was spring.) Immediately following my release from the cell, I was sent to work and was warned, 'If you give us any more trouble, you'll go right back to the isolation cell'! That was my camp 'initiation'. The camp zone was completely desolate. There was no vegetation, just placards, such as, 'Fulfilling the work quota is the law', or, 'Honest labor: the road home', and the like."

Here is thus an example of what you will find in the camps of *Voronezh* Region.

*

BRYANSK REGION
(area: 34 900 sq. km.; pop.: 1 600 000)

Bryansk Region is well known for its forests and, among prisoners, for its logging camps.

In *Kletnya, Zhukovka, Dyat'kovo,* and *Fokino,* all of which are located in the north of the region, there are altogether four intensified-regime camps of 800 to 900 prisoners each assigned to the logging industry. Directions: 25 to 50 kilometers by car or train from Bryansk.

In each of the camps in *Mglin* (90 kilometers west of Bryansk), *Pochep* (50 kilometers south of Bryansk), and *Surazh* (120 kilometers west of Bryansk, 1200 to 1500 prisoners are assigned to work in woodworking industrial plants and, to a lesser extent, in housing and industrial construction.

BRYANSK REGION

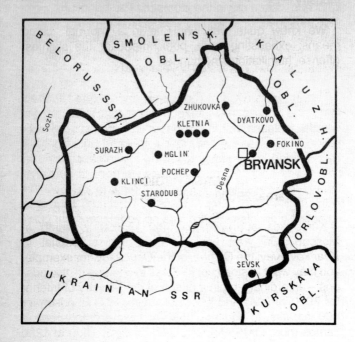

In each of the three strict-regime camps in *Sevsk, Starodub,* and *Klintsy,* all of which are located 150 to 200 kilometers south of Bryansk, 1000 prisoners are assigned to road construction, stone quarrying, or clay mining.

In *Bryansk* city (regional capital; pop.: 420000), you may visit a prison for both ordinary offenders and political prisoners as well as a camp in which 500 to 700 prisoners manufacture springs, scales, doorhandles, and locks for local industry.

We have no information on the treatment of prisoners in these facilities. Their everyday life, however, is, in our view, in itself horrifying.

Bryansk is by no means an atypical region of the Soviet Union. It lies no more than 300 kilometers from *Moscow.* In practically every city here, there are slave prisoners who are put to work "for the benefit of local industry".

We know quite well what life in a "normal" camp means: exhausting work, punishment for the slightest offense, humiliation, and hunger.

*

KURSK REGION
(area: 29 800 sq. km.; pop.: 1 500 000)

Kursk lies approximately 400 kilometers south of Moscow. On your way from the Soviet capital to *Khar'kov, Kiev,* the *Crimea,* or the *Caucasus,* for example, you may want to stop over in *Kursk* to observe its two prisons – an ordinary-regime prison of the Ministry of Interior for 2000 inmates and a special-regime K.G.B. prison for 800 inmates. In addition, there are two ordinary-regime camps (nos. OKh-30/1 and OKh-30/2) of 1000 to 1200 prisoners located on the outskirts of the city on the road to *Pryamintsyno.* Directions: bus nos. 34 and 36. Camp commanders are Major Kostyukov and Major Lyadov. You can see the prisoners early in the morning or late in the evening as they are taken to and from their work duties at various construction sites within the city in barred trucks.

In *Kozinovo,* located 20 kilometers from Kursk, approximately 20 to 25 Christians arrested for their belief in God, their perseverance in protesting the destruction of churches and monasteries in the Soviet Union, and their attempts to impart religious instruction to their children are confined in a strict-regime camp (no. OKh-30/3) among some 1000 ordinary prisoners.

In both *L'gov* and *Oboyan',* located 50 to 60 kilometers by train from Kursk, 600 to 700 prisoners are assigned to the woodworking industry.

In *Shchigry,* approximately 1000 prisoners in a strict-regime camp make slag blocks and bricks.

KURSK REGION

In *Fatezh,* 500 to 600 prisoners in an ordinary-regime camp are assigned to farm work.

In both *Zheleznogorsk* and *Ryl'sk,* there is an intensified-regime camp for 800 to 900 prisoners assigned to work in mechanics shops in local industry.

Altogether, we know of nine camps and two prisons in *Kursk* Region.

*

PSKOV REGION
(area: 55300 sq. km.; pop.: 900000)

On your way from *Leningrad* to *Minsk,* you may wish to make a stopover in *Pskov* city (regional capital; pop.: 170000), where you will find a prison for approximately 1200 inmates, including many who were arrested for practicing their religious convictions. Located on the outskirts of the city (on the right-hand side as you exit), this prison contains a pre-trial detention, transit, and or-

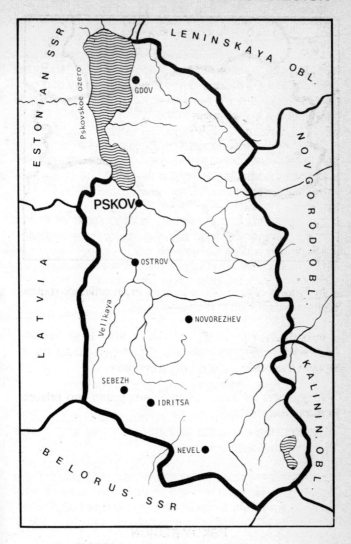

dinary-regime section. On the left, there is an ordinary-regime camp of 1000 to 1100 prisoners assigned to a woodworking plant and to housing construction projects within the city. Camp commander is Major Savelov.

Along the highway by-passing *Gdov,* which is located

north of Pskov, approximately 800 prisoners from an intensified-regime camp are assigned to construction in the military sector.

Driving south from *Pskov* along the highway past *Ostrov,* you will see a camp (address: p/ya 46/4) at the entrance to the road to *Slantsy.* Approximately 800 prisoners here work in a farm machinery repair shop. Camp commander is Captain Ivan'kov.

In *Novorzhev,* located 150 kilometers southeast of Pskov, 600 prisoners in a strict-regime camp mine clay or make bricks by hand without the use of any mechanized equipment whatsoever.

In both *Sebezh* and *Nevel',* located south of *Ostrov* on the Leningrad-Minsk highway, there is an ordinary-regime camp of approximately 500 prisoners assigned to farm work on sovkhozes. The prisoners thus replace those of the local population who chose to leave this region in order to escape the prevailing poverty here.

*

IVANOVO REGION
(area: 23 900 sq. km.; pop.: 1 400 000)

We know of only seven camps and one prison in *Ivanovo* Region, which is located east of and almost borders on Moscow Region.

In *Ivanovo* city (regional capital; pop.: 470 000), there is a prison for 1500 to 1600 inmates and a men's ordinary-regime camp of approximately 1600 to 1800 prisoners assigned to duties in construction and to a lesser extent in local industry.

In each of the three ordinary-regime camps located in *Kineshma, Zavolzhsk,* and *Yur'evets,* approximately 1000 prisoners work in woodworking industrial plants or are assigned to loading and rafting timber.

Approximately 500 prisoners in the camps in *Shuya, Yuzha,* and *An'kovo* are assigned to slave work on sovkhozes.

The longer our list of Soviet penal facilities becomes, the more dull and commonplace it appears. Yet that is precisely why it is so horrifying! Camps, watchtowers, and watchdogs are indeed commonplace features of everyday Soviet life.

The sufferings of the victims of forced-labor camp life must also be understood and remembered.

Here is the testimony of V. Sh., a former inmate of the prison in *Ivanovo* (1977): "We were brought to this prison at dawn. Because we were transit prisoners, we were not taken immediately to our cells. We stood in a room and observed the dirty, ragged 'short-timers' as they performed their prison duties by taking small mess dishes from the kitchen into the corridors of the facility. A group of women was led out to the guards' rooms and to the corridors to scrub the floors. The women were like witches, all tattered and wearing torn dresses. Some of them stood at the supervisor's office and shrieked out their demands. Two or three cried and pleaded for permission to return to their cells so that they could breast-feed their babies, whom they were forced to leave unattended.

"All this was for me, new to prison life as I was, like a painting by Goya – a portrait of horrible and misshapen shadows wallowing in filth."

Following his brief stay in *Ivanovo*, V.Sh. was brought to the camp in *Shuya*. His report: "The camp is located within the city on the road to Ivanovo. On arriving, we were greeted by Captain Lapin, the disciplinary officer of the camp, who announced, 'This may be an ordinary-regime camp, but I'll throw you into the isolation cell or into prison for the slightest infraction of the rules'! After his talk, we were taken to have our hair cut down to the scalp; we were issued old prison camp uniforms and then led to the barracks. The barracks were separated from one another by barbed-wire fencing. We were forbidden to move from one barracks to another. We had to fall into formation before going to work or to the mess hall. Among the criminals at the camp were informers whose red armbands indicated that they performed duties for the administration. We worked in sovkhoz fields; not, however, according to fixed but rather to daylight hours – from sunrise to sunset."

*

PENZA REGION
(area: 43 200 sq. km.; pop.: 1 600 000)

We know of two prisons in *Penza* city (regional capital; pop.: 450 000): a prison in the regional K.G.B. building for 800 to 900 inmates; a pre-trial detention and transit prison for 1500 to 1800 inmates.

In *Nikol'sk*, located 125 kilometers northeast of Penza, approximately 2000 prisoners from a strict-regime camp are assigned to logging or to woodworking in a lumber mill. Camp commander is Major Zotov.

In *Kuznetsk*, located 130 kilometers by car to the east of Penza, 800 to 900 prisoners from an ordinary-regime camp work on construction projects in the city.

322

In both *Sursk* and *Russkii Kameshkir,* there is a camp for 1000 prisoners assigned to quarry building stone and gravel or are given duties in a brick plant.

In *Nizhnii Lomov,* located 130 to 140 kilometers west of Penza, 1000 to 1100 prisoners from an ordinary-regime camp are assigned to construction. Camp commander is Captain Kartashov.

In *Kamenka,* located 80 kilometers west of Penza and accessible only by car, 700 to 800 prisoners in a special-regime camp wear striped and numbered prison camp uniforms and work in a quarry. Camp commander is Captain Laptev.

In *Serdobsk,* located approximately 85 kilometers southwest of Penza, about 1000 prisoners from an ordinary-regime camp are assigned to logging.

In *Belinskii,* located approximately 150 kilometers west of Penza, 1200 prisoners from an ordinary-regime camp are assigned to a woodworking industrial plant. Camp commander is Major Ozerov.

Altogether, we know of eight camps and two prisons in *Penza* Region.

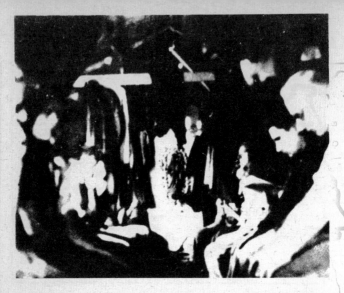

The camp barracks are overfilled. Some 500 prisoners live on plank-beds. Religious prisoners pray here, too. The photograph shows prisoners praying in a camp (photo 1977).

*

ORENBURG REGION
(area: 124000 sq. km.; pop.: 2100000)

In *Orenburg* city (regional capital; pop.: 450000), you may visit a camp of 1200 to 1500 prisoners assigned to construction projects in the military sector. You will also find a K.G.B. prison with approximately 600 inmates and a pre-trial detention and transit prison for 2500 inmates.

In the vicinity of *Buguruslan,* located 350 kilometers from Orenburg, there are three strict-regime camps of approximately 1000 to 1200 prisoners each, who are assigned to work in oilfields or on construction projects. You will also find here a prison for 800 to 1000 inmates convicted of committing a misdemeanor in one of the surrounding camps. The prison has in addition a pre-trial detention and a transit ward.

In *Sol'-Iletsk,* located 70 kilometers south of Orenburg,

and in the surrounding area, there are three strict-regime camps of 1500 inmates and a special strict-regime camp of approximately 800 prisoners, all of whom work in the salt mines. There is also a prison in *Sol'-Iletsk* for those prisoners convicted of additional crimes.

In the vicinity of *Mednogorsk* and *Orsk,* located approximately 300 kilometers southeast of Orenburg, there are several camps. We have precise evidence, however, of only six strict-regime or intensified-regime camps of 1000 to 1200 prisoners each. Work duties include copper, coal, and nickel mining, oil-refining, and construction in the military sector.

The work conditions in these camps are extremely harsh and hazardous to health. K.B., a former prisoner in a camp in *Orsk,* reports: "I was a transit prisoner in *Orsk* in early 1976. It was terribly cold, and there were horrible snowstorms. Located in a suburb, the camp was exposed to the wind from all directions. There were cracks in the walls of the barracks as well, which meant that it was cold inside. Towards morning, the buckets full of water in the buildings would freeze. We were herded to our work duties at the copper-smelting plant. The workshops were drafty, cold, and full of harmful fumes from the smelting of the copper. You could not stop coughing either during or after work. The food we were given was typical of that generally available in the camps – spoiled or frozen vegetables, spoiled herring. We were given no extra rations despite the hazardous work. Most of the inmates of the camp were ordinary criminals, but there were de facto political prisoners as well. Two were imprisoned for attempting to leave the country illegally. One was a sailor who was convicted for bringing proscribed books into the Soviet Union. He was accused of selling them. Ten or twelve of the prisoners were arrested for participating in prayer meetings that had not been registered with the authorities.

"The ordinary criminals were not as badly treated by the camp supervisors as we. Sometimes, they were even incited against us. It is interesting to note, however, that the criminals did not allow themselves to be duped by the provocations of the K.G.B. security officer but generally left us alone."

As you can see, the authorities tried to aggravate the living conditions for the political prisoners in the camp.

*

TAMBOV REGION
(area: 34 300 sq. km.; pop.: 1 500 000)

Tambov Region, which is located approximately 400 kilometers south of Moscow, is easily accessible both by train as well as by car.

In *Tambov* (regional capital; pop.: 275 000), there is a prison of the Ministry of Interior for 1500 to 1600 inmates. Next to it is an ordinary-regime camp of 800 to 900 prisoners assigned to construction work within the city. You may observe the prisoners in the morning and evening on the streets of the city as they are transported to and

---

from work. For an example of such transports, see the photograph in our *Guidebook*.

In *Kochetovka*, there is an intensified-regime camp for 1500 prisoners assigned to work in a machine plant where they manufacture steel springs for automobiles and metal fittings.

In *Kotovsk*, 1000 to 1100 prisoners in an ordinary-regime camp work in a woodworking plant. Camp commander is Major Sukhin.

In *Kamenka*, 450 to 500 prisoners from a special-regime camp work in a quarry. The prisoners here wear striped and numbered concentration camp uniforms and are thus not to be distinguished from those who were incarcerated in the camps of Nazi Germany.

A total of approximately 2300 to 2400 prisoners in the three intensified-regime camps in *Sosnovka, Uvarova,* and *Zherdevka* are assigned to the logging and wood-working industries.

In *Rasskazovo*, there is a camp hospital for 1300 to 1400 prisoners. This hospital is always filled to capacity as it draws its patients not only from *Tambov*, but also from other regions of the Soviet Union.

*

LIPETSK REGION
(area: 24100 sq. km.; pop.: 1300000)

In *Lipetsk* city (regional capital; pop.: 390000); there is a prison in which both military personnel as well as civilians are incarcerated. Within the military units stationed in and around the city, cases of personnel refusing to carry out orders or of committing some other misdemeanor frequently occur. Approximately 1000 inmates are confined in the prison.

Next to the prison is an ordinary-regime camp for 500 to 600 prisoners assigned to mechanics workshops. Camp commander is Major Peskov.

In *Elets*, there is a prison for 1000 to 1200 inmates and next to it a camp for 800 to 900 prisoners assigned to construction duties at the military garrisons in *Zarech'e*. Camp commander is Captain Semënov.

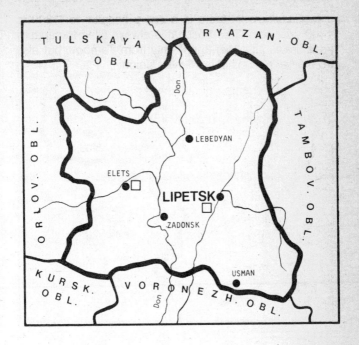

In *Lebedyan'*, 600 to 800 prisoners from a strict-regime camp work at a brick factory.

In both *Zadonsk* and *Usman'*, there is an ordinary-regime camp of 600 to 800 prisoners assigned to woodworking plants, sawmills, and to a lesser extent, to local sovkhozes where they participate in bringing in the harvest.

Altogether, therefore, we know of five camps and two prisons in this region, a rather "modest" number when compared to the more "developed" areas of the Soviet Union.

UL'YANOVSK REGION

UL'YANOVSK REGION
(area: 37300 sq. km.; pop.: 1300000)

This region lies approximately 700 kilometers east of Moscow and is easily accessible by all modes of transportation. The tourist will find things of interest to observe here.

In *Ul'yanovsk* city (regional capital; pop.: 470000), for example, approximately 600 women prisoners from camp no. YuP-78/2 make ferrite rings in the BSM computer plant. A number of the women maintain custody of their infant children.

I.T., an eyewitness, reports that the women are used for this work because there are no volunteers. The work represents a major health hazard. After about a year at the plant, the women prisoners become almost completely blind.

There is also a prison of the Ministry of Interior for 1800 inmates and a K.G.B. pre-trial detention isolation facility for 200 inmates in *Ul'yanovsk*.

In *Kandei,* located southwest of Ul'yanovsk, you may visit another camp for women and small children (no. YuP-78/4). Approximately 1500 prisoners work here as seamstresses. Camp commander is Major Volodin.

In *Melekess,* located southeast of Ul'yanovsk, there is a prison for 500 inmates transferred here from the camps as a punishment. Next to it is a camp hospital in which there are 1000 to 1200 prisoner patients.

In *Karsun,* 1800 to 2000 prisoners in an ordinary-regime camp (no. YuP-78/6) are assigned to a wood-working plant.

In *Sengilei,* approximately 1000 prisoners in camp no. YuP-78/5 work at a ship repair plant on the Kuibyshev Reservoir. Camp commander is Captain Komov.

In *Barysh,* approximately 1200 prisoners in an intensi-fied-regime camp (no. YuP-78/8) work in a brick plant.

In *Radishchevo,* located in the south of the region, 500 to 600 prisoners in a camp are assigned to farm work.

In *Dmitrovograd,* approximately 1000 prisoners from a strict-regime camp (no. YuP-78/5) quarry and break stone without the use of mechanized equipment. Many prisoners here were arrested for their belief in God or their participation in national liberation struggles. Sender *Levinzon,* for example, was imprisoned here as a result of his desire to emigrate to Israel. Camp commander is Major Sidorov.

CHITA REGION

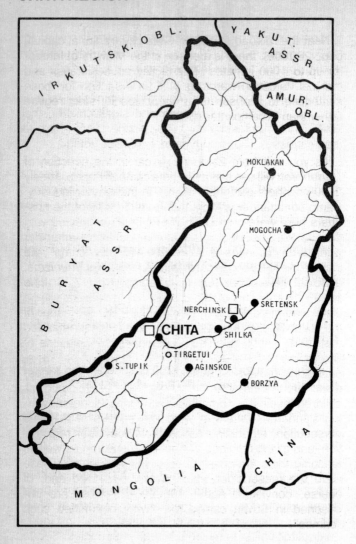

CHITA REGION
(area: 431 000 sq. km.; pop.: 1 200 000)

Located east of Lake Baikal and more than 5000 kilometers from Moscow, *Chita* Region is characterized by a harsh continental climate. A large part of its territory is uninhabitable.

Our information on this region is incomplete. We have knowledge of only nine camps and two prisons here.

Near the railroad station in *Chita* city (regional capital; pop.: 280000), there is a prison of the Ministry of Interior for up to 4000 inmates. This facility houses transit and pre-trial detention wards as well as a section for those sentenced to a prison term under special strict regime rather than to camp internment.

As you exit from *Zarech'e* by car in the direction of *Ugdan,* you will see a strict-regime camp of approximately 2500 prisoners assigned to work in the leather industry. Camp commander is Major Kostromin. Many of the prisoners here were convicted of a "crime" connected with their religious beliefs. In order to acquaint those unfamiliar with the peculiarities of Soviet life with this "crime", we include the following excerpt from *Znamya Kommunizma,* a Soviet newspaper (Odessa Region, No. 17, 6 June 1979): "A meeting of the citizens of *Vasil'evka* village discussed the antisocial activities of P. *Dimov,* leader of the local Baptist initiative group. Everyone demanded that he be called to order and tried for his violations of Soviet law: refusal to register his group of believers, organizing prayers at burials, leading religious processions through the village after the burials, forbidding his children to join the Komsomol and Young Pioneers, writing slanderous letters in which he speaks of religious persecution, organizing baptisms without prior registration, and giving religious instruction to children as well as teaching them the observance of religious rites." These were the reasons for which *Dimov* was tried and, of course, convicted. About 100000 Christians are imprisoned in Soviet camps for having committed such "crimes".

Two railroad lines and two strategic highways run south from *Chita* towards the Mongolian (and Chinese) border. Approximately 500 kilometers in length, these thoroughfares were built by prisoners from the camps in *Achinskoe, Shilka, Nerchinsk,* and *Sretensk.* Except for repair work on the completed roads, the 1500 to 1600 prisoners of each camp are now assigned to other projects as well: *Achinskoe* – housing construction; *Shilka* – coal mining, brick-making, production of reinforced-concrete blocks; *Nerchinsk* – duties in a lumber mill and a machine plant; and *Sretensk* – duties in a lumber mill.

In addition, there is a prison for 1200 to 1300 inmates in *Nerchinsk* for those punished for some misdemeanor in the camps.

In *Borzya,* located near the Mongolian border, approximately 2000 prisoners in a strict-regime camp are assigned to construction in the military sector.

A strict-regime camp with prisoners assigned to similar duties may be found in *Mogocha* near the Chinese border.

In *Tupik,* approximately 1500 prisoners from a special strict-regime camp work in a silicate factory or are assigned to grind mirrors. The prisoners, many of whom were arrested for their religious beliefs, are thus subject to serious health hazards.

In *Moklakan,* located in the northeastern part of the region, there is a special strict-regime camp. We do not know, however, the number of prisoners there or the work they do.

We believe that there are many more camps hidden in the mountains and dense forests of *Chita* Region, and with them, many human tragedies and ruined lives.

We know, for example, that somewhere in this region, there is a camp for foreigners placed on "missing-persons" lists. In this connection, see the notes on Raoul *Wallenberg,* the kidnapped Swedish diplomat who has spent the last 35 years in Soviet camps and prisons.

KHABAROVSK TERRITORY
(area: 824600 sq. km.; pop.: 1400000)

This remote territory in the Far East forms part of the Soviet Pacific coast line. It is accessible by both train and airplane.

In *Khabarovsk* (territorial capital; pop.: 540000), there is a prison of the Ministry of Interior for 2500 inmates and a special K.G.B. isolation prison for 300 to 400 inmates. As you exit the city in the direction of *Volochaevka,* you will see a strict-regime camp in which there are 3000 prisoners assigned to construction projects in the military sector. There are many Christians imprisoned here for practicing their religion.

In *Birobidzhan* (capital of the territory's Jewish Autonomous Region), there is a prison for 1200 inmates sentenced here to terms of various lengths for having violated regulations at the camp in which they were previously confined. Next to the prison is an ordinary-regime camp in which approximately 1500 prisoners are assigned to duties in a woodworking plant. In *Izvestkovyi,* there is a strict-regime camp for 2000 prisoners assigned to mining and lime-burning.

In *Komsomol'sk-na-Amure,* there is a prison of the Ministry of the Interior for 2000 inmates and an ordinary-regime camp for 1200 prisoners who work in shipyards. There is some inexact information available on other camps in *Komsomol'sk; we do not, however, have their addresses.*

Until 1956, there were up to ten camps and transit camps for 10000 to 15000 prisoners in *Sovetskaya Gavan'.* From here, transit prisoners were taken by ship to the prisons in *Kolyma, Sakhalin, Kamchatka,* and to the uranium mines of *Primorsk* Territory.

We know of two camps in *Sovetskaya Gavan':* a transit camp for 2000 prisoners awaiting transfer to a final station

KHABAROVSK TERRITORY

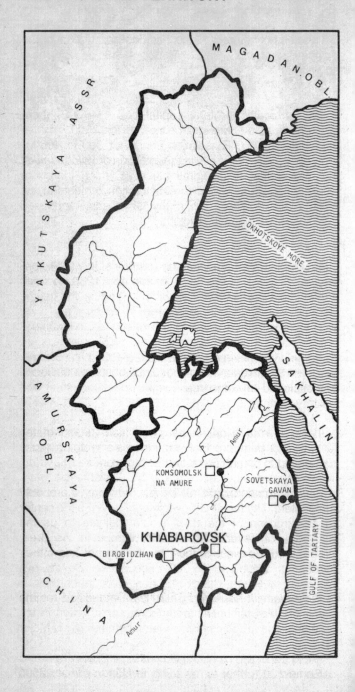

Work by prisoners on all construction sites, railroads, and canals in the U.S.S.R. is done by hand and without the aid of machinery (photo 1977).

to participate in the construction of the Baikal-Amur Railroad (BAM); an intensified-regime camp of 1 500 prisoners assigned to construction work in the industrial and military sectors.

There is also a prison here in which 2 500 inmates – including both pre-trial detainees as well as those sentenced to normal penal terms – are confined.

Our information on *Khabarovsk* Territory is probably incomplete. The fact that *Sovetskaya Gavan'* is the center of construction of the BAM would indicate to us the existence of several forced-labor camps in the area, probably to the west of the city. We do not know their location.

In *Nikolaevsk-na-Amure,* there is an intensified-regime camp of 1800 prisoners assigned to construction in the industrial and military sectors. Camp commander is Major Osipov.

Somewhat further to the south in *Bogorodskoe,* 2500

337

prisoners in a strict-regime camp are assigned to a wood-working plant. Camp commander is Major Kosach.

The many secrets and horrors of the camps and prisons of *Khabarovsk* Territory are kept closely guarded. Only the liquidation of the Soviet state would open up these mysterious regions of lawlessness to public view.

KALUGA REGION

KALUGA REGION
(area: 29 900 sq. km.; pop.: 1 000 000)

In *Kaluga* city (regional capital; pop. 270000), there is a prison for 1 800 to 2 000 inmates at the town exit on the road to *Yukhnov.* Both political prisoners and ordinary offenders are imprisoned here. Next to the prison is an ordinary-regime camp for 500 to 600 prisoners assigned to manufacture hardware items for local industry.

Political prisoners are also confined to the psychiatric hospital in *Kaluga.* Among them is Vladimir *Rozhdestvenskii,* who circulated leaflets protesting the absence of democracy in the Soviet Union.

In *Medyn',* there is a prison for 1000 to 1200 inmates as well as a camp of approximately 800 prisoners assigned to farm work, road repair, or to duties in a brick plant.

In *Maloyaroslavets,* there is a prison of approximately 1000 inmates sent here from the camps as a punishment. There is also an ordinary-regime camp of approximately 2500 prisoners assigned to various construction duties in the "atomic city" of *Obninsk.*

In *Sukhinichi,* there is a special strict-regime prison for 600 to 700 inmates sent here for having committed a misdemeanor at a camp. Next to the prison, 500 to 600 prisoners in a strict-regime camp make reinforced-concrete slabs.

In *Kozel'sk,* 800 to 900 prisoners in an ordinary-regime camp work in a sawmill.

In *Zhizdra,* there is a strict-regime camp for 1000 to 1200 prisoners assigned to the logging industry. In the prison in *Zhizdra,* there are 500 to 600 inmates.

Thus, there are six camps and five prisons in *Kaluga* Region, a "modest" sum for a population of 1 000 000. And it is not known whether there are more penal facilities here.

CHELYABINSK Region

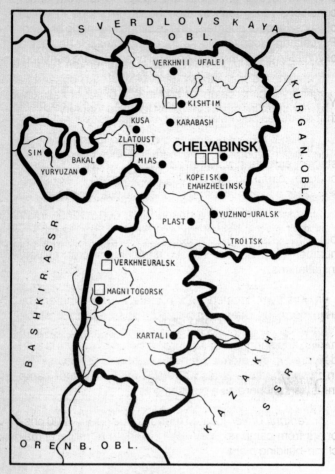

CHELYABINSK REGION
(area: 87 900 sq. km.; pop.: 3 600 000)

Chelyabinsk Region is located on the eastern slopes of the southern Urals.

We know of 18 camps and five prisons here. A short description of them follows.

In *Chelyabinsk* city itself (regional capital; pop.: 1 010 000), there is a K.G.B. prison for 1200 inmates and a prison of the Ministry of Interior for 3000 inmates. At the ordinary-regime camp located near the tractor plant in the city, 800 to 900 prisoners are assigned to work under conditions hazardous to their health in shops in which plastics, lacquer enamels, and castings are made or used. Psychiatric Hospital No. 2 in *Chelyabinsk* is in fact a psychiatric prison in which political prisoners are confined.

One thousand eight hundred prisoners in camp no. YaV-48/8, also located in *Chelyabinsk*, work in a plant that produces boilers and other, similar vessels.

Forty kilometers southeast of *Chelyabinsk* lies a restricted satellite city, Chelyabinsk-40, where 2000 prisoners in camp no. YaV-48/6 are assigned to construct a nuclear power reactor and an atomic warhead plant.

Fifty-one kilometers from *Chelyabinsk* lies *Chelyabinsk-51,* a second satellite city, where an undisclosed number of prisoners are constructing secret military installations.

In *Kyshtym,* located approximately 70 kilometers by train north of *Chelyabinsk,* 2500 prisoners in a strict-regime camp (no. YaV-48/7) are assigned to uranium mining and enrichment. The uranium from *Kyshtym* is then delivered to the atomic warhead plant in *Chelyabinsk*-40. In *Kyshtym,* there is also a prison for 500 former camp inmates sent here as a punishment.

In *Verkhnii Ufalei,* located further to the north, 1200 prisoners from camp no. YaV-48/12 work in a (military) machine-building plant.

In *Karabash,* there is a strict-regime camp for 800 to 900 prisoners assigned to work in quarries.

In *Zlatoust,* there is a prison for 2500 inmates. The facility includes a pre-trial detention section. One thousand five hundred prisoners in a camp here work in a metallurgical factory.

In *Miass,* approximately 1200 prisoners from a camp are assigned to industrial construction.

In *Bakal,* 1800 prisoners in an ordinary-regime camp (no. YaV-48/9) work in a machine-tool plant. (Two of the workshops here produce machine-tools; another ten manufacture weapons.)

In *Yuryuzan',* there is a camp hospital for 1500 prisoners.

In *Sim,* 600 to 700 prisoners in a strict-regime camp work in a quarry.

In *Kusa,* located 25 kilometers from *Zlatoust,* 1200 prisoners in an ordinary-regime camp are assigned to produce manufacture economizers in a machine-building plant.

In *Kopeisk,* located 15 kilometers east of *Chelyabinsk,* approximately 1600 prisoners in a strict-regime camp are assigned to a secret construction project in the military sphere.

In *Emanzhelinsk,* 2000 prisoners in an ordinary-regime camp (no. YaV-48/14) are assigned to a woodworking industrial plant. Camp commander is Major Sidorchuk.

In *Yuzhno-Ural'sk, Troitsk,* and *Plast,* there are three camps of aproximately 1200 prisoners each assigned to construction work.

In both *Verkhneural'sk* and *Magnitogorsk,* there is a camp of approximately 2500 prisoners who work under conditions hazardous to health in metallurgical plants or in the construction industry.

Both cities also have a prison of approximately 1500 to 1800 inmates.

In *Kartaly,* 3000 prisoners in an ordinary-regime camp are assigned to logging or timber-sawing.

As you can see, there is enough work for all the slaves.

YAKUTSK A.S.S.R.
(area: 3100000 sq. km.; pop.: 700000)

This part of the U.S.S.R. is 7 to 10000 kilometers from Moscow and can only be reached by air. We know of 21 camps and one prison in this region which clearly does not cover all the penal institutions in the wide open spaces of *Yakutiya,* with its rich deposits of gold, platinum, diamonds, poly-metal ores, coal, and oil. For example, we have discovered that there are camps used for oil-drilling and related construction sites to the south of *Yakutsk* city (*Pokrovskii* district) and to the north as well, (near *Kablyaya* and *Namtsy*) but we have no more specific information about these camps as yet. Therefore, we shall only tell of the sites with which we are more fully acquainted.

In the city of *Yakutsk* itself, there is a prison, newly

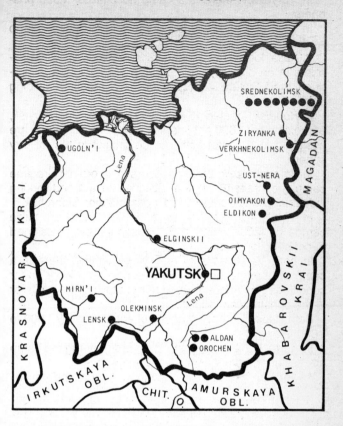

constructed by the Soviet authorities, which is able to hold 2000 prisoners as well as a camp (No. Ya D-40/3) for 1800 prisoners who are assigned to industrial construction sites and road-building.

In *Aldan,* in the southern part of the republic, there are two camps (No. Ya D-40/16 and No. Ya D-40/14); the approximately 1500 prisoners there are used in the mining of gold.

In *Orochen,* also in the south, there is a strict regime camp for 3000 prisoners. Part of them are assigned to gold-mining and the rest to construction sites.

In *Mirny,* in the west, prison labor is used to mine diamonds (strict-regime Camp No. Ya D-40/18; 1200 prisoners). The diamonds are polished by other prisoners in *Salekhard* (see under *Tyumen* Region).

In *Lensk,* there is an ordinary-regime camp and a hospital which can hold 1500 to 1600 prisoners.

In *Olekminsk,* there is a strict-regime camp containing 1800 prisoners assigned to industrial sites.

In the settlements at *Elginsky* and *Ist' Nera,* prisoners are assigned to military construction sites, but the number of prison camps and total prisoners has not yet been determined with any accuracy.

In *El'dikon* and *Oimiakon,* there are two strict-regime camps with 1600 to 1700 prisoners each assigned to gold mining.

At *Verkhnekolymsk* and *Zyrianka,* there are two camps (No. Ya D-40/12 and No. Ya D-40/15) holding 1200 to 1400 prisoners each who are assigned to the mining of gold and poly-metals. In *Srednekolymsk,* beyond the Arctic Circle, there is a group of 8 camps: Nos. Ya D-40/10, Ya D-40/19, Ya D-40/13, and Ya D-40/11 with about 1500 prisoners each assigned to gold mining. These are strict-regime camps.

In *Ugol'nyi,* in the far northwest corner of the republic, is a strict-regime camp whose 2500 prisoners mine coal and poly-metals. The camp commander is Major Esipenko.

This is the testimony of K.S. who worked there in 1977: "I was only able to observe the life of the prisoners at a distance since I was not a prisoner but worked in *Ugol'nyi* as a hired mining technician. But even the life of a hired technician was difficult. There were constant disruptions of basic supplies. When I would ask some of the prisoners how they fared, they would answer, "We chew on our fists," that is, there was nothing to eat. I would try to pass something to them but this was merely a drop in the bucket. Prisoners in *Ugol'nyi* work in the mines and at an ore-concentration plant in a three-shift rotation (both day and night). They live in prefabricated dwellings which they jokingly call "prefabricated draughts" since the wind constantly comes through the walls. The prisoners look extremely emaciated and some of them suffer from scurvy since there are no fresh fruits or vegetables in their diet. Many of them said to me, "Bring some onions or garlic: my teeth are loose." But we didn't have onions or garlic that often ourselves."

In the U.S.S.R., there is a sad joke: "What element in our economy is constant? Temporary difficulties."

Isolated *Yakutiya* is no exception to the general ethnic enmity found in the U.S.S.R.: on June 11, 1979, there were mass disorders and demonstrations demanding the right of withdrawal by *Yakutiya* from the U.S.S.R. As in the case of all other such demonstrations, this one was put down with troops. The Soviet regime "defends" itself.

THE USE OF
SOVIET PENAL LABOR

THE USE OF FORCED LABOR
IN THE SOVIET ARMS INDUSTRY

Official state budget reports submitted annually by the Soviet government indicate that funds appropriated for peaceful purposes greatly exceed those reserved for the military sphere. The deception will become obvious to all, however, who find the opportunity to observe the "peaceful" industrial plants of the Soviet Union.

In *Tula,* for example, we suggest that you go to the center of town, cross the bridge over the river as if you were driving in the direction of *Yasnaya Polyana,* the estate of *Lev Tolstoi,* and look immediately to the right. There you will see a huge factory. Officially, it is called a machine-building plant. You will be told that it produces machines designed to manufacture stockings. In fact, however, there are 38 workshops in the plant, designated as no. 535, that produce artillery weapons and only one in which machines for stockings are manufactured. This "peaceful" factory is officially financed not through the military budget but by the Ministry for Machine Construction. On the left side of the same bridge is a huge machine-building plant that manufactures Kalashnikov automatic firearms, which have been used to kill and continue to kill human beings in the free world. (Think of Vietnam, Africa, Rhodesia, the countless terrorists. The Kalashnikov is everywhere.) The plant is subsidized by non-military industry.

A similar situation reigns in other plants: in aviation plants in *Kuibyshev* (Kuibyshev Region) in which missiles are produced; in a motorcycle plant in *Izhevsk* in which armored personnel carriers are built; in an automobile plant in *Gor'kii* in which cross-country vehicles for the army are manufactured; or in the "peaceful" machine-building plants in *Chelyabinsk* (Chelyabinsk Region) in which warheads for strategic missiles are made.

Here is some information about the duties of prisoners in this infernal arms business.

1. In the Ukraine, you may observe the work of the enslaved prisoners in the "Arsenal" and "Kvarts" arms factories and the "Graviton" military helicopter plant; the same may be seen in the "Elektron" plant in *L'vov* and in *Khotin*. In *Zaparozh'e,* there are three aviation plants to which prisoners are brought in trucks. The prisoners can be seen from the outside during their transport. Tanks are made in the Malyshev plant (no. 75) in *Khar'kov.* Missiles are assembled in the vicinity of *Lesopark.* In the "Yuzhnoe Mashinostroenie" plant in *Dnepropetrovsk,* atomic warheads are manufactured. (A large part of the city is thus exposed to a high level of radiation, a matter that the population has not been informed of.) Similar conditions reign in a naval plant in *Kherson* and at the construction site of underground military airfields in *Borispol'* (Kiev Region).

2. Baltic states. In *Vilnius,* there is a plant (no. 555) in which special radios are made for the army and for spying purposes as well as the "Telekompanent" plant where radar installations are manufactured. In *Lirmunai,* there is an arms plant (address: Lapuno Street 7, p/ya 52). – On *Paldiski* Bay, prisoners are given the extremely dangerous duty of cleaning the nozzles of atomic-powered submarines.

3. Belorussian S.S.R. In *Vitebsk,* you will find prisoners in the following arms plants: "Elektroizmeritel'" (Khinskii Street 2), "Monolit", "Aviapribor", "Mashinostroitel'nyi", "Instrumental'nyi", and "Priborostroitel'nyi", all of which are innocuous names. In *Bobruisk,* prisoners are assigned to work at strictly secret construction sites (underground tank fields and airfields) and in two arms plants.

4. Moldavian S.S.R. In *Kishinev,* prisoners are among the workers in the "Stiral'nye mashiny" (washing machines) plant, which is in fact a highly secret arms factory. Prisoners in *Kishinev* also work in the "Signal" arms plant (near the Botanical Gardens), the "Luch" plant (military computers), the "Mezon" plant (Merenkovki area), and the "Vibropribor" plant (military optical equipment). In *Bel'tsy,* prisoners are assigned to hazardous

duties in the plastics and castings workshop in the naval equipment plant.

5. If we turn our attention to the cities of Siberia and the rest of Asia, we will find dozens of arms plants and special military construction sites where the slave labor of the prisoners is used: *Krasnoyarsk* p/ya 26, uranium enrichment plant and death camp; *Krasnoyarsk* p/ya 24, military construction sites and the "Krasmash", "Metallurgicheskii", "Steklozavod", and "Krasnoyarsk-9" plants; *Achinsk,* "Glinozemnyi" plant, a uranium enrichment plant in which prisoners become contaminated and eventually die. Camps assigned to uranium mining may be found in *Zeravshan, Fergana, Leninsk, Margilan, Amalyk* near Tashkent (all in Uzbek S.S.R.); in *Aksu* (Kazakh S.S.R.); and in many other cities. (See the map of the death camps in our *Guidebook*.)

6. Women prisoners are also used in the arms industry. In *Volgograd* and *Veseloe* (Volgograd Region), women sew uniforms as well as tank covers. In *Achinsk* and *Slyudyanka,* they are assigned to cleave mica. In *Ul'yanovsk,* they work in the "Vychislitel'nye mashiny" (computer machines) plant, which in fact is assigned to the military sector. In *Gor'kii,* they sew ammunition pouches and tank covers.

7. There are also special secret scientific research institutes and special construction bureaus to which prisoners are assigned: in *Leningrad,* the OKB-16 in *Kresty* Prison and another installation at the "Lomo" plant; in *Moscow,* the Institute of Petroleum Synthetics; in *Baku,* the Institute of Burning Materials, in which prisoners work on new kinds of rocket fuel and new kinds of napalm.

The list of arms plants and military research institutes in which prisoners work is long. Our information is nevertheless incomplete.

FORCED LABOR IN THE OIL FIELDS OF THE SOVIET UNION

In the ten years that I spent in the political camps of the Soviet Union, I met many prisoners who had been assigned to duties in the oil industry. I often heard from friends in other camps, moreover, about the work of prisoners in the production and refining of oil and the construction of oil pipelines.

I was in camp no. 3 of the *"Kamyshlag"* complex in *Omsk* in 1954. There were altogether four camps and a total of approximately 12 000 prisoners. We built oil-refining and oil-processing plants, a project that lasted until 1969. The other camps of the *"Kamyshlag"* complex built the Kuibyshev-Omsk pipeline. We also knew that the Kuibyshev-Moscow pipeline was constructed by prisoners as well.

From others who had been transferred to our camps, I learned about the work of about 10 000 prisoners in the facilities in *Angarsk (Irkutsk* Region, *"Ozerlag")* on the construction of a very large complex for the production of gasoline, a project that continued to 1970. When I was in prison in *Semipalatinsk* and *Ust'-Kamenogorsk,* I met many prisoners from the oil fields of the Kazakh S.S.R. as well as from those in the vicinity of *Astrakhan', Krasnovodsk,* and the *Mangyshlak* peninsula (all on the Caspian Sea). During my travels throughout the Soviet Union (1965–1970) following my release, I saw camps at the oil fields in Kirghizia *(Rybach'e,* Lake *Issyk-Kul')* and Azerbaidzhan *(Lenkoran', Baku).*

Working in Israel at the Research Center for the study of the camps, I received a wealth of information on those facilities now assigned to the oil industry and related fields from those who emigrated from the Soviet Union in the years 1976–1979. Such facilities may be found, for example, in *Ukhta* (Komi A.S.S.R.), *Gur'ev* (on the Caspian Sea), the areas north and south of *Yakutsk* city, and *Maikop, Neftegorsk,* and *Khadyzhensk* (Krasnodar Territory).

In *Sal'skie Stepi* and *Prikum'e,* prisoners in the camps in *Karabulak, Goiti-Kort, Solonchakovoe,* and *Sukhumskii* are also assigned to the oil industry.

We know of camps assigned to the oil industry in *Ishimbai, Ufa, Emba, Tuimazy,* and *Karaul-Bazar.* In Siberia, there are similar camps along the Enisei River, in *Turukhansk* District, and *Tyumen'* Region (*Shaim, Krasnopolyanskii, Surgutskii, Nizhnevartovskii,* and *Alexsandrovskii*). Forced labor from *D'yavol'skoe* is employed in oil production near the Tunguska River.

Along the Lena River, oil is produced in *Barabinsk* and in the extreme north in *Noril'sk.*

As you can see, forced labor is widely used in the Soviet oil industry. For lack of space, it would be impossible to list all the camps in the Soviet Union assigned to this important branch of industry.

SOUVENIRS FOR TOURISTS AND TRINKETS FOR EXPORT TO THE WEST ARE MANUFACTURED BY PRISONERS

Accompanying these notes is a photograph of a few souvenirs made by prisoners in the Soviet Union.

The prisoners manufacture wooden *matrëshki* (a wooden doll with similar, successively smaller ones inside), small jewel boxes sold as the work of "folk artists", and

Women prisoners from a concentration camp on Shikotan Island (Kurile Islands; seized from Japan by the Soviet Union in September 1945). More than 6000 women prisoners here, who have been torn away from their families and children, work in a fish-processing plant. The women process cartilaginous fish and black caviar and prepare crab and fish preservatives. The fish is caught by the Soviet Far East fleet. The products of the plant are exported to what is still the free world. These unfortunate women wish you "bon appétit!" (photo 1976).

decorated wooden spoons, which tourists display on their sideboards as mementos of the Soviet Union. These are in fact mementos of the prisoners. Your purchases, moreover, help the Soviet Union buy equipment abroad for its arms industry, which in turn manufactures weapons for use against the West.

Prisoners also make other kinds of souvenirs, such as bone carvings, antlers set in silver, or jewelry set with diamonds (mined in *Mirnyi* and processed in the camps in *Salekhard*. For details, see the section on *Tyumen'* Region).

Even sweets manufactured and packed in the Soviet Union are made by prisoners.

And that black caviar that you are regaled with (but only for hard currency!) is prepared in the Lenin industrial plant in *Gur'ev,* Kazakh S.S.R., which was built by prisoners. Red caviar and crabs, on the other hand, are processed by 6000 women prisoners in the camps on *Shikotan* Island (Kurile Islands – once Japanese territory

351

but now occupied by the Soviet Union; part of *Sakhalin* Region).

Last but not least, the mascot of the Summer Olympic Games in Moscow 1980, Mishka himself, is a product of prisoner labor.

THE KIDNAPPING OF RAOUL WALLENBERG

Raoul Wallenberg, a Swedish diplomat, was stationed in Hungary at the end of World War II. He successfully organized a whole series of measures that rescued the lives of Hungarian Jews. Thousands of Jews owe him their lives.

Soviet troops, however, soon entered Hungary. On 17 January, 1945, Wallenberg was summoned to the military headquarters of the Soviet army. In violation of international law, he was arrested, secretly taken into the Soviet Union, and incarcerated in *Lubyanka* Prison in Moscow. (See photograph of Lubyanka in this *Guidebook*).

In response to all queries of the Swedish government, the Soviet Union disclaimed any knowledge of the matter. In 1958, however, after having repeatedly been confronted with conclusive evidence that organs of the Soviet secret police had kidnapped Wallenberg, the Soviet government officially released a statement that "Raoul Wallenberg died in a Moscow prison in 1947"

After their return from several years' imprisonment in Soviet labor camps, many former German prisoners of war reported having seen Wallenberg in the Soviet Union after 1947.

E. *Moshinskii,* whom I met in Israel in 1972, was imprisoned in a camp on *Vrangel'* (Wrangel) Island, where he saw Wallenberg in 1962. Inquiries in Israel led to A. *Kalinskii,* who testifies that he saw Wallenberg in *Vladimir* prison in 1959.*

Wallenberg was also seen in Soviet camps by former prisoners from Hungary and Rumania between 1950 and 1960.

Yan *Kaplan,* an eyewitness, saw Wallenberg by chance in the hospital of Moscow's *Butyrka* Prison (see

*See the earlier discussion of this on page 248.

photograph of this facility in our *Guidebook*) in 1975. Wallenberg had then already spent 30 years in the camps and prisons of the Soviet Union. Kaplan conveyed this information to his daughter in Israel by telephone in 1978 following his release from prison. He subsequently sent a detailed letter to Israel about this meeting. The letter, however, was intercepted, as a result of which Kaplan was immediately arrested by the K.G.B. And so, the circle was closed. Wallenberg, a Christian, sacrificed himself in order to save thousands of Jews. He has been imprisoned in the Soviet Union for 35 years. Kaplan, a Jew, attempted to inform the free world about Wallenberg in the hope of rescuing him. As a result, he was immediately rearrested by the merciless K.G.B. in 1979.

You have the opportunity to help both of them. Demand their release! Do not remain silent! Learn about courage by following the examples of Raoul Wallenberg and Yan Kaplan.

ADDITIONAL INFORMATION
TO THE FIRST EDITION

on camps, prisons, and psychiatric prisons in the Soviet Union received after completion of research of the Guidebook.

1. *Azanka,* Tavda District, Sverdlovsk Region: camp no. 299/2-1; strict regime; approximately 1800 prisoners; logging.

2. *Golovino,* Sudogda District, Vladimir Region: camp no. OD-1/1; strict regime; approximately 1200 prisoners; brick plant.

3. *Khokhloma,* Ivanovo District, Ivanovo Region; camp no. OK-3; ordinary regime, mechanics workshops.

4. *Sukhobezvodnoe,* Semenov District, Gor'kii Region; camp no. UZ-62/2; strict regime; 2000 prisoners; machine plant.

5. *Osh,* Osh Region, Kirghiz S.S.R.: Uritskii Street 6; ITK for children, approximately 800 prisoners.

6. *Moldovanka,* Aledin District, Kirghiz S.S.R.: camp no. 36/1; ordinary regime; 500 to 600 prisoners; farm work.

7. *Perekrestovka,* Romny District, Sumy Region, Ukrainian S.S.R.: camp no. US-319/56; ordinary regime; 1500 prisoners; slag block production.

8. *Omsk,* Omsk Region: camp no. UKh-16/16-D; strict regime; 1800 prisoners; industrial construction.

9. *Nal'chik,* Kabaradinian-Balkarian A.S.S.R.: psychiatric hospital with special wards for political prisoners; located in the vicinity of "Dubka" (among the prisoners here is Yakov *Khotorskoi,* author of works on Soviet economy).

10. *Gur'ev,* Astrakhan' Region: camp no. UG-157/9; strict regime; 1500 prisoners; industrial construction.

11. *Khar'kov,* Ukrainian S.S.R.: Adoreiskii Lane 12;

camp no. YuZh-313/25; ordinary-regime; 1200 prisoners; construction work.

12. *Makerdovo,* Dnepropetrovsk Region, Ukrainian S.S.R.: camp no. 309/45; ordinary-regime; 600 to 700 prisoners; mechanical repair workshops.

13. *Prunkul,* Moldavian S.S.R.: strict-regime camp for 2500 prisoners assigned to work at a lime quarry.

14. *Narva,* Leningrad Region: srtict-regime camp for 3000 prisoners assigned to harvesting peat.

15. *Vinnitsa,* Vinnitsa Region, Ukrainian S.S.R.: prison no. IV-301/176, in which there are political prisoners (such as Sergei *Babich*); psychiatric hospital on Pirogov Street with special K.G.B. wards in which there are political prisoners. Camp no. IV-301/8 in which Ukrainian freedom fighters, such as *Mel'nichuk,* are imprisoned.

16. *Kommisarovka* (30 kilometers from *Debal'tsevo*), Donets Region, Ukrainian S.S.R.: strict-regime camp; 2000 prisoners; aviation plant.

17. *Berezniki,* Perm' Region; strict-regime camp; 2500 prisoners assigned to construct a chemical industrial plant for potassium fertilizers (in fact, however, for explosives).

18. *Obukhovo,* Leningrad Region; ordinary-regime camp; 2000 prisoners who work in the "Stroidetal'" plant.

19. *Ul'yanovka,* Leningrad Region: women's camp; 1500 prisoners; sewing industrial plant for special uniforms.

20. *Metallostroi,* Leningrad Region: intensified-regime camp; 2500 prisoners; metal-processing plant.

21. *Otar* (80 kilometers from Alma-Ata), Alma-Ata Region, Kazakh S.S.R.: special strict-regime camp; approximately 1000 prisoners; duties in stone and granite quarries.

22. *Ksani,* Georgian S.S.R.: ordinary-regime camp;

1000 prisoners; duties on tea plantations.

23. *Turinsk,* Sverdlovsk Region: special regime camp; 1000 to 1200 prisoners assigned to logging.

24. *Khar'kov,* Khar'kov Region, Ukrainian S.S.R.: prison on "Kholodnaya Gora" (Cold Mountain); special strict-regime camp; 1500 to 1600 prisoners.

25. *Derbent,* Daghestan A.S.S.R.: special prison for 600 inmates on corner of Lenin and Kabikovskaya Streets. Many religious citizens, including those who refused induction into the Soviet Army, are imprisoned here as well as servicemen who refused to obey orders.

26. *Bel'tsy,* Moldavian S.S.R.: prison on corner of Leningradskaya and Krasnaya Streets; 1000 to 1100 prisoners under special regime.

27. *Mar'ino,* Mari A.S.S.R.: camp no. OSh-25/1; strict-regime; 1500 prisoners; logging.

28. *Symgait* (suburb of *Baku*), Azerbaidzhan S.S.R.: camp no. UA-38/11; ordinary regime; 5000 prisoners assigned to the construction of a chemical industrial plant and a tuberolling mill.

29. *Petrov Val,* Volgograd Region: women's ordinary-regime camp; approximately 2000 prisoners; textile and knitwear production. Many of the women were arrested for their religious beliefs and denied their maternal rights for having given religious instruction to their children.

30. *Rafalovka,* Rovno Region, Ukrainian S.S.R.: camp no. OR-318/76; ordinary regime; number of prisoners and kinds of duties here unknown; among prisoners are dissidents, including *Namonyuk.*

31. *Gubakhap,* Perm' Region; camp no. VV-2017/13; regime, number of prisoners, and kinds of duties unknown. Among the prisoners here are Ukrainian freedom fighters, such as *Pidgorodetskii.*

32. *Kos'va,* Gashkov District, Perm' Region: camp p/ya 201/20; strict regime; logging. There are political prisoners here, including Miroslav *Simchich.* The camp ad-

ministration incites the ordinary criminals of the camp against Simchich.

33. *Kaunas*, Lithuanian S.S.R.: psychiatric hospital on Kuzmos Street in which there are special wards for male and female political prisoners. Ask about Anchela *Paskauskiene*, who distributed patriotic leaflets demanding the independence of Lithuania.

34. *Votkinsk*, Udmurt A.S.S.R.: children's intensified-regime camp for 800 to 900 prisoners; duties in mechanics workshops in which locks and springs are manufactured.

35. *"Bezymyanka"* (suburb of *Kuibyshev*), Kuibyshev Region; camp for 2000 prisoners assigned to construct an arms plant.

36. *Tabago*, Yakutsk A.S.S.R.: camp no. YaD-40/7; Georgii Vins, leader of the underground Baptist church in the Soviet Union, was held here until recently, when he was exchanged for Soviet spies imprisoned in the United States.

37. *Fergana*, Uzbek S.S.R.: strict-regime camp for 2500 prisoners assigned to uranium mining; exposed to contamination.

38. *Andizhan*, Uzbek S.S.R.: strict-regime camp for 2500 prisoners assigned to underground uranium mining; a death camp.

39. *Surgut*, in the north of Tyumen' Region: strict-regime camp; 200 prisoners; construction in the military sector.

40. *Lovozero*, Murmansk Region: strict-regime camp in which approximately 1000 prisoners manufacture special protective gloves made of steel threads and worn by fishermen when pulling in trawls.

41. *Balakovo*, Saratov' Region: ordinary-regime camp for 2000 prisoners assigned to construct a chemical industrial plant and work in those sections of the facility that have already been completed. (Production of poisonous gases for military purposes.)

ADDITIONAL INFORMATION
TO THE SECOND EDITION

1. In Dzhalalabad city (*Kirgiz S.S.R.*) right next to the local hotel is a building with a sign containing the letters— ACLC—Administration of Corrective Labor Camps.

Behind the sign, however, there is not an administrative office. There are more than 3000 prisoners laboring in a prison mechanical factory which produces "PZhD-40" boilers for military vehicles and armored transports using diesel fuel. The commanding officer of the camp is Major Perevertin and its chief engineer is named Bubel'. A civilian engineer who has worked at the factory has reported that the inmates of the camp live in cramped quarters where there are at times 400 to 500 persons in one barracks. Their earnings are paltry, and they suffer from hunger. He tells, for instance, of one prisoner working as an arc-welder who was responsible for the production of details indispensable for other operations. This worker was given 7 bonuses so that he would have enough "for at least a smoke". Prisoners sent to this camp have been given terms ranging from 10 to 15 years. The military administration of the factory desires a minimum "turnover" in their trained work force, on whom they depend for the fulfillment of their production plan. This camp now contains 20 prisoners being held for political reasons such as the wish to live outside the U.S.S.R., confession of religious faith, the instruction of children in faith in God, and the reading and distribution of forbidden books.

2. Marta Niklusa is a biologist and musician. A fighter for the independence of Estonia from the U.S.S.R., he has already spent 8 years in the camps and prisons for his fight for the freedom of his homeland (previous to 1966) and has recently been arrested again.

In January, 1981, after sentencing him to 10 years in the camps, the authorities sent him to a political prison camp in *Perm'*, but then moved him from there in March, 1981 to *Mordoviya*, where he was placed in a psychiatric hospital.

Pay a visit to his parents in the city of *Tartu* at Viker Kaare Street, 25. Mart Niklus has been on a hunger-strike for several months in protest against his illegal arrest.

3. In a prison in the city of *Tallin* on Kalarania Street 2,

Yurii Kukk has been held since January, 1981. He was arrested for demanding independence for Estonia and its separation from the U.S.S.R. He too has been participating in a hunger-strike. In March, 1981, Kukk was transferred to a camp in the *Murmansk* region where he died.

4. In *Nakhodka,* (Primorsk Territory) in a special prison, many members of the Pentecostal Church are being held after being arrested for their religious convictions and for distributing the Bible. Here are the names of these heroes and sufferers for their faith: Valentin Poleshchuk, Boris Perchatkin, Zinaida Perchatkina, Yurii Zherebilov, Vasilii Patrushev, Vitalii Istomin, Sergei Onishchenko. Unfortunately, we are not able to recount all the names of those who have been arrested.

5. Visit the Jewish activist in the struggle for his right to emigrate to Israel—Iosif Zasel's. He has been sentenced and thrown into a camp for common criminals in *Sokiryany,* Chernovits region (*RCh*-328/67). The K.G.B. is to arrange an additional frame-up against him inside the camp itself and to this end is fomenting provocations among the criminals and extorting false testimony against Zasel's. The commandant of this camp is a Captain Yakovlev, his assistant is Captain Krushel'nitskii, and the supervisor of the K.G.B. unit is Captain Chernei. In the Chernovity K.G.B. Administration, the man from whom to demand an accounting for the treatment of Iosif Zasel is Lieutenant Chekalov. This camp is under his direction.

6. In *Moscow* is the Psychiatric Hospital No. 14, Bekhterev Street 15. Here political prisoners are held in section No. 6 and are in the charge of "Dr." Vladimir Levitskii who has as yet escaped punishment for performing injections of goloperidol, thriftazine, aminazine on healthy people.

7. In *Yakutiya,* in the settlement *B. Morkha,* the well-known fighter for Ukrainian independence, V. Chornovil is being held in solitary confinement (P.O. Box IZ-16/1). He was re-arrested during his exile on a fabricated charge of rape. The goal of the K.G.B. is clearly to compromise a hero and fighter. V. Chornovil has now been transferred to the *Yakutsk* city prison.

8. In *B. Morkha,* also at the edge of the settlement, is a

camp containing 400 to 500 prisoners working at a brick factory. This is a strict-regime camp.

9. The human rights activist Mal'va Landa, an old woman and a pensioner, has been transferred in a prison railway car to a place of exile in the *Kazakh S.S.R.*, to the settlement of *Dzhezdy* in the *Dzerzhinsky* district. Visit her and write her.

10. In the *Lefortovo* prison in *Moscow*, the well-known defender of human rights in the U.S.S.R., the mathematician Alexander Lavut is being held for investigation after his arrest on April 29, 1980. His wife, Serafima Mostinskaya, lives in *Moscow* at 2 Troitskii pereulok No. 6, Apt. 16. Visit her and ask about the life of political prisoners.

11. In the *Volgograd* region (*Kamyshinsky* district), in the village of *Dvoryanskoye*, a new special psychiatric prison has been opened (Ya R-154/SPB). It consists of two concentration camps previously located there. There you may visit the political prisoner, Peteris Lazda, a lawyer who has defended the human rights of others and spoken out against the Russification of Latvia. His wife, Velta Lazda, lives with her daughter in *Tukums, Latvian S.S.R.* on Spartak Street No. 9 Apt. 35. Their telephone number is 2-60-22.

12. In the prison in *Tartu (Estonian S.S.R.)*, at 54 Ulikooli Street, one may find the political prisoner and Baptist Herbert Murd. He is "guilty" of having organized a private concert of religious music for young people in Estonia. He is a musician himself.

13. It has been established that in the Leningrad Psychiatric Hospital No. 5, political prisoners are being kept in sections No. 7 and No. 9.

14. In the *Dnepropetrovsk* region (*Sofievskii* district), in the village of *Makorty*, there is a concentration camp to which prisoners are taken who have become invalids (Uchr. YaE-309/45). There you can demand a meeting with the political prisoner F. Yaroslavsky, who has gone blind, and P. Savitsky. Not long ago the prisoner Proniuk died there. For the year 1980, 400 prisoners have died out of twelve hundred.

15. In *Uman'* (*Voronezh* region), there is a prison

(Uchr. YuU-323/L-B) where there are prisoners who fought for human rights in the U.S.S.R.

16. Mikhail Gorbal', a fighter for Ukrainian independence is being held in a camp in *Ol'shanskoye* (*Nikolaevskii* region, *Nikolaevskii* district, *Ukrainian S.S.R.*) since his sentencing in January, 1980. You may visit him on your way from Moscow to the Crimea or to Sochi.

17. Igor Korchnoi, the son of the famous chess-player, who requested political asylum in the West, is being held in Concentration Camp OF-2 at Prosvet Statin (*Ketovskii* district, *Chelyabinsk* region, not far from the city of Kurgan). He was arrested and sentenced in order to exert pressure on his father.

18. In *Chelyabinsk,* you may visit the German Gerhart Buterus who is being held for illegally attempting to leave the U.S.S.R. He is at Psychiatric Hospital No. 2, a prison in actual fact.

19. In *L'vov,* at the Psychiatric Hospital, in reality a prison, at 5 Kul'tparkovaya Street, you may visit another unsuccessful fugitive from the U.S.S.R.: Kazimir Gal'ko. Psychiatrists often diagnose as *non compos mentis* anyone who desires to leave the Soviet "paradise."

20. In the Special Psychiatrical Hospital of *Krasnodar,* the Baptist Fedor Sidenko is being held on a prison regimen after being convicted for his belief in God. You may visit him on your way to the resorts of Novorossiisk, Anapa, and Sochi.

21. At *Zima Junction* (*Irkutsk* region), a huge chemical factory has been in the process of construction since 1977 with the aid of machinery and equipment from the Federal Republic of Germany and the German Democratic Republic as well as the participation of their technical advisors. The construction work is done by camps situated around the construction site. They contain 10 000 guarded prisoners and 2 000 prisoners working without armed guards. Journalists may question the foreign advisors and obtain photographs of the camps from them.

22. In the *Irkutsk* region at the *Usol'e Sibirskoye Station,* a chemical factory has been under construction since 1970. This factory is being built by inmates of the nearby

strict-regime camp, a total of 3000 prisoners. The camp warden in Major Khomiakov.

23. In *Rovno (Ukraine),* there is a dormitory for 3000 prisoners at the "Azot" chemical factory which produces fertilizers. They work at the factory as prisoners without armed guards. Visit this open dormitory and speak with the prisoners. There is no permission required for this and travel to *Rovno* is quite simple. Among the prisoners are people who have been sentenced for their belief in God.

24. In *Al'malyk (Uzbek S.S.R.),* it is quite easy to locate the chemical factory where 3000 prisoners are working out of the ordinary regime camp located next to the factory. The camp warden is Lieutenant-Colonel Krasnov.

25. In *Shaikhali (Uzbek S.S.R., Karashi Station*-16), Camp UYa-64 is located. Here you may visit Yakov Kandinov who has been sentenced for Zionism.

26. In *Borodenka (Moscow* region, *Ruzskii* district) there is a psychiatric hospital (in reality a prison) whose inmates include political prisoners.

27. *Pokrovskoye,* which is near the Sheremet'evo International Airport outside of Moscow, is the location of Psychiatric Hospital No. 4. There you may visit in prison section No. 8, Yurii Valov, who was categorized as insane for his attempt to meet with American diplomats in Moscow.

28. In *Kerzhach (Vladimir* region) there is a prison containing prisoners serving terms for "infractions" committed while in camps. This prison has three floors and contains up to 600 prisoners. The prison is to be found as one leaves *Kerzhach* in the direction of the village of Turki. Next to the prison is a common-regime camp for 500 to 600 prisoners assigned to mechanical repair shops.

29. On the highway leading from the city of *Alma-Ata* towards the Ili River, about 75 km. from the city, is a strict-regime camp. It contains a wood-finishing plant, employing about 2500 prisoners. The head of the camp is Major Kopytin. This camp holds many prisoners sentenced for their belief in God.

30. In the city of *Novorossiisk* (*Krasnodarskii* territory) on the Black Sea, the city prison of 1 200 to 1 300 prisoners contains a special psychiatric hospital for dissidents (IZ-18-3). Ask for Fedor Sidenko while you are there, he is a completely normal person who has been thrown in with insane patients for his non-conformist views.

31. In the village of *Abramtsevo* (*Moscow* region), there is a psychiatric hospital. In 1979, the believers Alexander Pushkin (arrested in the city of *Mytishchi, Moscow* region) and Ivan Akinin (a novice at the Troitsko-Sergievskaya Lavra and a former doctor) were imprisoned in 1979. Visit them. This is not a prison camp, but "merely" a psychiatric hospital in a suburb of Moscow.

32. We have already mentioned in the section on *Leningrad* the Psychiatric Hospital No. 3 (*Skvortsov-Stepanov*). In 1980, it contained the dissident Vladimir Borisov. He is in the 8th section of the hospital which is located at No. 36 on the Fermsk Highway. Borisov is known for his heroic conduct during his previous arrests and incarcerations in special psychiatric hospitals in 1964 and 1966. Visit him or his wife in Moscow. Irina Kaplun lives with her child at No. 5 Apt. 37 on the Vorob'evskii Highway. His mother can be visited in Leningrad: Elena Borisova, Prospekt Vernosti No. 28, Korpus 1, Apt. 135—Telephone 249-87-19.

33. In the *Kuibyshev* region (*Stavropolskii* district) in the village of Verkhnyaya Belozerka, camp UR-65 is located. The political prisoner Vladislav Bebko has been sent among common criminals. By order of the local officials, these criminals give him regular, systematic beatings. Bebko has already suffered a brain concussion and instead of treatment the K.G.B. has transferred him to a psychiatric hospital. A letter about him can be addressed to the administration of the camp.

34. In the city of *Tol'yati,* (*Kuibyshev* region) the Italians built an automobile plant to meet the needs of the U.S.S.R. This is yet another prison camp-hospital, No. UR-65/16, to which prisoners are transported. If you are taken on a tour of the automobile factory, demand a tour of this terrible concentration camp.

35. There is a common-regime camp located at

Gorlovka Station 21 (*Donetsk* region). There you will find the political prisoner Gordienko.

36. In the *Kirgiz S.S.R.* in the village of *Moldavanka* (*Aladinskii* district), camp No. 36-1 contains many imprisoned Christians. The name of one of them is Gorpenyuk. You might write him.

37. In the settlement of *Arushevskoye* (*Rostov* region), is camp No. 398/6 where political prisoners are kept among common criminals; the name of one of them is Kharchenko.

38. In Camp Yu E-313/32 in the city of *Makeevka* (*Donets* region), many Pentecostals who have been sentenced for their belief in God are kept among common criminals; among them is Vladislav Zagumennyi.

39. Kirill Podrabinek, the brother of the man who exposed Soviet crimes in psychiatric hospitals, Alexander Podrabinek, is imprisoned in Common Prison No. Yu U-323 in *Kel'tse* (*Lipetskaya* region), although he is a political prisoner.

40. Il'ya Lepshin, a Jewish political prisoner, is being held in a camp in *Zerovshan (Usbek S.S.R.).* This is within an area exposed to uranium radiation. (See the map of the Extermination Camps.) He is also being persecuted for refusing to work on the Sabbath. His refusal is motivated by religious reasons.

41. In *Lithuania,* we have established the existence of one more common-regime camp in the city of *Vilenkionis* to the west of *Vil'nius.* It contains about 300 boys in ages up to 14 years old.

42. The political prisoner Stasevich is in a camp for common criminals in the *Kirov* region (*Verkhnekamskii* district) in the settlement of *Lesnoi.*

43. We are able to provide some additional information about the *Serbskii Institute* of Forensic Psychiatry in Moscow: Kropotkinskii pereulok No. 23 (metro to "Kropotkinskaya", see Note 23 to schematic plan of penal facilities in Moscow in Guidebook plus sketch of Kropotkinskaya Square). The director of the Institute is K.G.B. General Georgii Morozov; telephone No. 203-74-35.

The assistant director in charge of research is Alexander Kachaev, the coordinator of expertise is Tamara Pechernikova, the chairman of the Commission on Expertise is Yurii Il'inskii. He is also responsible for the *Chernyakhovsk* psychiatric prison. (See photo under Kaliningrad Region in *Guidebook*.) The administrator of the political prisoners section is Margarita Tal'tse.

Look again at the map of the Extermination Camps on pages 32 and 33 and remember that it is still not complete. We have recently established the existence of an additional camp in *Khaidarovka, Kirgiz S.S.R.*, where prisoners die while mining uranium among the fertile orchards of the Fergan Valley and another death camp with uranium mines in *Kul-Kuduk* in the deserts of Kara-Kuma. This brings the number of Extermination Camps to forty-three.

If we do not all struggle against the concentration camps of Communism that are threatening the world, then they shall become the future for both us and our children.

AFTERWORD TO THE FIRST EDITION

Thus, you have seen the manner in which the Soviet Union observes the Helsinki accords on the question of human rights and the United Nations Universal Declaration of Human Rights.

What was the purpose of this book? To frighten or astonish you? No. After the tragedies of Auschwitz and Maidanek, after the mass extermination of human beings in Cambodia and Vietnam, mankind will most unlikely be astonished by anything else.

If you have a conscience, however, consider, if you will, the fact that human beings have been systematically tortured and murdered in the Soviet Union for more than 60 years. More than 60 000 000 innocent human beings have perished in these camps. Today, what is left of free thinking or of the various "catacomb" churches in the Soviet Union is slowly being eradicated. The murderers are now looking in your direction!

Their tanks are now standing on the threshold of Europe, their divisions are marching east through Afghanistan, their missiles in Cuba are pointed in the direction of the United States, their warships are cruising in every major body of water, and their embassies have proscription lists of the intelligentsia in your country marked for "liquidation" for the day when they take power. The "leftists" in your country, who have been clearing the way for a Communist takeover, would be well advised to remember the fates of Russian and East European Socialists. They were the first to be killed by the secret police. The same will happen to you if you, too, remain indifferent to events in the Soviet Union and fail to join the active struggle against those who are preparing you and your children for a life of lawless camp slavery.

We have given you the facts. It is up to you to decide how you wish to take up the struggle. Your political leaders are now capitulating to the Soviet threat before the eyes of the entire world. The camps are getting closer and closer.

After having read this book, you will no longer be able to tell your children that no one warned you.

AFTERWORD TO THE SECOND EDITION

The Research Center for Prisons, Psychprisons, and Forced Labor Concentration Camps of the U.S.S.R. continued its work even after the publication of this Guidebook.

To our great distress, we have ascertained that in 1981 the authorities in the U.S.S.R. have sharply increased arrests, persecutions, and intimidation of dissidents, religious persons, and those attempting to emigrate from the U.S.S.R. We know of many cases of beatings and murders of both clergy and those who simply believe in God. It would seem probable that this increased activity is connected with the desire of the Soviet Union to have a "quiet home front" in the event that their world-wide aggression, and attempts to keep Poland in their hands, should provoke a military clash with the free world.

Here are a few examples which illustrate the actions of the Soviet authorities against individuals they do not find to their liking: a series of arrests were made in Estonia of people demanding the re-establishment of the independence of this state which was occupied by the U.S.S.R. in 1940; arrests have been made of Ukrainian and Lithuanian nationalists demanding their independence; arrests of Jewish activists demanding permission to emigrate to Israel have become a common occurence. Viktor Brailovskii has been arrested for publishing a journal on Jewish culture. The authorities' rage has led them to arrest well-known women defenders of the rights of persecuted people in the U.S.S.R. Following the arrest of Ida Nudel', they arrested Tatyana Osipova, who has been on a hunger strike in Moscow where she is being held at Novoslobodskaya Street 45 in a Special Psychiatric Reception Center for Women. Tatyana Velikanova, a middle-aged woman with grandchildren, Mal'va Landa, a pensioner, and Oksana Meshko, who is 75 years old, have also been arrested. The political prisoner Ol'ga Nozhak is wasting away in a Special Psychiatric Hospital in *Alma-Ata (Kazakh S.S.R.)* where she has been imprisoned among the insane for 25 years. This is the fate that awaits the heroic women arrested in 1980 if the world will not come to their defense.

The authorities have increased repressive measures against people who believe in God. Prayer meetings taking place in private homes and in the woods because their churches have been shut down, have been dispersed by the militia who used tear gas although the worshippers made no resistance. Such was the case in the city of *Stolbuny* in the Ukraine. There have been arrests of believers in God who have refused to register their faith. Doing so would put the "mark of Cain" on them and necessitate their submission to the authorities as well as to surveillance by the K.G.B. In Lithuania, during 1980, six priests were beaten, injured, and killed and more than twenty cathedrals were defaced.

Vladimir Shelkov spent 23 years in the camps and died in Siberia, in *Yakutiia,* Yurii Kukk died after a hunger strike in protest against his illegal arrest, Semen Bakholdin, imprisoned unjustly for his belief in God, died during a hunger strike in protest against the arbitrary measures of the K.G.B. in *Solikamsk* city. Alexander Ogorodnikov, a dissident who was sentenced to 6 years because he openly expressed his views, has been conducting a hunger strike since October, 1980. Veniamin Moiseev went blind "during the interrogation" and was sent to a psychiatric prison. In a children's camp in *Belaya Tserkov* city in the Ukraine, the miserable children rushed out into the street and marched in a column demanding that there be an end to their suffering and mistreatment. But troops herded the children back inside the camp and the "instigators" were arrested.

Some prisoners have been driven to the point where they tattoo slogans on their foreheads: "Death to Communism!" "Down with the Soviet regime!" Previously, these tattoos were cut out of their flesh, without any anesthesia. Now such offenders are tried in secret and shot.

In order to make clear to the entire world the full extent of the crimes committed in the U.S.S.R., it is our intention to publish an album of photographs containing original photographs made in the prisons and camps of the U.S.S.R. and to put out Part II of our documentary film series "Prisonland" which has already been exhibited in the free world. We also intend to publish an Information Guide explaining changes in the regimens of prisons and camps during the rule of Stalin, Khrushchev, and Brezhnev in order to give factual data about the so-called "improved" conditions.

We are also organizing the sending of parcels to the families of political prisoners in the U.S.S.R.

If you should desire to help us in this work, our bank account number is No. 30392 in the *Zikhron Yakov* branch of the Discount Bank in Israel.

It is our hope that this Guidebook, with its additions for the year 1981, will aid you and your friends to better understand the brutal essence of the Communist regime in the U.S.S.R.

Sources consulted

1. Interviews with eyewitness and their written testimonies: archive materials of the Research Center for Prisons, Psychprisons and Forced-Labor Concentration Camps of the U.S.S.R. Nos. 317-470, 677-835, 1639-1939; 14-p, 24-p, 36-p, 78-p, 79-p, 80-p, 112-p, 116-p, 139-p, 144-p, 156-p, 167-p, 270-p, 278-p, 314-p, 318-p, 410-p, 416-p, 419-p, 420-p, 421-p, 422-p, 434-p.

2. V. Artem'ev, *Rezhim i Okhrana ispravitel'no-trudovikh lagerei SSSR.* Munich: Institute for the Study of the U.S.S.R., 1956.

3. M. de Santerr. *Sovetskie poslevoennie kontslageri i ikh obitateli.* Munich: Institute for the Study of the U.S.S.R., 1960.

4. B. Yakovlev, *Concentration Camps in the U.S.S.R.* Munich: Institute for the Study of the History and Culture of the U.S.S.R., 1955.

5. *Uniform Crime Reports for the United States.* Washington: U.S. Department of Justice, 1977.

6. *The Voice of the Martyrs.* Jesus to the Communist World. Inc. 1967–1977. Box 11, Glendale, Calif. 91209, U.S.A.

7. *The Voice of the Martyrs.* Jesus to the Communist World. Inc. 1977–1979. Box 11, Glendale, Calif. 91209, U.S.A.

8. *Great World Atlas.* London: Reader's Digest Association.

9. *The Times Concise Atlas of the World.* Time Books.

10. A. Gaivoron, *Putevoditel' po Odesse.* Gosizdat SSSR.

11. *Guide to the map of Kiev.* Kiev: State publishing house.

12. *Putevoditel' po Kievu.* Kiev: State publishing house of political literature.

13. I. Myachin and V. Chernov, *Putevoditel' po Moskve.* Moscow: A.P.N.

14. N.T. Markova (ed.), *Atlas of highways of the U.S.S.R.* Moscow: State Department of geodesy and cartography of the Council of Ministers of the U.S.S.R.

15. *News Brief* (bimonthly), ed. by Cronid Lubarsky. Nos. 1–23. Brussels: Cahiers du Samizdat.

16. *E.L.T.A. Information Bulletin of the Supreme Committee for Liberation of Lithuania.* Washington: Lithuanian National Foundation, Inc.

17. *I.M.P.A. Internationale Märtyrer Presse-Agentur der Hilfsaktion Märtyrerkirche e.V.*

18. *Magazine of unregistered Soviet Baptists.* Samizdat, U.S.S.R.

19. *A.B.N. Correspondence. Bulletin of the Antibolshevik Bloc of Nations.* Munich.

20. *Sucasnist. Magazine of the Ukrainian Association.* Munich.

21. *The Ukrainian Review.* A quarterly magazine of the Association of Ukrainians in Great Britain, Ltd., the Organization of the Defence of Four Freedoms for the Ukraine, Inc. (USA), and the Canadian League for the Ukraine's Liberation.

22. *Volnoe Slovo.* A documentary serial. Frankfurt/Main: Possev-Verlag, issues of 1976–1979.

23. *Chronicle of Current Events.* Issues of 1977–1979.

24. *Khronika Arkhipelaga GULAG* (collection of documents). Frankfurt/Main: Possev-Verlag.

25. *Natsional'nyi Vopros v SSSR* (collection of documents). 1975.

374

26. Yurii Mal'tsev, *Reportazh iz sumashedshego doma.* Published by *The New Review,* 1974.

27. *Delo Dandarona.* Florence:Edizioni Aurora, 1974.

28. *Istoriya Bolezni Leonida Plyushch* (collection of documents). Amsterdam, 1974.

29. *Annals of Samizdat.* Amsterdam: Herzen Foundation.

30. *VSKHON* (collection of trial documents). Frankfurt/Main: Possev-Verlag, 1976.

31. U.S. Senate, *Abuse of Psychiatry for Political Repression in the Soviet Union* (hearings). Washington, 1972.

32. S. Rosefielde. *The Lessons of Solzhenitsyn's GULAG Archipelago,* 1979.

33. Mitchell Knisbacher, "Aliyah of Soviet Jews: Protection of the Right of Emigration under International Law." *Harvard International Law Journal.* Vol. XIV, no. 1, 1973.

34. A. Marchenko, *My Testimony.* La Presse Libre, 1969.

Index

A

377

379

The author, **Avraham Shifrin**, who was born in Minsk in 1923, lived in Moscow until 1941. There he was inducted into the Soviet Army and into active service in World War II. His father, Isaak Shifrin, had already been arrested for having told an anti-Stalin joke. He died after ten years imprisonment in a forced-labor camp.

As the son of a camp convict, Shifrin was assigned to a delinquent battalion. Wounded twice at the front, he was released from service as an █████. After the war, he studied law and became a legal adviser and at-██████ was arrested in 1953 and sentenced to death for anti-Soviet ██████ sentence was later commuted to 25 years camp imprison-███████ after ten years' camp internment and four years' exile, ██████████ advocate of Soviet Jews wishing to emigrate to Israel. ███████ in the distribution of Leon Uris' novel, *Exodus*, in the ███████ 0, he was permitted to emigrate to Israel, where he ██████ ooks, *The Fourth Dimension* and *Das Verhör* (The ██████ n's testimony before a U.S. Senate committee), he ██████ ences in Soviet prison camps. He produced an 80-███████ ary film, *Prisonland* (Prison Country), on the persecu-████████ ormist Soviet citizens. He has written numerous articles █████ pers and periodicals on the same subject.

██████ y, he is the director of "The Research Center for Prisons, Psych-█████ ons, and Forced-Labor Concentration Camps of the U.S.S.R."

This *Guidebook* has been three years in the making. The documentary materials used in its preparation were gathered from sources in the Soviet Union smuggled to the West through underground channels. In-formation on the location, conditions, etc. of Soviet penal facilities has also been drawn from Shifrin's numerous interviews with former camp and prison inmates and compiled in this *Guidebook*.

After publication by Stephanus Edition in September of 1980, Shifrin continued to compile information, much of which is included in this second edition, now published by Bantam Books.

Photo 1
Shifrin after his release
from camp imprisonment.

Photo 2
Shifrin in Israel.